Lecture Notes in Artificial Intelligence 1881

Subseries of Lecture Notes in Computer Science
Edited by J. G. Carbonell and J. Siekmann

Lecture Notes in Computer Science

Edited by G. Goos, J. Hartmanis and J. van Leeuwen

Springer

Berlin
Heidelberg
New York
Barcelona
Hong Kong
London
Milan
Paris
Singapore
Tokyo

Chengqi Zhang   Von-Wun Soo (Eds.)

Design and Applications of Intelligent Agents

Third Pacific Rim International Workshop
on Multi-Agents, PRIMA 2000
Melbourne, Australia, August 28 - 29, 2000
Proceedings

 Springer

Series Editors

Jaime G. Carbonell,Carnegie Mellon University, Pittsburgh, PA, USA
Jörg Siekmann, University of Saarland, Saarbrücken, Germany

Volume Editors

Chengqi Zhang
Deakin University
School of Computing and Mathematics
Geelong, Victoria 3217, Australia
E-mail: chengqi@deakin.edu.au

Von-Wun Soo
Department of Computer Science
National Tsing Hua University
Hsin-Chu City, 30043 Taiwan
E-mail: soo@cs.nthu.edu.tw

Cataloging-in-Publication Data applied for

Die Deutsche Bibliothek - CIP-Einheitsaufnahme

Design and applications of intelligent agents : proceedings / Third
Pacific Rim International Workshop on Multi-Agents, PRIMA 2000,
Melbourne, Australia, August 28 - 29, 2000. Chengqi Zhang ; Von-Wun
Soo (ed.). - Berlin ; Heidelberg ; New York ; Barcelona ; Hong Kong ;
London ; Milan ; Paris ; Singapore ; Tokyo : Springer, 2000
 (Lecture notes in computer science ; Vol. 1881 : Lecture notes in
 artificial intelligence)
 ISBN 3-540-67911-1

CR Subject Classification (1998): I.2.11, I.2, C.2, D.2.3, H.4, H.5, H.3

ISBN 3-540-67911-1 Springer-Verlag Berlin Heidelberg New York

Springer-Verlag Berlin Heidelberg New York
a member of BertelsmannSpringer Science+Business Media GmbH
© Springer-Verlag Berlin Heidelberg 2000
Printed in Germany

Typesetting: Camera-ready by author, data conversion by PTP-Berlin, Stefan Sossna
Printed on acid-free paper   SPIN 10722426   06/3142   5 4 3 2 1 0

Preface

PRIMA 2000 was the third in the series of Pacific Rim International Workshops on Multi-Agents. It was held on August 28-29, 2000, in Melbourne, Australia in conjunction with the Pacific Rim International Conference on Artificial Intelligence 2000. PRIMA is the main forum for the agent or multi-agent researchers in pacific rim countries to exchange and discuss their research results.

This volume contains selected papers from PRIMA 2000. It covers theory, design, and applications of intelligent agents. The specific aspects include coordination, negotiation, learning, architecture, specification, allocation, and application of intelligent agents. All papers are of high quality because each of them was reviewed and recommended by at least two international renowned program committee members.

Many people contributed to this volume. We would like to thank all the authors who submitted papers to the workshop. Many thanks also to the members of the program committee who diligently reviewed all the papers. Finally, we thank the editorial staff of Springer-Verlag for publishing this volume in the Lecture Notes in Artificial Intelligence series.

For more information about PRIMA, please check the following web pages:

PRIMA Web page   http://www.lab7.kuis.kyoto-u.ac.jp/prima/
PRIMA'99 Web page   http://www.lab7.kuis.kyoto-u.ac.jp/prima99/
PRIMA 2000 Web page http://www.lab7.kuis.kyoto-u.ac.jp/prima2000/

June 2000

Chengqi Zhang
Von-Wun Soo

PRIMA 2000 Committee Members

General Chair

Michael Georgeff
Agentis International
Melbourne, Australia
georgeff@agentis.com.au

Program Co-chairs

Chengqi Zhang
School of Computing and Mathematics
Deakin University
Geelong, Victoria 3217, Australia
chengqi@deakin.edu.au

Von-Wun Soo
Department of Computer Science
National Tsing Hua University
Hsin-Chu City, 30043, Taiwan
soo@cs.nthu.edu.tw

Publicity Chair

David Kinny
Department of Computer Science
University of Melbourne
Victoria 3010, Australia
Email: dnk@cs.mu.oz.au

Workshop Web Master

Kosuke Nakatsuka
Kyoto University
606-8501 Kyoto, Japan
Email: nakatuka@kuis.kyoto-u.ac.jp

Makoto Amamiya	Japan
Cristiano Castelfranchi	Italy
Brahim Chaib-draa	Canada
John Debenham	Australia
Tharam Dillon	China
Mark d'Inverno	UK
Ed Durfee	USA
Klaus Fisher	Germany
Norbert Glaser	Germany
Barbara Grosz	USA
Jieh Hsiang	Taiwan
Jane Hsu	Taiwan
Michael Huhns	USA
Toru Ishida	Japan
Minkoo Kim	Korea
David Kinny	Australia
Yasuhiko Kitamura	Japan
Kazuhiro Kuwabara	Japan
Jaeho Lee	Korea
Victor Lesser	USA
Ho-fung Leung	China
Jyi-shane Liu	Taiwan
Jian Lu	China
Michael Luck	UK
Xudong Luo	China
John Jules Meyer	The Netherlands
David Morley	Australia
Joerg Mueller	Germany
Hideyuki Nakashima	Japan
Tim Norman	UK
Ei-Ichi Osawa	Japan
Ichiro Osawa	Japan
Sascha Ossowski	Spain
Van Parunak	USA
Ramakoti Sadananda	Thailand
Abdul Satter	Australia
Sandip Sen	USA
Zhongzhi Shi	China
Leon Sterling	Australia
Peter Stone	USA
Toshiharu Sugawara	Japan
Ron Sun	USA
Lam Kwok Yan	Singapore
Makoto Yokoo	Japan
Xinhuo Yu	Australia
Soe-Tsyr Yuan	Taiwan
Minjie Zhang	Australia

Table of Contents

Coordination, Negotiation, and Learning

Architecture, Specification, and Allocation

Applications

Coordinating Distributed Decision Making Using Reusable Interaction Specifications

K.S. Barber, D.C. Han, and T.H. Liu

The University of Texas at Austin
Department of Electrical and Computer Engineering
24th and Speedway, ENS 240
barber@mail.utexas.edu

Abstract. The organization structure of Multi-Agent Systems (MAS) constrains the mechanisms that may be used for coordinating the agents' decision-making process. As researchers develop MAS that allow agents to dynamically re-organize how to interact with each other, the design of the agents must provide the ability to operate under different organizations. This paper investigates the issues involved in increasing the flexibility of agents' coordination capabilities. Applying the concepts of encapsulation and polymorphism, a representation of coordination strategies is presented as an abstraction that allows agents to easily switch coordination mechanisms and that allows coordination mechanisms to be applied to different domains.

1   Introduction

Agents can be generally described as independent entities equipped with some amount of decision-making power. A Multi-Agent System (MAS) can be seen as a group of entities interacting to achieve individual or collective goals. In the past two decades, researchers have developed various designs for MAS architectures; some of them are equipped with the ability to dynamically modify agent organizational structures [2,13,14,24]). Equipping agents with such abilities is motivated by the fact that one specific organizational structure is not suitable for all situations in dynamic environments [3]. Take Sensible Agents [6] for example, they are equipped with the capability to reason about and switch among levels of autonomy. Typical autonomy levels (which are assigned to goals instead of agents) include: command-driven, master, consensus, and locally autonomous. If the agent is at command-driven level, it does not make decisions and must obey orders given by a master agent. If the agent is at consensus level, it works as a team member, sharing decision-making tasks equally with other agents. If the agent is at locally autonomous or master levels, it makes decisions alone.

Coordination of the decision-making processes in such dynamically organized multi-agent systems must be flexible. The agents must have the ability to interact under any organization that they may find themselves in. Just as there is no best organization structure for all situations, there is no best coordination technique for all organizations. This paper describes our work in equipping agents

C. Zhang and V.-W. Soo (Eds.): PRIMA 2000, LNAI 1881, pp. 1–15, 2000.

with the ability to change the manner in which they coordinate their decision-making processes. Specifically, this paper discusses an abstract representation for specifying agent coordination techniques based on object oriented concepts (e.g. encapsulation and polymorphism) as well as the selection and usage of those techniques. The advantage of equipping agents with the ability to select proper strategies is the increased flexibility of MAS problem solving. As long as there exists a solution and a strategy that can reach the solution, agents will quickly (our research objective) and eventually follow that strategy to reach their goals.

The paper is organized as follows. Section 2 presents a brief overview of agent coordination and four common coordination mechanisms. Section 3 presents the representation of coordination strategies. Section 4 provides a description of reasoning for the purpose of strategy selection. Section 5 concludes the paper.

2   Agent Coordination

One of the strengths of an agent-based approach is the ability of the agents to cooperate in order to solve domain problems that they may not be able to solve individually. In order to collectively solve problems, each agent must have the ability to coordinate its decision-making processes as well as its actuations with the other agents. These decision-making processes include the ability to generate, allocate, integrate, and execute plans [4]. Generically, coordination is the process by which agents reason about and manage the interdependencies among their behaviors and try to ensure that every member of the system acts consistently [17].

Researchers have developed various coordination techniques for multi-agent systems. Some popular coordination techniques, namely, negotiation, arbitration, voting, and self-modification, are described below.

Negotiation is the most popular coordination technique for multi-agent systems. Game theory-based negotiation developed by Zlotkin and Rosenschein is a typical example [21]. It is assumed that all agents are rational and intelligent, which means they make decisions consistently to pursue their own goals. It is also assumed that each agent's objective is to maximize its expected payoff, which is measured by a utility scale [19]. Various negotiation approaches are developed, reflecting the rich diversity of humans' negotiation behavior under different contexts [9,26].

Arbitration is a technique in which conflicts are arbitrated by a third party. In arbitration, the decision of the third party (arbitrator) must be accepted by the coordinating agents. Usually an arbitrator is equipped with the authority, more complete knowledge and more solution-search capabilities than other agents involved in the dispute. The authority comes from the agreement of agents within the organizational structure [16,21].

Voting is another coordination technique used in human organizations. Researchers in distributed systems have applied this approach in Group Membership Problems (GMP) to eliminate conflicts about which agent should take over the manager position when the previous manager is disabled [20]. Steeb explored a similar method for multi-agent systems in air traffic control problems [23]. Voting can be used to achieve maximum social welfare in Ephrati and Rosenschein's approach [10]. By their method, each agent expresses its preferences and votes for candidate states that are generated based on each agent's goal to maximize the total satisfaction of the system. In addition, agents can use this approach to incrementally construct a plan that brings the society to a state of maximal social welfare [11]. Before each joint action, all agents reveal additional information about their goals and the candidate states keep expanding to form new sets of candidate states until the process reaches new constraints. Then every agent votes for the next joint action.

Self-modification is a technique used by an agent who does not want to interact with other agents. This technique is also named "Independence" [1]. Self-modification is simple and can be effective; except for modifying the agents' own behaviors, no extra effort/cost is required. For example, in multi-robot systems, a collision between robots is the result of conflicting robot path plans. Since collisions have serious effects on system functionality, it is necessary, and often more efficient, for robots to modify their positions/velocities to avoid collisions rather than request changes from others [8].

3   Coordination Strategy Representation

Given that the agents can dynamically change their organization structure, the agents should be equipped with the ability to change coordination techniques to match. The object-oriented concepts of encapsulation and polymorphism [7] provide appropriate and relevant methods with which to address this ability. Encapsulation minimizes the interdependencies between objects through intelligent selection of object boundaries. Encapsulation of the agent coordination mechanism separates it from the rest of the infrastructure that composes the agent, such as the manner in which sensing, modeling, and actuation are implemented as well as other reasoning processes that the agent may perform. Polymorphism allows objects that satisfy the same interface to be interchangeable. Encapsulating and making agent coordination mechanisms interchangeable, allows the agent to manage its interactions at a more abstract level, such as at the organizational level.

The strategy design pattern [12] was developed with the intent of defining a family of algorithms, encapsulating them, and making them interchangeable to the client. There are generally three participants in this design pattern: the *strategy base class, concrete strategy classes*, and the *context class*. The *strategy base class* describes the interface to the strategy. The *concrete strategy classes* implement this interface, hiding their implementation details from the client. The *context* acts as a go-between for the client and the strategies. It provides any information that the strategy requires and uses the interface described in the base strategy to control the concrete strategies. Details of the "strategy" design pattern can be found in [12]. The representation of coordination strategies is presented in terms of this design pattern, as shown in Figure 1, along with a representation for roles to compose the coordination mechanisms.

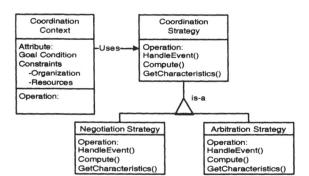

Fig. 1. Object Diagram describing the Coordination Strategy Representation

3.1   Coordination Context

The agent uses the context to both provide needed information for the coordination strategies as well as control their execution. First, the context provides
the strategy with the problem that this particular instance of coordination was
formed to solve, whether it is to plan to solve some domain objective or resolve
conflicts among agents. Second, the context provides the organization structure
in which the agent will address this goal. The organization structure is formulated in terms of constraints and requirements. These constraints and requirements
describe which agents have responsibility for planning for, or reasoning about,
the given problem and which agents have obligated themselves to execute the
solution. The context also provides the strategies with environmental information, as well as acting as a message router for inter-agent communication. For
this purpose, the context holds a translator to convert events produced by the
strategies into inter-agent communication messages. This abstracts the coordination mechanism away from any communication language or medium as well
as the infrastructure provided by the agent.

3.2   Coordination Strategy Construct

The coordination context has the ability to call two methods on the coordination
strategy interface. The context can 1) pass relevant events to the coordination
strategy that were events. The coordination strategy stores incoming events on
a queue until it receives the command from the context to process the events. As
every computational unit is triggered by some event, this allows the context to
control how much computation is performed by each coordination strategy, which
is useful when dealing with deadlines and a limited amount of computational
resources.

Coordination strategies can be constructed out of a set of computational
units. Just as roles can be used to describe and separate the functionality required of the agents for some domain problem [28], the same concepts can be
used to define the computational units needed to solve the domain independent
problem of achieving agreement among distributed agents (i.e. the coordination

strategy). These units will be referred to as the roles that agents can play in the coordination strategy. Possible roles that compose the coordination strategies include the following. **Solution Generators** produce solutions to the domain problem that the agents are addressing. Evaluation of the solutions can be performed by two different roles; **Solution Selectors** and evaluate the given solutions according to the agent's priorities to provide a quantitative measure of the quality of each solution from the agent's perspective and **Solution Acceptability Testers** provide a Boolean verdict on the acceptability of each solution to the given agent. There are managers for each type of coordination strategy, which direct the operation of the generators and evaluators. Finally, there are **Solution Implementers**, which execute the agent's portion of the solution.

Since a coordination strategy is an abstraction the agent can use to formulate different coordination approaches, each agent must recognize the roles they play and the interactions they should expect with other roles. The purpose of the coordination strategy construct is to provide a formal description of the interactions among roles. The strategy construct binds roles together, ensuring that the inputs to one role are provided as outputs from another. The strategy is also the vehicle through which the agent evaluates its situation and decides which roles to play in coordination. The representation of roles and a description of each of these roles in terms of that representation are presented in the next section, after the description of specific coordination strategies.

Examples of four common coordination mechanisms, Arbitration, Self Modification, Voting, and Negotiation, have been formulated as coordination strategies [5]. Figure 2 provides an example dataflow diagram describing the Negotiation strategy. Included in the diagram are cardinality values describing the number of agents that may play each role, where n is the total number of agents in the organization.

In this case, decision-making power is spread among the agents. Agents assume roles based on the constraints placed upon the agents by the organizational structure. Agents with responsibility to plan for the goal may assume the Solution Generator and Solution Acceptability Tester roles. Agents with responsibility to execute the solution may take on the Solution Implementer role. One

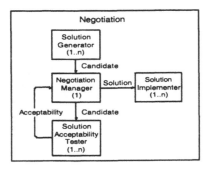

Fig. 2. Data Flow among the roles that compose Negotiation

of the agents will assume the role of Negotiation Manager, whose job is to route the candidate solutions among the agents and to keep track of which proposals are acceptable to which agents.

In order for the agents to control their respective roles, each agent needs to contain the following information, stored in the coordination strategy construct [5]:

1. Role Output/Input Event Mapping: The strategy must be able to receive events and route the information to the appropriate roles. To do this it must maintain a mapping, showing which output events correspond to which input events.
2. Role Interaction Mapping: The agent must decide which roles to play in the given interaction. Decisions on which role to play may sometimes require agreements from other agents. Some examples of these may include a default starting role or usage of trigger events for controlling the addition of new roles and the deletion of old roles.

Agents may concurrently play more than one role in a given coordination strategy. In many cases the input and output mapping of roles may pass information among roles being played by a single agent. Even in these cases, the roles still provide a conceptual division of the computational tasks that need to occur in each coordination strategy.

3.3   Role Construct

Roles encapsulate of the behaviors of each agent, simplifying the dependencies among agents. Using roles, agents do not require intimate knowledge of the internal workings of external agents, operating at a more abstract level. An example task flow for the role of Negotiation Manager is shown in Figure 3. This is presented in a format similar to state transition diagrams, but where each state corresponds to some reasoning or computational process as specified by the role description. The Negotiation Manager role controls the data flowing through the negotiation process, receiving and forwarding nominations, and receiving acceptance for each nomination. Once there is a single candidate solution that is

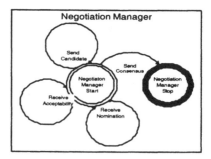

Fig. 3. Task Flow for the Negotiation Manager Role

acceptable to all agents, the Negotiation Manager announces the results to the agents responsible for executing the solution.

The purpose of a role is to define the actions that the agent is responsible for when interacting with other agents. These actions are defined by the input and output events. Because the role deals with generic events, the role interactions are independent from the implemented language or transport. The coordination process among agents is decomposed into roles, providing a blueprint for each agent to follow. Each role handles a section of the complete coordination protocol. The task flow is formulated as a state chart to represent the local view of the protocol with which the agents coordinate. As described in [5], the representation of roles includes:

1. Interface Specifications: The interface is the set of input and output events that the agent should recognize while playing this role. The output events correspond to actions that the agent may execute to change the state of the world (including speech acts). Input events correspond to sensor inputs, including speech acts or other detectable changes of world state. These interface specifications provide a syntax that the agent must follow to play out this role.
2. Reasoning Process Specifications: The interface specifies only the externally detectable events that occur among agents. The specifications for the internal processes, or computational units, the agent executes must also be defined in order to preserve the semantics of the role. Each step of the reasoning process is represented as a task or function the agent must execute.
3. Internal Agent Event Specification: When playing a role, events may be generated to deal with situations of importance internal to the agent. These events inform the agent of important situations, and are important for the interactions between the roles a single agent plays.
4. Task Flow: The order in which the reasoning processes are executed as well as the trigger events that starts and ends such reasoning processes must be defined. The task flow also defines when the internal events are triggered.

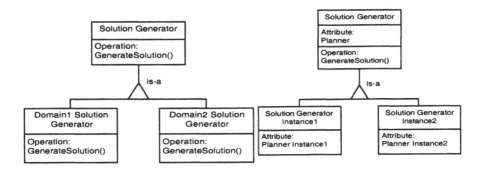

Fig. 4. Domain dependent derived classes and instances aid the transfer of coordination strategies across domains

The Task Flow provides direction for the role, leading the behavior of the agent to the goals associated with this role.

Using inheritance, it is possible to transfer and reuse coordination strategies across domains. As shown in Figure 4, by deriving Solution Generators classes (as well as other roles that require domain specific computation) for each domain, coordination strategies that make use of the Solution Generator role can be equipped to handle problems in that domain. In cases where a number of planners with similar attributes are available, a single Solution Generator class can be implemented to use an abstract planner, an instance of which can be supplied at runtime. These mechanisms allow the agent to reuse the coordination strategy definition to solve various problems in different domains.

4   Strategy Selection

For flexibility in the system, the agents must not only use multiple strategies, but have the ability to select the most appropriate strategy for each situation. Strategy selection can be thought of as polymorphism of coordination mechanisms. In object oriented programming, polymorphism provides for the execution of different methods as selected through some form of table lookup based on the type of object that is invoked. Strategy selection provides for the execution of different strategies based on reasoning processes more complex than a simple table lookup. Instead, it is based on an evaluation of the situation the agents face. The abstract representation of coordination strategies presented above is helpful not only in modeling, but is also operational, allowing for selection online, during runtime. The representation of coordination strategies allows us to treat all strategies in an abstract manner, giving the agents this ability to change strategies and incorporate new strategies as they are developed. Strategic decision-making [15] helps to select the appropriate strategy. Whether performed on-line or off-line by the MAS designer, decisions must be made with regard to which strategies are most appropriate for the given problem [4]. The selected strategy serves as a long-term guideline to assist selecting feasible and appropriate actions to take. Through executing actions, agents can provide the solutions to the problems that triggered the decision-making process. For MAS strategic decision-making, the characteristics to be considered include both domain dependent and independent characteristics [5]:

1. Requirement imposed by the strategy: Strategies may make use of different portions of an agent's abilities. Strategies may or may not require inter-agent communication. Strategies may also place constraints on the member agent's reasoning capabilities.
2. Cost of strategy execution: Execution of each strategy consumes a portion of the agent's resources. For example, some strategies may require a larger number of messages or a longer time. It is important to consider this factor when dealing with deadlines or limited agent resources.
3. Solution quality: Usage of different strategies may produce solutions of differing quality. Longer deliberation may produce a better solution. The agents

may have time to perform trade-off reasoning concerning the expected quality of the solution and the cost of strategy execution.

4. Domain requirements: Strategies may or may not be able to satisfy requirements imposed by the application domain itself, which may overlap the above characteristics.

Multiple approaches are applicable to the manner in which agents consider the above characteristics and select the most appropriate strategy. The difficulty is managing the trade-offs between multiple objectives [27,29]. Roughly, trade-off reasoning can be classified into the following two categories: (1) utility-based dynamic decision-making (or multiple attribute utility theory) [25], and (2) ranking relations (heuristic priority rules) [22]. A ranking problem will result in an objective solution only if all the separate criteria considered each yield the same ranking. Therefore, it is different from classic optimization problems (which search for some kind of hidden truth or objective best solution). Such trade-off reasoning usually results in comp romised solutions, which are highly dependent on the circumstances, methods, and preferences of decision-makers.

4.1   Strategy Characteristics Analysis

A quick description of some of the salient characteristics of strategies is provided in Table 1. Each coordination strategy will use some of the capabilities of the agent, thus the strategies that can be used by an agent are constrained by those capabilities. For example, coordination strategies may impose different computational loads on the various member agents. In dynamic environments, not all of the agent's resources will be available. If an agent's computational resources are overloaded for use in solving some other problems, it will be preferable or even necessary to enter a coordination strategy where it can assume less computational responsibility. Negotiation requires that agents can communicate with each other and have enough planning capability for searching and evaluating solutions. Voting requires that agents can communicate and will respect the majority opinion. Arbitration needs a knowledgeable and powerful arbitrator who can search, evaluate, and decide on solutions for other agents.

Table 1. Comparison of Coordination Strategies Characteristics

	Constraint	Cost	Quality
Negotiation	-Communication is required. -All agents have the authority to make decisions.	-As the number of involved agents increases, the complexity increases at $O(n^2)$.	-Not guaranteed to reach a solution. -May result in higher quality solutions -Cost maybe high.
Arbitration	-Communication is required. -An arbitrator agent is required. -All agents must obey the decisions of the arbitrator.	-As the number of involved agents increases, the complexity increases at $O(n)$.	-Guaranteed to reach a solution. -May result in low quality solutions
Voting	-Communication is required. -Agents have the right to vote. -All agents must obey the results of voting.	-As the number of involved agents increases, the complexity increases at $O(n)$	-Not guaranteed to reach a solution. -May result in low quality solutions
Self-modification	-All agents have the authority to make decisions.	-Constant $O(1)$	-Not guaranteed to reach a solution. -May result in low quality solutions -Cost maybe high.

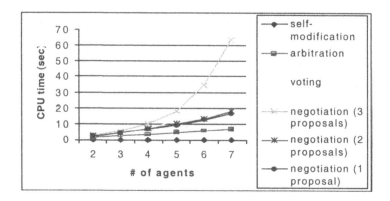

Fig. 5. A comparison of the CPU time required by different strategies

The first cost characteristic we consider is the number of (inter-role) messages, which refers to each output/input event binding, required for each strategy. If each message requires the same amount of time to deliver and process, then more messages implies that the strategy needs more time to execute. In the best case where the first proposal is accepted, Negotiation starts with a lower message requirement than Voting. If there is more than one proposal, the number of messages Negotiation requires increases to be more than required by any other strategy. Self-modification always requires the least number of messages: one. Self-modification is just a special case of Arbitration where a single agent plays both the Solution Generator and Solution Implementer roles. Because the same agent plays both roles, this strategy does not require inter-agent communication. For arbitration, the number of messages is linear to the number of agents. Interested readers can fined more details in [5].

The second cost characteristic we consider is the required time. Figure 5 shows the CPU time consumption for each strategy. The CPU time shown in the figure is the accumulated CPU time that the agent requires to execute the strategies, excluding the time used to deliver the messages. We can observe that the curves associated with negotiations involving one and two proposals are close to the curve of voting. The reason is that they require similar amounts of messages passing; voting needs to propose candidates, announce the candidates, vote, and announce the results, while negotiation needs to propose, reply, counter-propose, and agree. Negotiation with three proposals grows very fast, especially when four or more agents are involved. The explanation is the number of messages increase as $O(n^2)$, where n is the number of agents. Therefore the time to process messages grows abruptly.

Another cost to be considered is the time taken for each individual decision to be made. This includes both search and evaluation of solutions. For this analysis, we simplify the functions to constant values S and D respectively, but in general these values will be dependent on the situation. Using these two constants, we can analyze the strategies in the following way: for voting, it includes nS (when agents search for candidates to vote) and nD (when agents vote for candidates),

Table 2. Decision Making Costs for each Coordination Strategy

	Time required by decision making and searching
Arbitration	$1 \times D + 1 \times S$ (or $1 \times D + n \times S$, if every agents searches for solutions)
Negotiation	$p \times (n \times D + 1 \times S)$
Mediation	$p \times ((n-1) \times D + 1 \times S)$
Voting	$n \times D + n \times S$
Self-Modification	$1 \times D + 1 \times S$

where n is the number of agents. For mediation, for each proposal from the mediator, there is $1S$ (when the mediator searches for search for solutions) and nD (when agents decide whether or not to accept the proposal), where n is the number of agents not including the mediator. For arbitration, there is $1S$ (if only the arbitrator searches for solutions, or possible nS, if every agent searches for solutions) and $1D$ (the arbitrator makes the decision). For self-modification, there is only $1S$ and $1D$, that is the agent executing the strategy needs to search the solutions and to make the decision. For negotiation, each proposal involves with $1S$ (the agent that proposes) and nD (every agent needs to evaluate the proposal). The values of D and S could be provided by functions with proper domain knowledge. Therefore, the agents still follow the same strategic decision making algorithms as long as proper domain dependent functions and values are provided. Table 2 summarizes the formulas, where n is the number of agents and p is the number of proposals.

Now that cost related concerns have been addressed, the next step is to analyze the solution quality. Solution quality is highly dependent upon the actual (possibly domain dependent) decision-making capabilities possessed by each agent. If all agents possess the same capabilities, then the quality of the solution candidates produced by each agent is dependent only on their respective knowledge bases. If the agents are heterogeneous, then the quality of solution candidates may vary widely across the agents. One possible measure of quality is the number of agents whose input can impact the final solution. The assumption behind this measure is that a solution is deemed "better" if a larger percentage of the involved agents are required by the strategy to approve the solution. Negotiation will not terminate until all involved agents have approved the final solution. Voting requires only a majority, greater than 50%, of the agents to

$$Cost^i_{\text{Strategy } k} = \sum_j w_j \times Cost_{\text{Strategy } k}(y_j)$$

where y_j is attribute j under consideration, $j = 1$ to m,
w_j is the weight function for characteristic j,
$Cost_{\text{Strategy } k}(y_j)$ is the cost value of strategy k for characteristic j.

Equation 1. Cost of applying coordination strategies to reach a decision

approve the final solution. The minority has given their commitment to abide by the communal decision, but may have to sacrifice their local priorities for the communal good. Arbitration requires only a single agent to approve the final solution. As the number of involved agents increases, the percentage involved in the approval process decreases. This quality measure does not capture all the possible concerns about solution quality. It only serves as an illustrative example of the type of analysis that can be performed in terms of quality. In practice, solutions may range from unacceptable, to acceptable, to very favorable to each agent. Other metrics may be generated that incorporate these features.

4.2   Selection Mechanism

Agents may use utility to evaluate both potential solutions and coordination strategies (e.g. negotiation, voting, arbitration, and self-modification). In order to select an appropriate strategy, the agent must conduct some trade-off reasoning between among the strategies. Equation 1 shows how an agent can estimate the cost of applying strategies based on the characteristics described in section 4.1. The following data was recorded using coordination strategies to resolve conflicts [18].

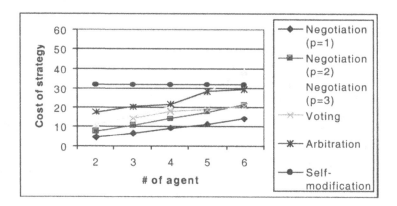

Fig. 6. Total estimated cost for each strategy compared to the # of agents

Figure 6 shows the total cost for strategies where agents are in a consensus organization (i.e. all agents wield equal amounts of decision making power). The control variables are the number of agents and conditions under which the agents operate. The dependent variables are the cost of the coordination strategies. Since negotiation and voting can be applied within consensus, these two strategies are promoted (i.e. they have lower cost values because they do not require the overhead of changing organizational structures). As the number of agents increases, the cost of negotiation increases rapidly such that voting and arbitration becomes cheaper for six agents and more than three proposals, even though the cost of arbitration includes the cost to modify the organizational structure from consensus to master-command driven (i.e. a hierarchical organization structure).

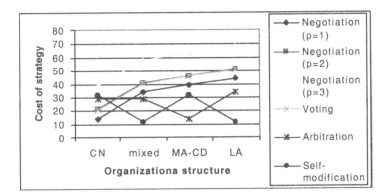

Fig. 7. Total estimated cost for each strategy compared with their starting organization structure

Figure 7 shows that the cost of coordination strategies for six agents in different organizational structures, consensus (CN), master/command driven (MA-CD), locally autonomous (LA), and a mixture of the above. Due to the constraints imposed by each strategy, the cost of modifying the organizational structure must also be considered. Including this cost recommends different strategies for different conditions.

5 Conclusion

This paper presents current progress to equip agents with the ability to operate using a variety of coordination mechanisms and problem solving techniques. A representation of coordination strategies described in this paper has been implemented, providing a uniform platform to assist agents in evaluating alternative strategies with the objective of letting agents dynamically select strategies to increase flexibility under dynamically organized MAS. There are generally three participants in this design pattern: the strategy base class, concrete strategy classes, and the context class.

The design of the coordination strategy representation using the concepts of encapsulation and polymorphism lends itself to operation in multiple domains. Whereas the representation is domain-independent, coordination strategies can easily be applied towards new domains through the replacement of domain specific computational units as roles.

The representation also allows a comparison of techniques using a constant framework as well as the incorporation of newly developed techniques to be added at later time. Experimental and analytical data on a number of characteristics differentiate the coordination strategies. Each strategy can be classified as "best" only in the context of the situation. Quantitatively comparing constraint, cost, and quality characteristics of strategies allows the agent to select appropriate strategies and change strategies when situations change, improving the overall performance.

Acknowledgements. This research is sponsored in part by the Texas Higher Education Coordinating Board # 003658-0188-1999.

References

[1] Adler, M. R., Davis, A. B., Weihmayer, R., and Worrest, R. W. Conflict-Resolution Strategies for Nonhierarchical Distributed Agents. In Distributed Artificial Intelligence II, Gasser, L. and Huhns, M. N., (eds.). Pitman Publishing, London, (1989) 139-161.
[2] Barber, K. S.: The Architecture for Sensible Agents. In Proceedings of International Multidisciplinary Conference, Intelligent Systems: A Semiotic Perspective (Gaithersburg, MD, 1996) National Institute of Standards and Technology, 49-54.
[3] Barber, K. S., Goel, A., and Martin, C. E. The Motivation for Dynamic Adaptive Autonomy in Agent-based Systems. In Proceedings of the 1st Asia-Pacific Conference on IAT, Hong Kong, December 14-17, 1999., Liu, J. and Zhong, N., (eds.). 131-140.
[4] Barber, K. S., Liu, T. H., and Han, D. C. Agent-Oriented Design. In Multi-Agent System Engineering. Lecture Notes in Artificial Intelligence, Garijo, F. J. and Boman, M., (eds.). Springer, Berlin, (1999) 28-40.
[5] Barber, K. S., Liu, T. H., and Han, D. C.: Strategy Selection-based Meta-level Reasoning, accepted to Agent Oriented Software Engineering 2000, Limerick, England, 2000,.
[6] Barber, K. S. and Martin, C. E. Agent Autonomy: Specification, Measurement, and Dynamic Adjustment, Technical Report. TR99-UT-LIPS-AGENTS-09, The University of Texas at Austin, Austin, TX, 1999.
[7] Booch, G. Object Oriented Design with Applications. Benjamin Cummings, Redwood City, CA, 1991.
[8] Chang, C., Chung, M. J., and Lee, B. H.: Collision Avoidance of Two General Robot Manipulators by Minimum Delay Time. IEEE Transactions on SMC, (1994) 517-522.
[9] Conry, S. E., Meyer, R. A., and Lesser, V. R. Multistage Negotiation in Distributed Planning. In Readings in Distributed Artificial Intelligence, Bond, A. H. and Gasser, L., (eds.). Morgan Kaufmann Publishers Inc., San Mateo, CA, (1988) 367-384.
[10] Ephrati, E. and Rosenschein, J. S.: The Clarke Tax as a Consensus Mechanism Among Automated Agents. In Proceedings of the Ninth Conference on Artificial Intelligence (Anaheim, CA. 1991) 173-178.
[11] Ephrati, E. and Rosenschein, J. S.: Multi-Agents Planning as a Dynamic Search for Social Consensus. In Proceedings of the 13th International Joint Conference on Artificial Intelligence (1993) 423-429.
[12] Gamma, E., Helm, R., Johnson, R., and Vlisside, J. Design Patterns: Elements of Reusable Object-Oriented Software. Addison-Wesley, Reading, Massachusetts, 1995.

[13] Gasser, L. and Ishida, T.: A Dynamic Organizational Architecture for Adaptive Problem Solving. In Proceedings of Ninth National Conference on Artificial Intelligence, (Anaheim, CA, 1991) 185-190.

[14] Glaser, N. and Morignot, P. The Reorganization of Societies of Autonomous Agents. In Multi-agent Rationality. Lecture notes in artificial intelligence, Boman, M. and van de Velde, W., (eds.). Springer-Verlag, Berlin, (1997) 98-111.

[15] Grant, R. M. Contemporary Strategy Analysis. Blackwell Publishers Inc, Oxford, UK, 1995.

[16] Ioannidis, Y. E. and Sellis, T. K.: Conflict Resolution of Rules Assigning Values to Virtual Attributes. In Proceedings of the 1989 ACM International Conference on the Managment of Data (Portland, Oregon., 1989) 205-214.

[17] Jennings, N. R. Coordination Techniques for Distributed Artificial Intelligence. In Foundations of Distributed Artificial Intelligence. Sixth-Generation Computer Technology Series, O'Hare, G. M. P. and Jennings, N. R., (eds.). John Wiley & Sons, Inc., New York, (1996) 187-210.

[18] Liu, T. H. Domain Independent Conflict Resolution for Dynamically Organized Multi-Agent Systems. PhD Dissertation, Electrical and Computer Engineering, The University of Texas at Austin, 2000.

[19] Myerson, R. B. Game Theory : Analysis of Conflict. Harvard University Press, Cambridge Massachusetts, 1991.

[20] Ricciardi, A. M. and Birman, K. P. Process Membership in Asynchronous Environments. TR93-1328, Cornell University, 1995.

[21] Rosenschein, J. S. and Zlotkin, G. Rules of Encounter: Designing Conventions for Automated Negotiation Among Computers. The MIT Press, Cambridge, Massachusetts, 1994.

[22] Roy, B. From Optimization to Multicriteria Decision Aid: Three Main Operational Attitudes. In Multiple Criteria Decision Making, Thiriez, H. and Zionts, S.(eds.). Springer-Verlag(1976) 1-32.

[23] Steeb, R., Cammarata, S., Hayes-Roth, F. A., Thorndyke, P. W., and Wesson, R. B. Architectures for Distributed Intelligence for Air Fleet Control. Technical Report R-2728-ARPA, Rand Corp., Santa Monica CA, 1981.

[24] Steels, L. Cooperation Between Distributed Agents through Self-organization. In Decentralized A.I. Demazeau, Y. and Müller, J.-P., (eds.). Elsevier Science, Amsterdam, (1990) 175-196.

[25] Sycara, K. P.: Utility Theory In Conflict Resolution. Annals of Operation Research, 12 (1988) 65-84.

[26] Sycara, K. P. Multiagent Compromise via Negotiation. In Distributed Artificial Intelligence II, Gasser, L. and Huhns, M. N., (eds.). Pitman Publishing, London, (1989) 119-137.

[27] Vincke, P., Gassner, M., and Roy, B. Multicriteria Decision-aid. John Wiley & Sons., Chichester, 1989.

[28] Wooldridge, M. J., Jennings, N. R., and Kinny, D.: A Methodology for Agent-Oriented Analysis and Design. In Proceedings of Third International Conference on Autonomous Agents (Seattle, WA, 1999) ACM Press, 69 - 83.

[29] Yu, P. L. Multiple-Criteria Decison Making: Concepts, Techniques, and Extensions. Plenum Press, New York, NY, 1985.

Dynamic Properties of Multiagents Based on a Mechanism of Loose Coalition

Takashi Katoh, Tetsuo Kinoshita, and Norio Shiratori

Research Institute of Electrical Communication, Tohoku University, Sendai, Japan
{p-katoh,kino,norio}@shiratori.riec.tohoku.ac.jp

Abstract. In this paper, we propose a method of coalition formation for assigning tasks to appropriate agents to improve the efficiency of multiagent systems. To form a coalition, we introduce *subjective information* to agents, which are the internal information of the agents. The subjective information reflect the agents' cooperative behavior of the past. Next, we introduce *loose coalition*, a concept of a coalition of agents based on the subjective information. Using the agents' sense of values defined by their subjective information, each agent can give priority to the loose coalitions to ask for the working status or to assign tasks. Thus loose coalitions with higher priority will be better cooperating candidates. Furthermore, loose coalitions enable agents to collect information (e.g. busyness of loose coalitions) for task assignment efficiently. Therefore, the agents on the system can decide its behavior properly, depending on the current status of the system, and thus the efficiency of the system can be improved. Then, we observe dynamic properties of system under several settings of agents to derive a guideline for designing effective multiagent systems based on loose coalitions.

1 Introduction

To realize an effective distributed system existing large amount of agents, it is needed to compose organizations consisting of several agents and to cooperate with each other. Therefore agents are required to know other agents' trait or current status via inter-agent communication and assign tasks based on the information.

In this paper, we propose *subjective information* and a concept of *loose coalition*. Each agent determines its behavior based on its subjective information, which are internal information of agents to be used as criteria of decision making. And the loose coalition, which represents relations between an agent and the neighboring agents, is defined based on the basis of subjective information. This relationship may change from time to time and by exchanging information about a loose coalition, an agent can know a situation of the peer's surroundings. Therefore, an agent can grasp information from a wider range by communicating only with a specific peer agent.

There are several works regarding cooperation among agents, e.g. Contract Net Protocol [1] and Multistage Negotiation Protocol [2]. They try to decide a

C. Zhang and V.-W. Soo (Eds.): PRIMA 2000, LNAI 1881, pp. 16–30, 2000.

role of an agent to do some fixed tasks (goals). These methods can be regarded as a way to compose organizations consisting of several agents. However, the amount of communication required for composing organizations or cooperated problem solving will increase if the number of agents on the system increases. As a result, the efficiency of the system may be degraded. On this account, the contract net protocol may cause much traffic because the agent issues its task announcements by broadcasting to all agents and has no way to select the most suitable agent based on its own sense of values.

There are several works on formation of coalitions [3,4]. These works try to improve the efficiency by grouping all agents on the system into several groups and allocating each task to each group. But this method divides the whole system into the number of tasks and processes each task in each group when several tasks exist. It is efficient when it is enough just to process only those tasks. However, it may not work well with a real multiagent system if tasks occur irregularly. Also the overloads of this method may become too large because this method is needed to form coalitions whenever it is given new tasks to the system. Therefore, this is not always a suitable method in a real multiagent system.

On the other hand, methods of the agents' dynamic organization formation based on the concept social awareness [5,6] or other task allocation methods [7,8] are being suggested in recent years. In these methods, the benefit is introduced explicitly and agents decide their behavior based on it. In case of agents which process actual tasks, however, it is difficult to apply this idea to the system because the time needed to perform the task, in general, is not known a priori.

We propose a new mechanism for organizing agents based on subjective information. Our main interests are to study (1) a method to utilize the subjective information as information of agents to make an organization, (2) how the loose coalitions are formed and affected the efficiency of the system, and (3) how to utilize loose coalitions to improve the behavior of the system, that is the configuration of the loose coalitions.

The rest of the paper is organized as follows. We define the subjective information of agents and model of agents' behavior in Sect. 2. Section 3 describes the proposed coalition formation based on subjective information and the behavior of coalitions. We show experimental results in Sect. 4, and conclude our work in Sect. 5.

2   Agent Model Based on Subjective Information

2.1   Subjective Information

In multiagent systems, behavior of a whole system may be determined based on its own states in the environment. Agents are required to behave flexibly not only to realize a desirable behavior of a multiagent system as a whole but also to work effectively. Thus each agent should have criteria of the decision making and determine its behavior based on the criteria.

In this section, we introduce *subjective information* as criteria of decision making. Each agent possesses, for example, the opponents' reliabilities based on the results of the previous negotiations.

Definition 1. Subjective information *is information maintained by an agent i internally and is used when an agent deals with subject S, which is a matter that an agent deals with (e.g. problems, concerning agents). Subjective information is defined as follows, i.e.,*

$$\langle S, \text{attribute}, \text{val} \rangle_i \ ,$$

where attribute is an identifier to specify a subjective information and val is its value.   □

In this paper, we discuss the behavior of agents which cooperatively distribute tasks.

An example of both the subjects and the attributes of subjective information is shown in Table 1.

Table 1. Example of subjects and attributes of subjective information

Subjects	Attributes of Subjective Information
agent	Reliability
	Busyness
	Satisfaction
	Ability
task	Priority
	Importance

For example, a subjective information $\langle \text{agent } B, Reliability, 10 \rangle_A$ means "agent A has a subjective information regarding *Reliability* of agent B and its current value is 10."

In addition, a content of agent i's subjective information concerning subject S can be referred as follows, i.e.,

$$\text{attribute}_i(S) = \text{val} \ .$$

[*Examples of definition of Busyness and Satisfaction*] A subjective information $Busyness_j(i)$, which represents the working status of an agent, is defined as follows:

$$Busyness_j(i) = \frac{n_t}{n_{\max}} \ , \tag{1}$$

where n_t is the number of current tasks and $n_{\max}$ is the maximum number of tasks that agent i can proceed at a time. In particular, for an agent which can process only one task at a time,

$$Busyness_i(i) = \begin{cases} 1 & \text{(if it is processing task)} \\ 0 & \text{(otherwise)} \end{cases}$$

Satisfaction of agent i is defined as follows:

$$Satisfaction_j(i) = \frac{\sum_{k=1}^n a_i(k)}{n} , \qquad (2)$$

where $a_i(k)$ is an accomplishment rate of the k-th task requested to agent i, and n is the number of requests issued to agent i. This subjective information represents agent i's actual ability to perform tasks.   □

2.2 Behavior of Agents Based on Subjective Information

(1) Behavior Model of Agent. Agents communicate with each other via interagent communication to allocate tasks. An agent with subjective information, in general, behaves as follows: (i) Interprets the received messages, (ii) Updates its subjective information, (iii) Selects the next action based on both the received messages and its own subjective information, (iv) Executes the selected action. Here, an action is defined as the domain specific behavior, e.g. "search for specified information" in the case of information retrieval agents.

Next, we discuss the details of (ii) and (iii), which are the important parts of our model.

(2) Updating Subjective Information. Each agent updates its subjective information based on the received messages.

Assume that agent j asks for processing a task to agent i. The behavior is defined as:

$$Reliability_j(i) \leftarrow \begin{cases} Reliability_j(i) + \alpha & \text{if ACCEPTed} \\ Reliability_j(i) - \beta & \text{if REFUSEd} \end{cases} , \qquad (3)$$

where α and β are terms defined with respect to the agents. An agent j increases its $Reliability_j(i)$ to agent i when the result is an ACCEPT and decreases its $Reliability_j(i)$ when the result is a REFUSE. This implies that the subjective information of agents reflect the agent's behavioral history.

The $Reliability_j(i)$ can be utilized as a criterion to select the most relevant opponent to send a request because a rate of returning an ACCEPT decreases when an agent become busy and the $Reliability_j(i)$ will also be gradually decreased. By changing agents' own subjective information depending on the results of repetitive communication, the agents can know the opponents' current status or situation of a group of agents.

(3) Decision Making of Agent. It is desirable that an agent selects the best opponent based on its experiences (e.g. previous results of requests) when the agent assigns tasks. This can be realized by using subjective information in the following way.

To send a request of a task t, an agent j selects another agent which maximizes a function of subjective information

$$f_i^{(j)}(\{m_j(i)\}) \ ,$$

where $m_j(i)$ is agent j's subjective information m to agent i, and $\{m_j(i)\}$ is a set of agent j's subjective information to agent i. This is agent j's evaluation function of agent i, and this function is defined with respect to the agents (j) as follows.

[*Example of definition of $f_i^{(j)}$*] When $Reliability_j(i)$ is used as basis to determine an agent to be issued a request, the agent which issues a request selects the agent whose $Reliability_j(i)$ is the highest, i.e. $f_i^{(j)}$ is defined by

$$f_i^{(j)} : \{m_j(i)\} \mapsto Reliability_j(i) \ , \tag{4}$$

and an agent i which maximizes $f_i^{(j)}(\{m_j(i)\})$, thus which satisfies

$$\max_i \{Reliability_j(i)\} \tag{5}$$

will be selected.

Furthermore if an agent j has a subjective information $Ability$, which represents the performable tasks of the agent, the candidates to send a request can previously be reduced only to a set of agents which satisfies[1] $t \in Ability_j(i)$. Using this information, an agent also satisfying condition (5) will be selected.

If an agent has a subjective information $Satisfaction$ (2) too, the agent can select an opponent appropriately by adding a condition of candidates:

$$f_i^{(j)} : \{m_j(i)\} \mapsto k_{rel}Reliability_j(i) + k_{sat}Satisfaction_j(i) \ ,$$

where k_{rel} and k_{sat} are constants defined with respect to the agents. As a result, the agent can cooperate with other suitable agents depending on their situations.

□

3   Loose Coalition for Multiagent Systems

3.1   Definition of Loose Coalition

In this section, we propose a concept of a group of agents, called *loose coalition*, to define a method for obtaining information of a multiagent system and selecting suitable agents to cooperate with. A loose coalition represents the relations of cooperation among agents. By exchanging information of a loose coalition, an agent can know a situation of the peer's surroundings.

---

[1]   This is equivalent to adding $\alpha = \begin{cases} 0 & (t \in Ability_j(i)) \\ -\infty & (\text{otherwise}) \end{cases}$ to the right side of (4).

Definition 2. Loose coalition *of an agent i is a set of agents C_i that satisfy the following condition:*

$$C_i = \{j \mid F(\{m_i(j)\}) > \theta\} \ ,$$

where $\{m_i(j)\}$ is a set of agent i's subjective information to agent j, F is a function of subjective information and θ is a threshold of $F(\{m_i(j)\})$. A function F and threshold θ is defined with respect to the agents. □

F is a function to evaluate agent whether it should cooperate or not. Loose coalitions help each agent to determine the appropriate partners to cooperate with.

Next, we define information about a loose coalition $M(C_i)$ to be exchanged between an agent and a loose coalition.

Definition 3. Information of a loose coalition $M(C_i)$ *is defined by:*

$$M(C_i) = \begin{cases} \dfrac{1}{|C_i|} \displaystyle\sum_{j \in C_i} m_i(j) & \text{(if } m_i(j) \text{ takes numerical value)} \\[2ex] \displaystyle\bigcup_{j \in C_i} m_i(j) & \text{(if } m_i(j) \text{ takes non-numerical value)} \end{cases} ,$$

where $|C_i|$ is the number of members of loose coalition C_i. □

For example, the busyness of loose coalition C_i, $C\_Busyness(C_i)$, can be calculated using (1):

$$C\_Busyness(C_i) = \frac{1}{|C_i|} \sum_{j \in C_i} Busyness_i(j) \ .$$

$C\_Ability(C_i)$, which represents C_i's ability of performing tasks, is union of $Ability_i(j)$ of the members of C_i:

$$C\_Ability(C_i) = \bigcup_{j \in C_i} Ability_i(j) \ .$$

3.2 Behavior of Multiagent Systems Based on Loose Coalition

We explain a method that agents form loose coalitions, gather the system's information based on the loose coalitions of other agents and assign tasks using the information of its loose coalition.

(1) Formation of Loose Coalition. According to the above definitions, loose coalitions are formed in the following manner. As described in Sect. 2.2, the agents communicate with each other and update their subjective information based on the results of communication. For example, to form loose coalitions

based on the $Reliability_i(j)$ described in Sect. 2.2, we just modify the condition
part of Definition 2 $(F(\{m_i(j)\}) > \theta)$ as follows, i.e.,

$$Reliability_i(j) > \theta \ .$$

If a $Reliability_i(j)$ is changed in the same manner described in Sect. 2.2, the loose
coalition can also be changed dynamically because a value of $Reliability_i(j)$ may
increase or decrease due to the repetitive negotiations among agents.

(2) Gathering the System's Information. It is possible to get information of unknown (new) agents based on information of loose coalitions. As the example
shown in Fig. 1, agent E may be an unknown agent for agent A. By communicating with members of its loose coalition (agent B, C), agent A can get
information of loose coalitions which these agents (B, C) belong to (C_B, C_C).

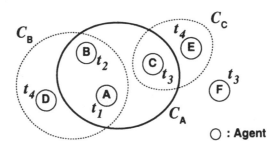

Fig. 1. Example of loose coalition

Here agent A receives information of not all agents but only the agents which
have close relationship with agent B or C, that is the agents which might be
also useful for agent A.

On account of this, the view of agent A will spread by agent communication,
and as a result, it can form a new loose coalition of wider range.

(3) Task Assignment. Next, we discuss a method of task assignment using information of loose coalitions.

When some agent selects the most suitable loose coalition to issue a task
request, the agent selects a loose coalition which maximizes a function of information of loose coalition:

$$g(\{M(C_i)\}) \ .$$

[Example of definition of g] When $C\_Busyness(C_i)$ is used as basis to determine
a loose coalition to be issued a request, the agent selects the loose coalition whose
$C\_Busyness(C_i)$ is the lowest, i.e. a loose coalition C_i which maximizes

$$g(\{M(C_i)\}) \equiv 1 - C\_Busyness(C_i) \ .$$

Furthermore if an agent utilizes ability of loose coalitions, define g as

$$g(\{M(C_i)\}) \equiv P_{C_i} \times (1 - C\_Busyness(C_i)) \ , \tag{6}$$

where P_{C_i} is a rate of performable subtasks and is calculated using $C\_Ability(C_i)$.

$\square$

[*Example of utilizing g*] Here, we assume the same situation shown in Fig. 1. Now, if we take a close look at agent A, a loose coalition of agent A is C_A, and its members are agent A, B and C:

$$C_A = \{A, B, C\} \ .$$

Agent A can get information of other loose coalitions $C\_Busyness(C_B)$, $C\_Ability(C_B)$, $C\_Busyness(C_C)$, $C\_Ability(C_C)$ from other members of C_A, i.e. Agent B, C. Agent A now can calculate the value of $g(\{M(C_i)\})$ (e.g. (6)) and select the most suitable loose coalition to issue a request.

4   Experiment on Dynamics of Multiagent System Based on Loose Coalition

In this section, we demonstrate the experimental results and discuss the dynamics of the multiagent system based on loose coalition.

In our previous work [9], we showed the efficiency of system based on loose coalition. Hence, the aim of experiment in this paper is to study the effect of the settings of agents' behavior etc. to forming of loose coalitions.

The agents of our experimental multiagent system have been implemented using Perl and executed on AT compatible computers of FreeBSD 2.2.8R and Sun Ultra SparcStations of Solaris 2.5.1.

4.1   Properties and Functions of Agents

In our experiment, a multiagent system consists of task agents and user agents as shown in Fig. 2. A user provides a task T to this system via a user agent. Task agent divides a task received from user agent into subtasks and processes the subtasks if the agent can perform the subtask by itself, otherwise tries to assign other agents. User agent assigns task received from user to this multiagent system.

The behavior of each agent is described below.

(1) User Agent. A user agent receives a task from a task from a user. The duty of a user agent is to select a task agent which has the highest *Reliability* value and to forward the task to the selected task agent.

(2) Task Agent. The experiments were executed under the following eight different settings of task agents.

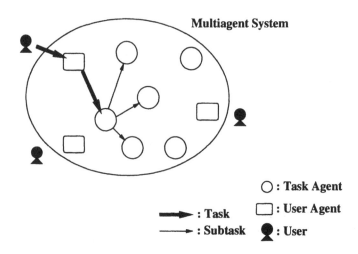

Fig. 2. Configuration of an experimental multiagent systems

(Setting A) Basic Property. (T1) When a task agent receives a request of task T from a user agent, (T1-1) the task agent divides the task into subtasks and distributes the subtasks to other task agents (candidate agents) considering their abilities. An assignment of subtasks ends up with a failure if there exists no candidate agents with required ability of performing the given subtask. (T1-2) The task agent updates its subjective information depending on the reply message as described in Sect. 2.2. Here we define α and β appeared in (3) as follows:

$$\alpha = \beta = 1 \ ,$$

i.e. when the result is an ACCEPT, the agent increases the *Reliability* of the candidate agent by $+1$, and when the result is a REFUSE, it decreases the *Reliability* of the candidate agent by -1. (T1-3) The task agent updates the list of known agents. The default value of *Reliability* to a new agent is 0.

(T2) When a task agent receives a request to perform subtask from another task agent (requester agent), (T2-1) the agent returns an ACCEPT if it is currently free, or returns a REFUSE if it is not free (dealing with another subtask). (T2-2) Along with the reply message (ACCEPT or REFUSE), the agent discloses information about its loose coalition and their abilities to the requester agent.

(Setting B) Reflects the Processing Time of the Tasks. In this setting, we have considered processing time as a parameter of *Reliability*. We define α and β appeared in (3) as $\alpha = (t_m - t)/t_m$ and $\beta = 1$, thus

$$Reliability_j(i) \leftarrow \begin{cases} Reliability_j(i) + \left(1 + \dfrac{t_m - t}{t_m}\right) & \text{if ACCEPTed} \\ Reliability_j(i) - 1 & \text{if REFUSEd} \end{cases} \ ,$$

where t_m is the mean time to process subtasks in the system, i.e. $t_m = 30$ in this experiment, and t is processing time of the subtask. That is, *Reliability* will also be affected by the processing time (*Reliability* will be even bigger if the processing time is less than the mean processing time).

Although the mean time to process subtasks t_m, in general, is not known a priori in real multiagent system, we assume t_m is known to the agents on the system to observe the effect of the modification of the way to update mental states.

(Setting C) Give-and-take. The receiver agent of the subtask gives information about its loose coalition members to the requester agent along with the reply message in setting A. In this setting, the information about members of loose coalition will be also given to the receiver agent by the requester agent when the subtask is ACCEPTed.

(Setting D) Accepts Other Agents' Sense of Values. A new agent (j) can be introduced by an interacting agent (k). *Reliability* to the new agent is 0 in setting A. In this setting, the *Reliability* to the new agent is heuristically set by

$$Reliability_i(j) \leftarrow \frac{Reliability_k(j)}{2} \quad .$$

We have also considered the possible combinations of the above settings.

(Setting B+C) Apply Settings B and C Simultaneously.

(Setting B+D) Apply Settings B and D Simultaneously.

(Setting C+D) Apply Settings C and D Simultaneously.

(Setting B+C+D) Apply Settings B, C and D Simultaneously.

4.2   System Configuration

In our experiment, a multiagent system consists of 30 task agents and four user agents. A user provides a task T to this system via a user agent in every 50 clocks. Each task T is a combination of randomly selected (one or more) subtasks $(t_1, \ldots, t_6)$ and each subtask cannot be subdivided anymore.

There exists five agents which can perform each of the subtasks in the experiment, and the agents take 10, 20, 30, 40 and 50 clocks to process the subtask respectively.

We have set up the following initial conditions: (1) User agents know the existence of all task agents but not their abilities, (2) Task agent knows only two other randomly selected agents and their abilities, (3) There exists no loose coalitions of agents in the initial state.

4.3 Experimental Results

We have carried out experiments three times with different task sequences. The following results show the average figures.

The number of successful tasks, the average success rates, the number of proceeded subtasks and the processing time per subtasks are summarized in Table 2. To evaluate the behavior of the system during formation of loose coalition, we summarized these values for first 500 tasks in Table 3. The transition of average size of loose coalitions (the average number of members of loose coalition) is depicted in Fig. 3.

Table 2. Performance of System in Long Period (for 5000 tasks)

Setting	A	B	C	D
number of successful tasks (for 5000 tasks)	4712.7	4532.3	4762.7	4718.3
average success rates	0.9766	0.9643	0.9737	0.9757
number of proceeded subtasks	17021.3	16826.0	16991.3	17038.0
processing time per subtasks	23.617	22.075	23.280	22.725

Setting	B+C	B+D	C+D	B+C+D
number of successful tasks (for 5000 tasks)	4828.7	4821.0	4759.3	4814.3
average success rates	0.9827	0.9823	0.9737	0.9810
number of proceeded subtasks	17151.0	17144.3	16991.7	17124.7
processing time per subtasks	19.698	20.290	22.103	18.772

Table 3. Performance of System at First Stage (for the First 500 Tasks)

Setting	A	B	C	D
number of successful tasks (for 500 tasks)	312.0	312.3	364.3	343.7
average success rates	0.8103	0.8120	0.8630	0.8300
number of proceeded subtasks	1407.3	1407.0	1500.3	1449.7
processing time per subtasks	25.929	25.378	25.853	25.108

Setting	B+C	B+D	C+D	B+C+D
number of successful tasks (for 500 tasks)	357.0	349.7	368.3	366.7
average success rates	0.8543	0.8597	0.8600	0.8630
number of proceeded subtasks	1482.7	1457.7	1499.3	1498.7
processing time per subtasks	23.893	22.315	24.322	20.536

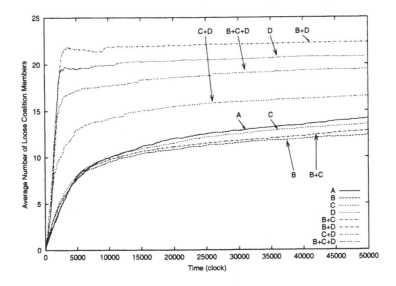

Fig. 3. Transition of average size of loose coalitions

4.4   Evaluation

- Comparing the results of setting A...D in Table 2, the number of successful tasks of setting C is higher than those of other settings. On the contrary, the processing time per subtasks of setting B is shorter than those of other settings. Thus setting C is suitable for the system to process tasks steadily, and setting B will be considered when rapid processing of tasks is more important than the quality of result of the tasks.
- The results of setting B+C...B+C+D in Table 2 shows that the combination of these settings (A...D) increases the performance of the system. Especially, in setting B+C, both of the number of successful tasks and the processing time are comparatively superior. Moreover, in case of setting B+C+D, the processing time is shorter than the other settings. This result indicates that the combination of setting A...D enables agents to make decision based on overall information.
- Comparing the results of setting B+C, C+D and B+C+D, the values of the number of successful tasks make little difference. The values of processing time, however, is the shortest in case of setting B+C+D.

  Furthermore, according to Fig. 3, the average number of loose coalition members of setting B+C+D is the least in these settings (B+C, C+D and B+C+D).

  These results imply that decision based on overall information of agents can increase the performance of system with necessary and sufficient number of loose coalition member.

- Figure 3 shows that members of loose coalition inflate in an early stage (0 ∼ 2500 clock) in case of settings D, B+D, C+D and B+C+D, i.e. settings including D.

  This inflation of loose coalition members can be explained as follows: In case of these settings, newly known agents (informed by other agent) are also added to the members of its loose coalition at the same time. This is because *Reliability* of the newly known agents had been greater than 0 under the condition *Reliability* > 0 to form loose coalition.

  Note that, the information about process time of subtasks is not exchanged among agents.

  Thus the desirable results of these settings in Table 3 (the average success rate) take place not because of inflation of members of loose coalition, but because the agents could know about the agents with higher *Reliability* at early stage.

- Figure 3 also shows that the numbers of loose coalition members do not vary drastically after 15000 clock in all settings. This can be considered that the loose coalitions are almost settled up to this point.

  This result implies that the differences of settings (i.e. exchanged information about agents) have less influence to the system in a (quasi-)steady state.

From these results, we can derive the following guideline for designing efficient multiagent systems based on loose coalition: It is important to propagate information of agents with higher *Reliability* as soon as possible to design efficient multiagent systems based on loose coalition. Moreover, the system works desirably even under the simple settings, e.g. setting A...D, after the sufficient communication among agents. Thus the concept of loose coalition seems effective, especially for the system such that agents on the system varies frequently, and we are planning to do further experiment to verify it.

5   Conclusion

To realize an effective distributed system existing large amount of agents, it is required to compose organizations consisting of several agents and cooperate with each other. Therefore agents are required to know other agents' trait or current status via inter-agent communication and assign tasks based on the information.

In this paper, we introduce the *subjective information* to agents, which are the internal information of the agents. The subjective information reflect the agents' cooperative behavior of the past and are used as criteria of agents' decision making. We also proposed a concept of *loose coalition*. A loose coalition represents relations between an agent and the neighboring agents, and it is defined on the basis of subjective information. This relationship may change from time to time and an agent can know a situation of the peer's surroundings by exchanging information about a loose coalition. Therefore, an agent can grasp information from a wider range by communicating with a specific peer agent.

We carried out an experiment by using four user agents and 30 task agents with different capabilities. From the results of this experiment, we can say that it is important to propagate information of agents with higher *Reliability* in a minimum time to design efficient multiagent systems based on a loose coalition.

The future works includes experimenting with other different settings, e.g. adding or deleting agents from the system while running the experiment and considering the coexistence of agents of various settings in the same system.

References

1. Reid G. Smith. The contract net protocol: High-level communication and control in a distributed problem solver. *IEEE Transactions on Computers*, C-29(12):1104–1113, December 1980.
2. Susan E. Conry, Kazuhiro Kuwabara, Victor R. Lesser, and Robert A. Meyer. Multistage negotiation for distributed constraint satisfaction. *IEEE Transactions on Systems, Man, and Cybernetics*, 21(6):1462–1477, November/December 1991.
3. Onn Shehory and Sarit Kraus. Task allocation via coalition formation among autonomous agents. In Chris S. Mellish, editor, *Proceedings of the International Joint Conference on Artificial Intelligence, 1995 (IJCAI-95)*, volume I, pages 655–661, Denver, Colorado, August 1995. International Joint Conferences on Artificial Intelligence, Inc., Professional Book Center.
4. Onn Shehory and Sarit Kraus. Methods for task allocation via agent coalition formation. *Artificial Intelligence*, 101:165–200, 1998.
5. L. M. Hogg and N. R. Jennings. Socially rational agents. In *Proc. AAAI Fall symposium on Socially Intelligent Agents*, pages 61–63. AAAI, November 1997.
6. S. Kalenka and N. R. Jennings. Socially responsible decision making by autonomous agents. In *Proceedings of Fifth International Colloquium on Cognitive Science (ICCS-97)*, May 1997. San Sebastian, Spain.
7. Martin R. Andersson and Tuomas W. Sandholm. Contract types for satisficing task allocation: II Experimental results. In *Proc. AAAI 1998 Spring Symposium on Satisficing Models*. AAAI, March 1998.
8. Tuomas W. Sandholm. Contract types for satisficing task allocation: I Theoretical results. In *Proc. AAAI 1998 Spring Symposium on Satisficing Models*. AAAI, March 1998.
9. Takashi Katoh, Tetsuo Kinoshita, and Norio Shiratori. A model of coalition formation based on agents' mental states. In *The Second Pacific Rim International Workshop on Multi-Agents (PRIMA99)*, pages 149–163, January 1999.
10. Takashi Katoh, Hideki Hara, Tetsuo Kinoshita, Kenji Sugawara, and Norio Shiratori. Behavior of agents based on mental states. In *Proceedings of the 12th International Conference on Information Networking (ICOIN12)*, pages 199–204. IEEE, January 1998.
11. Takashi Katoh, Tetsuo Kinoshita, and Norio Shiratori. Coalition formation of agents based on mental states. In *Proceedings of the 13th International Conference on Information Networking (ICOIN13)*, volume II, pages 6B-3.1–6. IEEE, January 1999.
12. N. R. Jennings and J. R. Campos. Towards a social level characterisation of socially responsible agents. In *IEE Proceedings on Software Engineering*, pages 11–25, 1997.
13. Steven Ketchpel. Forming. In *Proceedings of the Twelfth National Conference on Artificial Intelligence*, volume I, pages 414–419. AAAI, July, August 1994.

14. Matthias Klusch and Onn Shehory. Coalition formation among rational information agents. In W. Van de Velde and J. W. Perram, editors, *Agents Breaking Away*, number 1038 in Lecture Notes in Artificial Intelligence, pages 204–217. Springer, 1996.
15. Eric Malville and Francois Bourdon. Task allocation: A group self design approach. In *Proceedings of International Conference on Multi Agent Systems (ICMAS)*, pages 166–173. IEEE, July 1998.
16. Tuomas W. Sandholm and Victor R. Lesser. Coalition formation among bounded rational agents. In Chris S. Mellish, editor, *IJCAI-95*, volume I, pages 662–669, Denver, Colorado, August 1995. International Joint Conferences on Artificial Intelligence, Inc., Professional Book Center.
17. Onn Shehory and Sarit Kraus. A kernel-oriented model for coalition-formation in general environment: Implementation and results. In *Proceedings of AAAI-96*, volume I, pages 134–140, 1996.
18. Yoav Shoham. Agent-oriented programming. *Artificial Intelligence 60*, pages 51–92, 1993.

Agent Negotiation under Uncertainty and Risk

Von-Wun Soo

Department of Computer Science
National Tsing Hua University
Hsin Chu Taiwan 300
soo@cs.nthu.edu.tw

Abstract. Traditional game theoretic reasoning for agent negotiation usually base on the assumption of rationality of agents who are expected utility maximizers. The utility functions that express preferences of agents over goods, states or money are essential in decision making of rational agents. However, the utility functions are very sensitive to agent's wealth levels. To obtain the utility functions and wealth levels of other agents during the negotiation are extremely difficult. In this paper, we propose a way of getting around the problems by assuming the game theoretic decision making of rational agents be based on a monetary payoff game matrix instead of a utility payoff matrix. We regard utility functions and wealth levels of agents as private information while treating the monetary payoff game matrix as public information that is available to each agent. Rational agents of different risk preference types (e.g. risk averse, risk neutral and risk seeking) must negotiate to find a stable state using only the public information. We therefore extend the work of Wu and Soo who developed the negotiation mechanisms with a trusted third party as a mediator for agents to reach a stable equilibrium state under uncertain games. We discuss how the negotiation results based on the monetary payoff game matrix may be affected by different risk preferences of negotiating rational agents.

1 Introduction

In game theoretical based negotiation [7,9,10,13,14,16], rational agents will try to reach the Nash equilibrium that is a stable state for each agent. When agents reach such a state they will not leave it because whoever leaves it alone will get a less payoff. However, unique Nash equilibrium may not always exist, even it may, it might not be an optimal solution. In uncertain games, where payoffs of game outcomes can be uncertain due to the nature move, the decision making to reach an optimal and stable state for rational agents become a challenging task.

To understand how people make decision under uncertainty, previous work on both psychological and economic study has contributed a lot. The risk that a person feels in an uncertain game situation depends not only on the expected payoff in the game but also on the total amount of one's wealth [1]. Fabrycky and Thuesen [2] argued that risk preference (risk aversion) could be a mix-weighted combination of three criteria: 1. Maximizing the expected value, 2. Minimizing the expected variance, and 3. Minimizing the probability of a too low value. Machina [3] reported controversial views between economists and psychologists over interpretation of uncertainty and risk. Many controversial phenomena on human risk preference Fanning out problems

C. Zhang and V.-W. Soo (Eds.): PRIMA 2000, LNAI 1881, pp. 31- 45, 2000.

(Allais Paradox) which violates the linearity in probabilities were reported. To deal with uncertainty and risk, Sandholm and Lesser [12] proposed a leveled commitment contracting approach that took de-commitment with punishment into account in unpredictable future events.

Wu and Soo [11] showed how risk control could be taken into consideration in a trusted third party mediated negotiation games using negotiation protocol with compensation and guarantee communication actions. They showed that the final equilibrium of the uncertain game could end up with different strategy combinations after negotiation depending on different risk preference types of agents involved. However, in their discussion, only agents of extreme risk preference types can be discussed. Further more, they did not distinguish the difference between the utility payoffs and monetary payoff that is important in defining risk preference.

We argue that the utility functions are very sensitive to agent's wealth levels [1] and to obtain the utility functions and wealth levels of other agents during the negotiation are extremely difficult tasks that are almost impractical in reality. We might be able to estimate the cost in a given game situation in terms of money, but we might not be able to know precisely what it is valued by a given agent individually. Therefore, we propose a way of get around with the problems by assuming the game theoretic decision making of rational agents are based on a monetary payoff game matrix. In other words, we regard utility functions and wealth levels of agents as private information and assume instead that the monetary payoff game matrix is available to each agent as public information. We develop the negotiation mechanisms with trusted third party as a mediator for agents of different risk preference types (e.g. risk averse, risk neutral and risk seeking) based on merely on public information. We will discuss how the negotiation results based on the monetary payoff game matrix might be affected by risk preference of negotiating rational agents.

In section 2 we discuss the general settings and assumptions of agent negotiation under uncertain games with a trusted third party and define the risk preference in terms of Bernoulli utility functions. In section 3 we describe the communication mechanisms and negotiation protocol for agent to reach a stable agreement. In section 4 we illustrate a typical example to show the scenario of how different risk preference agents conduct the negotiation under an uncertain game. In section 5, we discuss the results and in section 6 we make the conclusion.

2   Assumptions under Trusted Third Party Mediated Uncertain Games

In the theoretical settings of a trusted third party mediated one-shot uncertain negotiation game, we must make following assumptions:

The rational agents are supposed to be expected utility maximizers and they regard each as mutually rational also. But they do not know other's risk preference and wealth levels.

A trusted third party exists and is known and trusted by both agents, the trusted third party is really trustworthy and can carry out the enforcing mechanism of paying the guarantee and compensation payoffs.

Each agent can obtain the payoff information in terms of money payoff at each outcome, but could not know the utility of the money payoff of other agents. Namely, the utility payoffs are private information while monetary payoffs are public information.

The scale of money in the monetary game matrix is the same for both agents.

The utility function of each agent belongs to the type of a von Neumann-Morgenstern expected utility function [5]. The von Neumann-Morgenstern expected utility function is defined in terms of lotteries whose counterpart is a Bernoulli utility function that is defined in terms of monetary payoffs. Let u(x) be a Bernoulli utility function over money payoff, and F($\bullet$) is a lottery function.

Definition 1 A risk-averse agent can then be defined as

$$\int u(x)dF(x) < u\left(\int xdF(x)\right) \quad \text{for all F($\bullet$)} \quad (1)$$

A risk-neutral agent can be defined as

$$\int u(x)dF(x) = u\left(\int xdF(x)\right) \quad \text{for all F($\bullet$)} \quad (2)$$

While a risk-seeking agent can be defined as

$$\int u(x)dF(x) > u\left(\int xdF(x)\right) \quad \text{for all F($\bullet$)} \quad (3)$$

Definition 2 The certainty equivalent of a given lottery F(.) with respected to an agent with a given utility function u(.) is defined as the amount of money for which the agent is indifferent from the lottery F(.) and the amount c(F,u). Namely, $u(c(F,u)) = \int u(x)dF(x)$. For example, if an agent cannot make any difference between an uncertain payoff F with 0.5 probability of getting 10 and 0.5 probability of getting 6 and a certain payoff C= 9, then we could say the certainty equivalent of the uncertain payoff F is equal to 9. Thus, the certainty equivalent can be computed as

$$c(F,u) = u^{-1}\left(\int u(x)dF(x)\right) \qquad (4)$$

where u^{-1} is the inverse function of u.

For risk averse agents the certainty equivalent of a lottery F(.) tend to be less than the expected monetary payoffs of the given lottery namely, $c(F,u) < \int xdF(x)$.

Furthermore, if agent A is more risk averse than agent B then agent A's certainty equivalent is not greater than that of B. Likewise we could define for risk neutral and risk seeking agents, the certainty equivalents for risk neutral and risk seeking agents are equal and greater than the expected monetary payoffs respectively.

Also we assume all Bernoulli utility functions of risk averse, risk neutral, and risk seeking agents are monotonic increasing. Namely, $\forall x_1, x_2$ if $x_2 > x_1$ then $u(x_2) > u(x_1)$.

3 The Communication Mechanisms and Negotiation Protocol

With a trusted third party mediating the game, Wu and Soo [11] proposed two communication actions of asking guarantee and offering compensation that can help to coordinate rational agents. The guarantee communication action is adopted when an agent want to prevent other agents from playing strategies that will lead to a worse result for other agents. It normally is used to create a Nash equilibrium. If P doesn't want Q to play a strategy that will lead to a less payoff result for P. P may ask Q to deposit some guarantee at a trusted third party to ensure the strategy that leads to the undesirable state will not be played. If Q keeps his/her commitment, the guarantee will be returned. The compensation communication action, on the other hand, is used to persuade other agents to play certain strategy that can lead to a desirable state. P may offer some compensation to Q in order to persuade him play certain strategy toward a better state for P. The compensation is deposited at a trusted third party and will be sent to Q if Q does play the strategy asked.

Since the guarantee communication actions do not actually change the agent's monetary payoff, we can use it at a later stage when both agents has reached a state of agreement using compensation communication actions. This is because no matter which agent pays the guarantee, it can be returned anyway if the agent does keep its promise. Therefore in negotiation process, the negotiating agents can concentrate on the compensation communication action first that is used to persuade the other agents to agree with his/her desirable state. If a state is agreed then the second stage of guarantee negotiation can be carried out.

3.1 The General Negotiation Protocol

The steps of a general negotiation protocol proceed as the following:
1) Each agent ranks the state preference according to its expected utility as its offering set.
2) Repeat the compensation negotiation until succeeds or the set is empty.
   2.1) Agent i offers a particular state with/without proper compensation,
   2.2) Agent $-i$ accepts the offer or proposes a counter offer.
   2.2) The compensation negotiation ends with a compromise or fails when no more offers can be suggested at each side.
3) Repeat the guarantee negotiation until succeeds or fails.
   3.1) Agent i making guarantee offer for the particular state in order to bind the commitment of both sides according to the expected monetary payoff matrix.
   3.2) Agent $-i$ accepts or proposes a counter offer.
   3.3) The guarantee negotiation ends with a compromise or a failure.

3.2 Negotiation Protocol – Make an Offer

It proceeds at two stages, the compensation and guarantee stages.
<u>At the compensation stage:</u>
Select the state with the maximal expected utility from the offering set.
Offer the state to the other agent.

If the other agent accepts then succeed and go to the stage of the guarantee negotiation stage.

Else offer small proper quantum of compensation to the other agent to persuade it to the state unless the utility of the monetary equivalent has reached the state that has the next highest expected utility for itself.

If the other agent accepts then succeed and go to the stage of the guarantee negotiation stage.

If the monetary equivalent has reached the next highest expected utility state, and the compensation offer is not accepted then suspend the current state offer and switch to the next highest expected utility state. Go to step 2.
<u>At the guarantee stage:</u>
Compute the amount of guarantee that could bind the commitments of both agents, and make the offer.

3.3 Negotiation Protocol -- Accept/Reject/Counter Offer

It proceeds also at two stages, the compensation and guarantee stages.
<u>At the compensation stage:</u>
If state of the compensation offer by the other agent satisfies the agent's preference (namely the maximal utility state) or the expected payoff of the offer is higher than itself can offer then accept the offer, else reject the offer and make a counter offer according to the offering procedure if possible else fail.
<u>At the guarantee stage:</u>
If the agent believes the guarantee is sufficient to bind the commitments of other agent according to the monetary payoff matrix then accept the offer, else reject and make a counter offer if possible.

4 A Scenario of Negotiation in an Uncertain Game with Different Risk Preference Agents

Suppose there is an uncertain game between two negotiating agents P and Q with probabilistic outcomes is expressed in terms of montary payoff as shown in Fig. 1 (a).

The expected monetary payoff matrix in Fig. 1(b) indicates that the game has no Nash equilibrium for the risk neutral agents. If both agents are risk neutral, we could simulate the negotiation protocol as discussed in section 3 as follows:

P and Q each ranks with the state preferences according to the expected monetary payoffs which is linearly proportional to the expected utility payoffs. P's preference is (B,D) > (B,C) > (A,C) > (A,D) while Q's preference is (A,D) > (B,C) > (A, C) > (B,D).

P starts with offering state (B,D) but Q rejects and makes a counter offers of (A,D). And of course P rejects too.

Loop of P offering compensation at state (B,D) by adding a certain small amount of compensation while Q rejecting and counter offering by adding the amount of compensation to P at the state (A,D), until Q reaches the amount of 19 which is the same amount as the state (B,C) for Q to get the next highest payoff. But P still rejects, because it has better offer 1 to Q and have 29 for itself at the state (A,D). Q switches to the state (B,C).

(a)

(b)

Fig. 1 (a) an uncertain game with probabilistic monetary payoffs, where the entry x/y represents payoff x with probability y. (b) the corresponding payoff matrix in terms of expected monetary payoffs.

Loop of Q offering compensation to P by adding small amount at the state (B,C) while P does it opposite at the state (A,D), until Q reaches the amount of paying 3 to P (P becomes getting payoff 27) while keeps 16 for itself, this offering is better than

P's offering of 3 to Q (Q gets only 13) while keeps 27 for itself, therefore P accepts and an agreement of the compensation stage is reached.

However, although the agreement is for P and Q to play (B,C) and Q pay compensation 3 to P so that P gets payoff of 27 and Q 16, P still has the chance to play D to get a more profitable payoff 30 if Q plays B. Therefore the subsequent negotiation for guarantee is for P to pay guarantee at least 3 at the trusted third party in order to bind P's commitment at (B,C).

The final negotiation result is to play (B,C) while P deposits guarantee at least 3 to play B, and Q pays P compensation 3.

But the above example is only for the case of both agents being risk neutral. The situations may become more complex if both are different types of agents. To understand more about the behaviors of agents with different risk preference, we use the same uncertain game as an example and elaborate the negotiation process a little bit.

The expected utilities of different outcomes for different agents in the uncertain game can be computed according to the table 1.

Table 1. The expected utilities of different outcomes, where w is the wealth level of the negotiating agent, u(.) is the Bernoulli utility function.

	Expected utility for P	Expected utility for Q
(A,C)	.5*u(w+0)+.5*u(w+40)	.8*u(w+5)+.2*u(w+40)
(A,D)	.5*u(w+10)+.5*u(w+20)	.33*u(w+0)+.67*u(w+30)
(B,C)	.4*u(w+15)+.6*u(w+30)	.1*u(w+10)+.9*u(w+20)
(B,D)	.4*u(w+15)+.6*u(w+40)	.75*u(w+0)+.25*u(w+40)

Without loosing of generality, we assume the risk-averse, risk-neutral and risk-seeking agents have such typical Bernoulli utility functions as $u_a(x) = \sqrt{x}$, $u_n(x)=x$ and $u_s(x)=x^2$ respectively. When we have different risk preference negotiating agents, there can be ways of transforming the monetary payoff matrix into different game matrices that conform with each agent's risk preference types. Of course, each negotiating agent cannot have such information because they don't know their counterpart's risk preference type not to mention their utility function and the original wealth level w. For simplicity of illustration here, we could assume that the original wealth levels are both 100 and 10 respectively. However, they could share the information of the original uncertain monetary payoff matrix and the expected monetary payoff matrix. In table 2 (a), (b), (c) and (d), we show expected utility payoff matrix calculated for different risk preference agents at different wealth levels. The numbers in parenthesis represent the certainty equivalents of the uncertain outcomes computed according to (4) in section 2 for different risk preferences.

Table 2 (a) Expected utility payoffs at different states for P with wealth level at 100.

	P risk neutral w=100 $u_n(x)=x$	P risk averse w=100 $u_a(x) = \sqrt{x}$	P risk seeking w=100 $u_s(x)=x^2$
(A,C)	120 (20)	10.91 (19.03)	14800 (21.66)
(A,D)	115 (15)	10.72 (14.92)	13250 (15.11)
(B,C)	124 (24)	11.13 (23.88)	15430 (24.22)
(B,D)	130 (30)	11.39 (29.73)	17050 (30.58)

Table 2 (b) Expected utility payoffs at different states for Q with wealth level at 100.

	Q risk neutral w=100 $u_n(x)=x$	Q risk averse w=100 $u_a(x) = \sqrt{x}$	Q risk seeking w=100 $u_s(x)=x^2$
(A,C)	112 (12)	10.56 (11.51)	12740 (12.87)
(A,D)	120 (20)	10.94 (19.68)	14623 (20.93)
(B,C)	119 (19)	10.91 (19.03)	14170 (19.04)
(B,D)	110 (10)	10.46 (10.88)	12400 (11.36)

Table 2 (c) Expected utility payoffs at different states for P with wealth level at 10.

	P risk neutral w=10 $u_n(x)=x$	P risk averse w=10 $u_a(x) = \sqrt{x}$	P risk seeking w=10 $u_s(x)=x^2$
(A,C)	30 (20)	5.12 (16.21)	1300 (26.06)
(A,D)	25 (15)	4.97 (14.70)	650 (15.50)
(B,C)	34 (24)	5.79 (23.52)	1210 (24.79)
(B,D)	40 (30)	6.24 (28.69)	1750 (31.83)

Table 2 (d) Expected utility payoffs at different states for Q with wealth level at 10.

	Q risk neutral w=10 $u_n(x)=x$	Q risk averse w=10 $u_a(x)=\sqrt{x}$	Q risk seeking w=10 $u_s(x)=x^2$
(A,C)	22 (12)	4.51 (10.34)	680 (16.07)
(A,D)	30 (20)	5.28 (17.88)	1105 (23.24)
(B,C)	29 (19)	5.38 (18.94)	850 (19.15)
(B,D)	20 (10)	4.14 (7.14)	700 (16.46)

As in the tables 2 (a), (b), (c) and (d), the certainty equivalents for risk averse agents tend to be smaller in comparison to those of risk neutral agents, while those of risk seeking agents tend to be larger. The orders of state preference for P and Q at higher wealth level (w=100) are not affected by different risk preference types. But it does have some effects at the lower wealth level (w=10). In risk seeking P agent, the state preference order is (B,D) > (A,C) > (B,C) > (A,D) that is different from that of risk neutral and risk averse P agent which is (B,D) > (B,C) > (A,C) > (A,D). Similar findings are found for agent Q. In risk averse agent Q, the state preference order for (A,D) and (B,C) is swapped, while the risk seeking agent Q, the state preference order for (A,C) and (B,D) is also swapped in comparison to risk neutral agent Q.

The following is a trace of compensation negotiation program when P and Q are both risk seeking. Both are at wealth level w=100 with compensation quantum = 1.
Memo1
STRAT :
Agent P wants to play (B,D)
Agent Q wants to play (A,D)
----------start negotiation----------
Agent P makes an offer 1
The P currently total offer is 1
and agent P will take 29.5800910634037
and agent Q will take 12.3432240947357

Agent Q makes a counter offer 1
The Q currently total offer is 1
and agent Q will take 19.9324810049388
and agent P will take 16.1077086157504

Agent P makes an offer 1
The P currently total offer is 2
and agent P will take 28.5846024996772
and agent Q will take 13.3313725320575

Agent Q makes a counter offer 1
The Q currently total offer is 2
and agent Q will take 18.939480409156
and agent P will take 17.1067888723792
Agent Q switch to state (B,C) and totally offer becomes 0

Agent P makes an offer 1
The P currently total offer is 3
and agent P will take 27.5891844946115
and agent Q will take 14.3197270815497

Agent Q makes a counter offer 1
The Q currently total offer is 1
and agent Q will take 18.0381294328235
and agent P will take 25.2158136977914

Agent P makes an offer 1
The P currently total offer is 4
and agent P will take 26.5938387126325
and agent Q will take 15.3082824431966

Agent Q makes a counter offer 1
The Q currently total offer is 2
and agent Q will take 17.038455218787
and agent P will take 26.2141038077758

Agent P makes an offer 1
The P currently total offer is 5
and agent P will take 25.5985668708047
and agent Q will take 16.2970334961301
Agent P switch to state (B,C) and poffer becomes 0

Agent Q makes a counter offer 1
The Q currently total offer is 3
and agent Q will take 16.0387866189577
and agent P will take 27.2124207772181
---end with q's offer-------
negotiation ends with a compromise !
and the compensation is 3

The following is a trace of compensation negotiation program when P is risk seeking at wealth level = 100 and Q are risk averse at wealth level = 10 with the compensation quantum =1:
Memo:
STRAT :

Agent P wants to play (B,D)
Agent Q wants to play (B,C)

----------start negotiation----------
Agent P makes an offer 1
The P currently total offer is 1
and agent P will take 29.58009106340337
and agent Q will take 8.25703946174526

Agent Q makes a counter offer 1
The Q currently total offer is 1
and agent Q will take 17.90521005395
and agent P will take 25.2158136977914

Agent P makes an offer 1
The P currently total offer is 2
and agent P will take 28.5846024996772
and agent Q will take 9.3674969975976

Agent Q makes a counter offer 1
The Q currently total offer is 2
and agent Q will take 16.9009899777159
and agent P will take 26.2141038077758

Agent P makes an offer 1
The P currently total offer is 3
and agent P will take 27.5891844946115
and agent Q will take 10.468303561305

Agent Q makes a counter offer 1
The Q currently total offer is 3
and agent Q will take 15.8963713514131
and agent P will take 27.2124207772181

Agent P makes an offer 1
The P currently total offer is 4
and agent P will take 26.5938387126325
and agent Q will take 11.5607953136506
Agent P switch to state (B,C) and poffer becomes 0

Agent Q makes a counter offer 1
The Q currently total offer is 4
and agent Q will take 14.8912940497868
and agent P will take 28.2107639786925
---end with q's offer-------
negotiation ends with a compromise !
and the compensation is 4

The above two traces show that different risk preference types of agents indeed will end up with different negotiation results (different compensations but the same final state) even at the same uncertain game. The negotiation compensation quantum is set to jump by an increment of 1. If the compensation quantum is chosen at a smaller amount, the final compensation offers at two different runs will be closer.

5 Discussion

5.1 The Effects of Different Risk Preferences on the Negotiation Results

According to (2) in section 2, the expected utility payoff is the same as the expected monetary payoff for risk neutral agents. When a risk-neutral agent offers compensation to another risk-neutral agent, the amount of compensation in terms of money is linearly proportional to the expected utility of both agents. Therefore the decision-making based on the expected monetary payoff matrix will be the same as that on the expected utility payoff matrix. However, if either one of the agents is not risk-neutral, the expected monetary payoff matrix can not longer be treated as the expected utility matrix of agents. The negotiation results can be affected. Therefore we need to understand the effects of how the risk preferences of agents can affect the negotiation results.

According to section 2, a risk-averse agent tends to have a certainty equivalent less than that of a risk neutral agent while a risk-seeking agent may have a higher one. Due to this reason, if two negotiating agents other than risk-neutral who are negotiating based on an expected monetary payoff matrix, the amount of compensation and guarantee offered can be to some extent distorted from the actual expected utility. Even if rational negotiating agents may not know each other's risk preference, making risk neutral assumption of others can be totally wrong if not unwise.

It turns out that offering compensation to a risk aversion agent it will normally take much more amount than to a risk neutral on. On the other hand, offering compensation to a risk-seeking agent, one might not need to pay as much the amount as to the risk neutral agent before a compromised agreement can be reached. The similar situation applies to the offering guarantee also. Since we could not have exact expected utility payoff matrix, negotiating agents who used expected monetary payoff matrix to propose the amount of guarantee to bind the commitment of other negotiating agents may not sometimes turn out to be successful. This is because there might be a higher expected utility state that is underestimated by the negotiating agent based on the expected monetary payoff matrix.

5.2 The Properties of Negotiation Protocol

The convergence property of the negotiation protocol holds since the negotiating set is finite and the number of alternatives is decreasing while both agent offering compensation. But the question is can the negotiation protocol lead to a stable and Pareto-efficient Nash equilibrium? Is it always possible?

Since each negotiating agent might not know other's wealth level and utility functions therefore they must propose best standing from their own perspective while trying to bind other's commitment via negotiation by taking advantage of the trusted third party. The only information they can base on is the probabilistic monetary payoff matrix. The decision making based on the expected monetary payoff matrix applies only if both agents are risk neutral. The negotiation protocol could reach very nice result as a Pareto-efficient Nash equilibrium. Unfortunately, heterogeneous types of agents are often encountered in real world, as discussed above, the guarantee paid might sometimes turn out to be not enough. Therefore, the nice property of "truly Nash" might not hold. Pareto-efficient property holds since the solution reached is the best possible offer for each side at all possible states. If a given offer is not the best for one side, the negotiating agent will reject it and make a better counter offer anyhow.

Order independent properties of negotiation may not apply either in the negotiation protocol, because agents with different utility function and wealth levels will tend to either reach agreement earlier with a less amount of compensation or postpone the agreement to a higher amount of compensation. Therefore the negotiation protocol cannot guarantee to lead to the same results if agents initiate the negotiation in different order.

The negotiation compensation quantum could assumed to be the smallest unit that could be represented in the negotiation. However, if the compensation quantum is too small, the negotiation process will take very long time before it reached agreement. On the other hand, if the compensation quantum is larger, then the negotiation might ends faster. However, the final compensation offer would either have a tolerance bound in comparison to that of the final agreement when the quantum is ideally small or it could end up with other states.

6 Conclusion

We distinguish monetary payoff from utility payoff that is an important issue for agent negotiation to be feasible in practice because utility functions of agents are difficult to obtain. We show how agents could negotiate via a trusted third party and find an equilibrium state based on an uncertain game matrix in terms of monetary payoff. The role of a trusted third party is to ensure the binding of the commitment of negotiating agents. The negotiation mechanism we propose runs at two stages that are different from that of Wu and Soo's [14,15] previous proposal. However, due to the lack of the precise information of other agent's risk preference, the guarantee paid to bind the agent's commitment can sometimes turn out to be not enough.

In the future work we need to investigate more subtle binding mechanisms for used in the negotiation protocol in order for negotiating agents to find a truly stable Nash as well as the Pareto-efficient state in uncertain games. We could also incorporate learning in the negotiation mechanism in order for the negotiating agents to learn the risk preference of other agents during the negotiation process as [17]. If it allows iterated games such as [6] rather than one-shot in this case, the negotiating agents could somehow infer or learn the other agent's utility functions or wealth levels. Also we have not take into consideration the cost of communication actions of guarantee and compensation via trusted third party [4]. It could become a complicated market economy if trusted third parties make charges and also participate in the negotiation protocol.

Acknowledgment

This work was financially supported by the National Science Council, Taiwan, Republic of China, under the grant No. NSC 89-2213-E-007 –066 and also by Program for Promoting Academic Excellence of Universities under grant number 89-E-FA04-1-4. Thanks go to Mr. Chun-An Hung to write the negotiation program.

References

[1] Bernoulli, D., Exposition of a New Theory of the Measurement of Risk, Econometrica, Vol. 22, pp. 23-36, 1954.

[2] Fabrycky, W. J., Thuesen, G. J., Decision Making Involving Risk, Chap 10 in Economic Decision Analysis, 2nd ed., 1980.

[3] Machina, M. J., Choice under Uncertainty: Problem Solved and Unsolved, Economic Perspective, Vol. 1, No. 1, pp 121-145, Summer, 1997.

[4] Gmytrasiewicz, P. J., Durfee, E. H., and Wehe, D. K., The Utility of Communication in Coordinating Intelligent Agents, In proceedings of AAAI, 1991.

[5] Mas-Colell, A., Whinston, M. D., and Green, J. R., Microeconomic Theory, Oxford University Press, 1995.

[6] Matsubara, S. and Yokoo, M., Cooperative Behavior in Iterated Game with a Change of the Payoff Values, In Proceedings of ICMAS, 1996.

[7] Nash, J. F., Non-Cooperative Games, Ann. Of Math., 54, pp. 286-295, 1951.

[8] Pratt, J. W., Risk Aversion in the Small and in the Large, Econometrica, Vol. 32, No. 1-2, Jan.-Apr., 1964.

[9] Rasmusen, E., *Games and Information: An Introduction to Game Theory*, Basil Blackwell, Oxford, 1989.

[10] Rosenschein, J. and Genensereth, M. R., Deals among Rational Agents, In Proceedings of IJCAI, 1985.

[11] Rosenschein, J. and Zlotkin, G., Rules of Encounter, MIT press, Cambridge, 1994.

[12] Sandholm T. W., and Lesser, V. R., Advantage of a Leveled Commitment Contracting Protocol, In Proceedings of AAAI, 1996.

[13] Tennenholtz, M., On stable Social Laws and Qualitative Equilibria, Artificial Intelligence, vol. 102, pp. 1-20, 1998.

[14] Wu, S. H. and Soo, V. W., Game Theoretic Approach to Multi-Agent Coordination by Negotiation with a Trusted Third Party, In Proceeding of the Third International Conference on Autonomous Agents, 1999.

[15] Wu, S. H. and Soo, V. W., Risk Control in Multi-agent Coordination by Negotiation with a Trusted Third Party, In Proceedings of IJCAI, 1999.

[16] Wu, S. H. and Soo, V. W., Making Rational Decisions in N-by-N Negotiation Games with a Trusted Third Party, In Proceedings of PRIMA, 1999.

[17] Zeng, D. and Sycara, K., Benefits of Learning in Negotiation, In Pro ceedings of AAAI, 1997.

Argumentation as a Social Computing Paradigm

Yuichi Umeda, Massashi Yamashita, Masanobu Inagaki, and Hajime Sawamura

Dept. of Information Engineering and Graduate School of
Science and Engineering, Niigata University,
8050, Ninocho, Ikarashi, Niigata, 950-2181 JAPAN
{umeda, masashi, inagaki, sawamura}@cs.ie.niigata-u.ac.jp

Abstract. In this paper, we claim that argumentation is a novel and prominent computing principle and provides a unified approach to technologies needed in agent-oriented computing, where social concepts play important roles in computation. Viewed as the reasoning methods of attaining a consensus, they can be roughly classified into three categories: (i) conflict-resolving reasoning, (ii) dialectical reasoning, and (iii) cooperative reasoning. We describe these formally in a unified manner, and build an argument-based agent system with those argument-based reasoning capabilities. Finally, we show its potential usefulness and feasibility in a convincing manner by applying it to a wide variety of the contemporary application domains.

Keywords: argumentation, agent, dialectics, Aufheben, compromise, concession, cooperation

1 Introduction

We can see a historical process of the birth of many kinds of computing principles or programming paradigms in our computing world. Various computability such as Turing machine, recursive function theory, lambda calculus, etc., were born in the field of mathematical logic. Programming paradigms such as structured programming in procedural languages, functional programming, logic programming, object-oriented programming, etc., were devised in the field of computer science. Most recently, genetic programming, chemical computing, quantum computing, DNA computing, etc., are attracting scientists' and technologists' attention to as a new generation computing principle that are expected to make it possible to drastically overcome the contemporary computing bottlenecks. A lesson learned from these computing phenomena is that the traditional major subjects such as mathematics, physics, chemistry, biology yield sources of computing principles. Apart from these traditional disciplines, why not other subjects such as sociology, economics, politics, literature, philosophy and so on? (The significance and classification of objects in object-oriented computing dates back to the category theory of Aristotle and Porphyrios in western ancient philosophy, and of Maticandra in Indian ancient philosophy. Interestingly, the number of object categories is 10 in both cases)

Sociology and economics are exceptions and have promoted 'agent-oriented computing' based on a societal view of computation. Then what is a fundamental leading principle of the agent-oriented computing? Our answer is above all

C. Zhang and V.-W. Soo (Eds.): PRIMA 2000, LNAI 1881, pp. 46–60, 2000.

'Argumentation'. Then what is the argumentation? According to linguists, sociologist, philosophers, and so on, "it is a verbal and social activity of reason carried out by a speaker or writer concerned with increasing (or decreasing) the acceptability of a controversial standpoint for a listener or reader, by putting forward a constellation of propositions intended to justify (or refute) the standpoint before a rational judge." [1][3]. We, computer scientists, would say that it is a social computing principle at which we arrived by taking into consideration the very nature of information [17][7][15], and we have already proposed some argument-based agent systems that we believe are a new form of information processing particularly in the new world connected by the world-wide network (whether it is real or virtual). And we claimed that argumentation could be a novel and prominent computing principle in the new era of the information processing, and provide a unified approach to technologies needed in agent-oriented computing, where social concepts play important roles in computation, such as negotiation, compromise, cooperation, coordination, collaboration, conflict resolution and management, and so on. Viewed as the reasoning methods of attaining a consensus, these social mechanisms can be roughly classified into three categories: (i) conflict-resolving reasoning, (ii) dialectical reasoning, and (iii) cooperative reasoning.

In this paper, we propose 'argumentation' as a fundamental computational principle or mechanism for dealing with these three in a unified manner. In doing so, we introduce an idea of multi-paradigm logic which allows for an interplay between logics. The logics we use here are the dialectical logic [13] and the logic of the extended logic programming [11]. In terms of the extended logic programming, arguments and counterarguments are formed from each agent's knowledge base. Put it differently, it is a source of contradictory propositions. They turn out to trigger cooperative reasoning and dialectical reasoning, resulting in producing better and more persuasive arguments, and higher-order agreements such as Aufheben, compromise, concession, etc. In the latter half of the paper, we describe an argument-based agent system with those argument-based reasoning capabilities, and show its potential usefulness and feasibility in a convincing manner by applying it to a wide variety of the contemporary application domains.

The paper is organized as follows. In the next section, first of all, we introduce an argumentation framework which consists of knowledge representation and argument for the succeeding sections. In Section 3, we discuss an idea of multi-paradigm logic. In Section 4, we describe the three types of argument-based reasoning one by one, in the form of inference rules. In Section 5, we integrate them into one argumentation protocol, with the illustrations of the argumentation flow. In Section 6, we list a variety of application domains where the argument-based agent system turns out to play a central role, and discuss its actual or potential usefulness and feasibility. The final section includes some intriguing future works.

2   An Argumentation Framework

In order to reflect the argument form that can be seen in our everyday life very often, we suppose the following very natural and inevitable premises, taking into account the network environment in modeling argumentation: (1) Knowledge base is distributed and not shared in general. That is, each agent has her/his own knowledge base, (2) The knowledge base of each agent or its combined one may be inconsistent, but an agent always exploits a consistent subset in her/his knowledge base (e. g., maximally consistent subset) in making arguments and counterarguments, (3) each agent has her/his own argument strategy as a proper way of reasoning [17], (4) not only two agents (one proponent and one opponent) but also n agents can attend to an argument.

The past argumentation frameworks proposed in the fields of philosophy and computer science (e. g., [5][10][8][4][2][11]) are, in a sense, so restrictive that they have not paid much attention to these premises of argumentation. And yet there has not been an actually implemented argument-based agent system with compromise, concession, dialectical reasoning ability and so on, as remarkable constituents of argumentation.

The purposes of argumentation in artificial intelligence generally and in agent-oriented computing specifically are twofold: (i) to resolve contradictions and choose one from them as an agreement, and (ii) to attain a consensus by making better arguments.

The first is similar to that of nonmonotonic logic. Non-monotonic logic, however, is more concerned with maintaining the consistency of knowledge bases, while argumentation is more concerned about argument process and superiority of arguments from logical, verbal and social point of view. The second is a kind of cooperation and collaboration. If a goal is kept unchangeable, it is a problem of argument or proof transformation. If a goal may be relaxed or modified, it is a sort of compromise, concession, and so on.

In the following subsections, we formally introduce various definitions on the knowledge representation, argument, compromise and concession.

2.1 Knowledge Representation

For our model of argumentation, we borrow some definitions from Prakken and Sartor [11]. The object language for knowledge representation is based on the extended logic programming with two negations: $\sim$ (negation as failure) called *weak negation* and $\neg$ (classical negation) called *strong negation*. A strong literal is an atomic formula or a formula preceded by strong negation $\neg$, and a weak literal is a literal of the form $\sim L$, where L is a strong literal. Then a rule has the form of $L_0 \Leftarrow L_1, ..., L_j, \sim L_k, ..., \sim L_n$, where each L_i $(0 \leq i \leq n)$ is an atomic formula or formula negated by $\neg$. The rule is called a *defeasible rule* and has the *assumptions* $\neg L_k, ..., \neg L_n$. The rule without any weak literal is called a *strict rule*. The roles of the weak literals in knowledge representation and argumentation are twofold: (i) one is that it allows to represent incomplete information by default and hence does not require grounds for them (see the next subsection on arguments), (ii) the other is that the existence of weak literals promotes cooperation with other agents, allowing to build better arguments satisfactory to the both parties (see the subsection 4.3).

2.2 Argument

An *argument* is a finite sequence, $r_0, ..., r_n$, of ground instances of rules such that (i) for every i $(0 \leq i \leq n)$ and for every strong literal L_j in the antecedent of r_i,

there is a $k < i$ such that L_j is the consequent of r_k, and
(ii) no two distinct rules in the sequence have the same consequent.

Let A_1 and A_2 be two arguments. Then a consequent L of a rule in A_1 can *attack* A_2 in such a way that:
(i) it *rebuts* the consequent $\neg L$ of a rule in A_2 (head conflict), or
(ii) it *undercuts* $\sim L$ in the antecedent of a rule in A_2 since this rule has an assumption $\neg L$.

An argument is said to be *coherent* if it does not attack itself. For example, the argument $p \Leftarrow \sim p$ is not coherent.

Let A_1 and A_2 be two coherent arguments. Then A_1 *defeats* A_2 iff
(i) A_1 undercuts A_2 or
(ii) A_1 rebuts A_2 and A_2 does not undercut A_1.
A_1 *strictly defeats* A_2 iff A_1 defeats A_2 and A_2 does not defeat A_1.

In this paper, we are concerned with the procedural semantics for the extended logic programs, just as the ordinary logic programming language Prolog relies upon it. This is due to the reason that it allows for a computationally feasible and practical reasoning. Under this semantics, we define two concepts: justified and overruled as follows. An argument A by Agent a is *justified* if each argument defeating A is strictly defeated by the arguments of Agent a. An argument A by Agent a is *overruled* if A is attacked by a justified argument of Agent b. (Note that Prakken and Sarter defined them in terms of their fixpoint semantics [11].)

Let us consider a pathological argument example here. Suppose that $p \Leftarrow \sim q$ is an argument constructed from Agent a's knowledge and $q \Leftarrow \sim p$ an argument constructed from Agent b's knowledge. Then Agent a defeats Agent b and vice versa, and hence neither Agent a nor Agent b strictly defeats one another. The Agent a's argument is not justified, nor overruled. A natural way for settling this indeterminateness would be to introduce argument strategies or argument controls based on appropriate argumentation protocols. In Section 5, we will propose an argumentation protocol (see also [17][7] for the argument strategies).

3   Multi-paradigm Logic

We have in mind such an assumption that in a multi-agent world like in our society, there exist many agents who think differently based on their own knowledge bases and thinking abilities and methods. In other words, the agents world is not homogeneous (like the race problem in the modern society), and hence the logic governing it can not be unique. We think that this applies to the multi-agent world as well, and should seek a multi-paradigm logic or so to speak a multiple logic for agents.

In this paper, for the time being, we consider the underlying logic for the argument-based agent system that consists of two logics: the logic of the extended logic programming (ELP) below [11] and the dialectical logics [13]. In terms of the extended logic programming, arguments and counterarguments are formed from each agent's knowledge base. Put it differently, it is a source of contradictory propositions. Those contradictory propositions, for example A and $\neg A$, are corresponded to the special constants p_i and $\neg p_i$ respectively in **DL** and **DM**

[13][15][18]. **DL** and **DM** are logics that admit existence of conflicting propositions such as p_i and $\neg p_i$, and in fact they are axioms and valid, keeping the systems absolutely consistent [13]. They turn out to trigger dialectical reasoning described below, resulting in higher-order agreements such as Aufheben, compromise, concession, etc. For example, suppose that agent a holds the issue $A \wedge \neg B$ with its argument and agent b holds the issue $\neg A \wedge B$ with its argument. Then we have the contradictory propositions, p_1 and $\neg p_1$, and p_2 and $\neg p_2$ in **DL** and **DM**, that are viewed as the axioms $p_1 \wedge \neg p_1$ and $p_2 \wedge \neg p_2$. Then by the following dialectical inference rule described in detail in the next section:

$$\frac{A \wedge \neg B \quad \neg A \wedge B}{A \wedge B},$$

we could get to a higher-order agreement $A \wedge B$ via $p_1 \wedge p_2$.

The co-existence of two logics may be well characterized as a problem solving by multi-paradigm logic where two logics interplay, switching one to another and vice versa. This reminds us of multi-paradigm programming in software development. We naturally can see such a phenomenon in our brains and society as well very often. In what follows, we consider three reasoning methods proper to argument-based agent systems, which are to be carried out in the framework of **DL** and **DM** [13][15][18], switching from that of the extended logic programming. We depict the overall story on the multi-paradigm logic through argumentation in Figure 1.

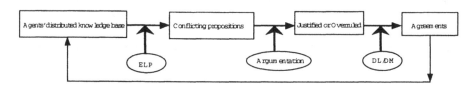

Fig. 1. Multi-paradigm logic and knowledge evolution

4   Argument-Based Reasoning

In this paper, we view argumentation as the reasoning methods of attaining a consensus. It, however, does not intend to exclude other views such that argumentation is a communication and influencing strategy, and does not necessarily start from a point of conflict. For the time being, we confine ourselves to narrow but computationally effective and feasible views on it. Below three aspects of it are distinguished: (i) conflict-resolving reasoning, (ii) dialectical reasoning, and (iii) cooperative reasoning.

4.1   Conflict-Resolving Reasoning

The primary goal of argumentation is to resolve contradictions by choosing one from them as a result of argumentation. Schematically, we represent the settlement from the contradictory arguments as follows.

Definition 1 (Conflict-resolution scheme).

$$\frac{A \quad \neg A}{A}, \frac{A \quad \neg A}{\neg A}$$

In classical logics, they do not make sense in the consistent theories although they are admissible. However, in the dialectical logics **DL** and **DM** [13][15][18] where existence of conflicting propositions is admitted, as mentioned above, they are worthy to be explicitly described as inference rules with a significant role. Of course, it is by the defeat relation of arguments above and argument strategies employed in the argumentation protocol described in the next section (see [17] and [7] for the argument strategy) that the choice is made from the two contradictory propositions. In actual arguments, the social role, standpoint, etc. of agents might be involved in the determination as well. But these are left as the important subjects to be studied in the future.

4.2   Dialectical Reasoning

If an argument has not been settled in the above, it might be better or necessary for the both sides to attain an agreement (consensus) satisfactory to some extent rather than leaving it unsettled. And also in confrontational situations, we often try to think of possible ways to resolve them by compromise, reconciliation, etc. These can be viewed as a form of dialectical reasoning[13][15][14][18]. Dialectical logic deserves attention to a logical study of higher-order aspects of argumentation [12][3][1] and a reasoning mode proper to agent-oriented computing (see [15][18] for the detailed discussions). In fact, dialectics may be the last inference pattern that has been forgotten for a long time in the studies of artificial intelligence as well as in our society. We now believe that it should be reincarnated in the agent world. Dialectics is obviously a way to reach truth by arguments (dialogue), and is sort of an inventive and/or creative social process in the sense that they can not be attained by any types of reasoning except for dialectics [18].

Below we attempt to give the definitions of compromise and concession, which are to be effectively used in our argumentation protocol described in the next section.

Definition 2 (Compromise). *Given two conflicting propositions, A and B, a proposition C is said to be a compromise attained by A and B if neither $\vdash A \rightarrow C$ nor $\vdash B \rightarrow C$.*

Although the proposition C above is too less restrictive enough to capture our intuition on compromise in the present form, we illustrate it through some persuasive examples in which a sort of the variable sharing property in relevant logics is tacitly supposed. (1) $A \wedge \neg B$ is a compromise from $A \wedge B$ and $\neg B$. Actually, it is not the case that $\vdash A \wedge B \rightarrow A \wedge \neg B$ and $\vdash \neg B \rightarrow A \wedge \neg B$ in the dialectical logics DL and DM [13][15], and even in classical logic. Note that the compromise shares the atomic propositions A and B with the two contradictory propositions respectively. (2) $A \wedge B$ is a compromise from $A \wedge \neg B$ and $\neg A \wedge B$ by the same reason as above. Diagrammatically, we can represent this as in Figure 2.

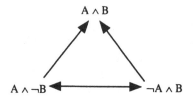

Fig. 2. Compromise scheme

Definition 3 (Concession). *Given two conflicting propositions, A and B, a proposition C is said to be a concession attained by A and B if it is not the case that* $\vdash A \rightarrow C$ *and it is the case that* $\vdash B \rightarrow C$, *or it is the case that* $\vdash A \rightarrow C$ *and it is not the case that* $\vdash B \rightarrow C$.

For example, (3) $A \wedge B$ is a concession obtained from $A \wedge B$ and $A \wedge \neg B$. Actually, it is not the case that $\vdash A \wedge \neg B \rightarrow A \wedge B$ but obviously it is the case that $\vdash A \wedge B \rightarrow A \wedge B$, in the dialectical logics DL and DM, and even in classical logic.

It should be noted that in both the compromise and concession above, the conclusion is a common knowledge that evolved from the conflicting propositions and hence agents could share (a form of knowledge evolution). It is, however, not a logical consequence from each agent's knowledge base. For example, in the example (2), the part of A in the compromise $A \wedge B$ is guaranteed by one agent and the part of B is not since the agent holds an argument on $\neg B$. On the other hand, the part of B in the compromise $A \wedge B$ is guaranteed by another agent and the part of A is not since the agent holds an argument on $\neg A$. However, they turn to have the compromise $A \wedge B$ as a shared common knowledge that should be kept separately from their original knowledge bases. (An alternative would be to accept all arguments of the compromise and concession even if it leads to an inconsistent knowledge base, since in fact we permit it in our argumentation framework and then we always employ its consistent subsets whenever making arguments.)

Those examples of conjunctive forms are highly compatible with the extended logic programming. We define them as elementary dialectical reasoning schemes as follows.

Definition 4 (Elementary dialectical reasoning scheme of conjunctive form).

$$\frac{A \wedge \neg B \quad \neg A \wedge B}{A \wedge B} \ , \ \frac{A \wedge B \quad \neg B}{A \wedge \neg B} \ , \ \frac{A \wedge B \quad A \wedge \neg B}{A \wedge B}$$

4.3 Cooperative Reasoning

The defeasible rule $L_0 \Leftarrow L_1, ..., L_j, \sim L_k, ..., \sim L_n$ has the *assumptions* $\neg L_k, ...,$ $\neg L_n$. This means agents are allowed to submit arguments without any grounds for those weak literals, as defined in the subsection 2.1. However, we could reinforce arguments or make them better if the assumptions of weak literals were replaced by other agents' arguments with those assumptions as rule heads. This obviously captures one aspect of cooperation offered by other agents.

So we introduce the definition of cooperation in the following form.

Definition 5 (Cooperation). *Let A_1 and A_2 be two arguments by Agent a and Agent b respectively, and let $L_0 \Leftarrow L_1, ..., L_j, \sim L_k, ..., \sim L_n$ in A_1 and $\neg L_i \Leftarrow M_1, ..., M_m$ in A_2 ($k \le i \le n$). Then the following is called a cooperation scheme with Agent a and Agent b (we call the conclusion the reinforced one or reinforcement simply):*

$$\frac{L_0 \Leftarrow L_1, ..., L_j, \sim L_k, ..., \sim L_i, ..., \sim L_n \quad \neg L_i \Leftarrow M_1, ..., M_k}{L_0 \Leftarrow L_1, ..., L_j, \sim L_k, ..., M_1, ..., M_k, ..., \sim L_n}$$

For example, the cooperation is best illustrated by representing arguments in a tree form, as in Figure 3.

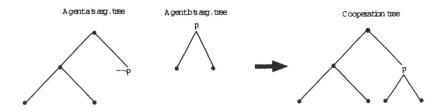

Fig. 3. Cooperative argument

5 Integrating Three Reasoning Methods into the Argumentation Protocol

Given an issue to be settled, arguments usually proceeds with mutually casting arguments and counterarguments that are constructed from each agent's knowledge base. Arguments usually result in 'justified' (sort of 'win') or 'overruled' (sort of 'lose') of the either side, based on the defeat relation of arguments above and argument strategies employed in the argumentation protocol (see [17] and [7] for the details of the argument strategy).

In this section, we give a flow of the argumentation. For simplicity and easiness of its description, we describe it only for argumentation among four agents and one special agent called Mediator agent who directs and mediates argumentation. Let agent P1 and agent P2 be proponents and agent O1 and agent O2 be opponents. Suppose that the order of speaking a voice is agent P1 and then agent P2, and the same for agent O1 and agent O2. Furthermore, issues to be argued are of the conjunctive form of strong literals such as A, B, C. Then, Mediator agent takes one conjunction at a time and passes it to the agent who attempts to argue about A, then argue about B and so on. Finally, Mediator agent makes a general agreement from each result. The argumentation protocol of our argument-based agent system basically consists of three phases: (i) Phase 1: making arguments and counterarguments, (ii) Phase 2: making cooperation, and (iii) Phase 3: making dialectical agreements, as described in the following (see Figure 4(b) for the overall structure of the flow).

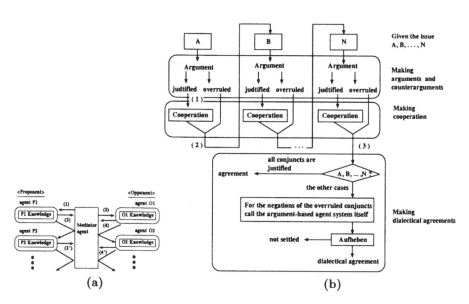

Fig. 4. (a): Phase 1's flow of argumentation (b): The overall flow of the argument-based agent system

[Phase 1. Making arguments and counterarguments]

Step 1. Mediator agent takes the first conjunct from the given issue and sends it to agent P1 and asks to make an argument on it ((1) in Figure 4(a)).

Step 2. Agent P1 tries to make an argument on the given conjunct from P1's knowledge base. If succeeds in making an argument, this will become the first main subject and be sent to Mediator agent ((2) in Figure 4(a)). Otherwise, agent P2 instead tries to make an argument on it ((2') in Figure 4(a)). If any proponent can not make an argument, then the system ends with no argument possible.

Step 3. Mediator agent sends agent Pi's argument to the opponent side, requesting to make a counterargument to it ((3) in Figure 4(a)).

Step 4. The first agent in the opponent side, agent O1, tries to make a counterargument to defeat the argument sent to it. If succeeds, it sends the counterargument to Mediator agent ((4) in Figure 4(a)), and then go to Step 5. If fails, the proposed argument is returned to Mediator agent and resent to another opponent agent O2, requesting to defeat it ((4') in Figure 4(a)). If no opponents succeed in the counterargument, the proposed argument is *justified* in the sense that there have been no attacks to it. Then, Mediator-agent records this result and asks any one of agent Ois if it can cooperate with the proposer to make a better argument than the proposed argument by reinforcing it with the help of Oi's knowledge (see the subsection 4.3) and then go to **Step 7** in **Phase 2** ((1) in Figure 4(b)).

Step 5. Mediator-agent sends the counterargument to agent P1 and requests it to make a counterargument to the counterargument from agent Oj.

Step 6. Agent P1 tries to make an counterargument in such a way that Agent P1 defeats the argument by agent Oj. If possible, agent P1 returns it to Mediator agent. Otherwise, like **Step 2** above, the next agent in the proponent side tries to make a counterargument. If no one in the proponent side can make a counterargument, the main subject is *overruled*. Then, Mediator-agent records this result. If there exist conjuncts which have not been argued yet, then go to **Step 2** where Mediator-agent takes the next conjunct, sends it to agent P1, asking to make an argument on it ((2) in Figure 4(b)). If all the conjuncts have already been argued, go to **Step 10** in **Phase 3** ((3) in Figure 4(b)).

[Phase 2. Making cooperation]

Step 7. Agent O1 pays attention to weak literals of the form ∼L appearing in the proposed argument by agent Pi, and tries to reinforce it according to the scheme in the subsection 4.3, using agent O1's knowledge base. If succeeds, agent O1 chooses the strongest argument from many possible alternatives in the sense that the number of the weak literals in that argument is minimal, and sends it to Mediator agent, going to Step 8. Otherwise, agent O2 instead tries to make a reinforcement on the argument. If no opponent can give its cooperation, go to **Step 2** in **Phase 1** where Mediator agent takes the next conjunct which has not been argued and sends it to agent P1 and asks to make an argument on it ((2) in Figure 4(b)). If all the conjuncts have already been argued, go to **Step 10** in **Phase 3** ((3) in Figure 4(b)).

Step 8. Mediator agent sends the reinforced argument to agent Pi.

Step 9. Agent Pi accepts the cooperation if the number of weak literals in the reinforcement is less than or equal to that in the original defeasible rule, otherwise agent Pi refuses it since adding this reinforcement to the original argument will result in increasing weak literals (incomplete information) in the original argument and hence weakening it. Agent Pi tells the refusal to the opponent via the Mediator agent and other opponents (for example, agent O2) instead try to cooperate with Agent Pi. If any opponent fails in the cooperation, then there is no cooperation between opponents and proponents. If all the conjuncts have already been argued, go to **Step 10** in **Phase 3** ((3) in Figure 4(b)). Otherwise go to **Step 2** in **Phase 1** where Mediator agent takes another conjunct which has not been argued and sends as the next conjunct to agent P1 and asks to make an argument on it ((2) in Figure 4(b)).

[Phase 3. Making dialectical agreements]
   Step 10. Mediator agent inspects all the results. If all the conjuncts are *justified*, the system ends with the agreement. If some or all conjuncts are *overruled*, call the argument-based agent system itself for the negations of overruled conjuncts to invoke the Aufheben process (see the subsection 4.2). For example, suppose that the issue is of the form A&B, and the first part is justified, but second part is overruled. If ¬B is justified by an opponent, the Aufheben process lifts up the contradiction and propose A&¬B as a dialectical agreement. Otherwise, the issue is left unsettled.

   It is noted that the argumentation process terminates in a finite number of steps since the proponents are not allowed to repeat the same arguments [17], or the system terminates if the proponents can not make arguments against the opponents and vice versa [17]. Moreover, the argumentation protocol is obviously fair in the sense that chances to speak a voice are given alternatively for both the proponent and opponent sides, and of course no conspiracy at all [17].

   The readers might have noticed that the argumentation protocol described above is not simply a protocol for arguing with other agents, but one for reaching an understanding with them. In a sense, we think that it might reflect an eastern way how talking with persons about matters and doing things. We might well say that we here presented such a protocol that avoids confrontational situations as possible as we can. We would say agents can not help but involving culture. East vs. West is a typical one. Western culture tends to begin with discussing a matter by making conflicting points thoroughly explicit, as seen in formal debate.

   As an alternative way of the argumentation protocol, we also built an argument-based agent system directed by the contract net protocol (CNP), where arguments are coordinated and mediated by a neutral agent called a judge who plays a role of a manager in CNP. Then s/he applies to the judgement various selection criteria with social meanings [7][16].

6   A Variety of Applications

In this section, we show that our model of argument-based agent system could allow to deal with various application domains in the networked computer environment, because of its versatility.

6.1   Applications of Conflict-Resolving Reasoning

[1] Application to a social issue: Example of $\vdash A$, $\vdash \neg A \Rightarrow \vdash \neg A$
   This is concerned with the real dispute on the issue: Is the nuclear power plant necessary or not at a local town of Japan? The knowledge base is made

from articles appeared in the newspapers, without putting any bias on the both sides. It includes right and wrong or propriety on various issues on the nuke construction (see [17] for the details of the knowledge base and the actual argument flow). The first agent's knowledge base (assent side) is mainly concerned about the issues on safety, disposal of effluent and pollution. The second agent's knowledge base (assent side) is mainly concerned about the issues on the need of energy, subsidy and local promotion. The third agent's knowledge base (dissent side) is mainly concerned about the issues on safety, accident and crop. The fourth agent's knowledge base (dissent side) is mainly concerned about the issues on information hiding and trust.

[2] Application to electronic commerce (traveling salesman agent, shopping agent, auction, etc.)

It would be an intriguing question how argument-based agent system can be applied to such a contemporary topic as electronic commerce with a high demand. We have realized (a) a shopping agent who wants to buy something by discounting, (b) auction agents, and (c) traveling salesman agent. Obviously, the discounting, auction and selling activities can be viewed as a sort of negotiation process of argumentation form. In particular, we realized a traveling salesman avatar as a mobile argument-based agent, who can visit (move around) the agent places on the network with her/his own knowledge base and argument (inference) engine and sell cars by negotiating the prices, quality, and so on with buyers through argumentation. After having finished the task, s/he comes back to her/his proprietor and report the result.

6.2   Applications of Dialectical Reasoning

[3] Application to a software design: Example of a compromise $\vdash A \& B$, $\vdash \neg B \Rightarrow \vdash A \& \neg B$

This is concerned with a dispute in designing software systems like our argument systems themselves. The confrontational issue is that one asserts 'Java and Lisp' for the choice of the implementation language, and the other asserts 'Prolog'. Then, our system reached a compromise as an agreement, 'Java and Prolog' after the argument, assuming that 'Lisp' is 'not Prolog'.

[4] Application to a Knowledge-based qualitative meeting scheduling agent system: Example of a compromise $A \wedge B$ from $A \wedge \neg B$ and $\neg A \wedge B$.

There have been many attempts to meeting scheduling agent systems. However, they are ones that schedules are coordinated quantitatively using some sort of a utility function and so on. Our argument-based approach is very different from them, and brings us unique advantages coming from the facts that it exploits knowledge base and hence allows highly qualitative decisions on the time and place for a meeting.

6.3   Applications of Cooperative Reasoning

[5] Application to cooperative theorem proving
We here chose a mini proof checker as the focus of a cooperative problem solving by argumentation. We deal with a reasoning task (issue) that arises in distributed environments where no agent has complete knowledge. In fact, the two agents below have incomplete knowledge about the logic respectively although their combined knowledge becomes complete. The issue to cooperatively solve is to examine whether the following sequence of formulas is a proof or not,

```
proof( [(((p -> p) -> (p -> p)) -> (p -> p)) -> (p -> p),
            ((p -> p) -> (p -> p)) -> (p -> p), p -> p] ),
```

under the following knowledge of Agent a and Agent b.

Agent a's knowledge (Agent a might forget the axioms):

```
proof(L) <= proof_checker(L, []).
proof_checker([], _) <= write('This is a proof').
proof_checker([H|T], Stack) <= ~ not axiom(H),
                        proof_checker(T, [H|Stack]).
proof_checker([H|T], Stack) <= derived(H, Stack),
                        proof_checker(T, [H|Stack]).
derived(G, Stack) <= modus_ponens(E, F, G),
                        member(E, Stack), member(F, Stack).
modus_ponens(A -> B, A, B).
member(X, [X|Xs]).
member(X, [Y|Ys]) :- member(X, Ys).
```

Agent b's knowledge (Agent b only knows what the axioms are.):

```
axiom((A -> B) -> ((B -> C) -> (A -> C))).
axiom(((A -> A) -> B) -> B).
axiom((A -> (A -> B)) -> (A -> B)).
```

Agent a can ascertain that it is a proof under her/his belief on the axioms although s/he forgets them, for two reasons. First, the weak literal $\sim$not axiom(H) is used in Agent a's knowledge, and this means that Agent a believes axiom(H) without its verification, in other words, axiom(H) is Agent a's assumption by default. Second, there is no counterargument from Agent b for Agent a's proposed argument (proof). Then Agent b might feel inclined to make a better proof and cooperate with Agent a, persuading Agent a to guarantee that it is certainly a proof if Agent b's knowledge is provided.

Interestingly, if the issue is something like

```
proof( [(((p -> p) -> (p -> p)) -> (p -> p)) -> (p -> p), q, p -> p] ),
```

the agents could have a corrected proof as the result of argument and cooperation.

We have described the cases where the reasoning leads to a success whether it is a true proof or putative one. In the case of the argument' failures that actually occur very often, we have not given an appropriate idea, but this can be viewed as sort of distributed problem solving such as distributed automated reasoning [6].

7   Concluding Remarks

In this paper, we claimed that argumentation is a social computing paradigm or principle, by revealing three kinds of reasoning triggered by arguments among agents: (i) conflict-resolving reasoning, (ii) dialectical reasoning, and (iii) cooperative reasoning. We built an argument-based agent system by incorporating these reasoning methods into the argumentation protocol. Finally, we showed its potential usefulness and feasibility in a convincing manner by applying it to a wide variety of the contemporary application domains.

Although what we have done is still at the initial stage, we believe that this could yield a completely new direction to making agents versatile and bring a new insight to agent studies from now on.

It is planned to extend our argument-based agent model to various directions: (i) an agent that can change its mental states like humans during argumentation, (ii) an agent that can reason quantitatively as well as qualitatively, and (iii) an agent to be able to attend computer-mediated conference. Then we would need to take into account various results and considerations from social psychology.

Acknowledgments. We would like to express our gratitude to Prof. M. Toda, a project leader of the interdisciplinary research group (on Attaining a Consensus in a Virtual Society over the Network) of Niigata University and the other members. We also would like to thank the anonymous reviewers for many profound comments on an earlier version of this paper.

References

1. Benthem, J. van et al. (eds.): *Logic and Argumentation*, Proc. of the Colloquium 'Logic and Argumentation', Royal Netherlands Academy of Arts and Sciences, 1994.
2. Dung, P. M.: *An Argumentational Semantics for Logic Programming with Classical Negation*, Proc. of Tenth Int. Conf. on Logic Programming, MIT Press, pp. 616-630, 1993.
3. Eemeren, F. H., Grootendorst, R., Henkmans, A. F. S., et al.: *Fundamentals of Argumentation Theory, A Handbook of Historical Backgrounds and Contemporary Developments*, Lawrence Erlbaum, 1996.
4. Krause, P., Ambler, S., Goransson, M. E. and Fox, J.: *A Logic of Argumentation for Reasoning under Uncertainty*, Computational Intelligence, Vol. 11, No. 1, pp. 113-131, 1995.
5. Loui, R. P.: *Defeat among Arguments: a System of Defeasible Inference*, Computational Intelligence, Vol.2, pp. 100-106, 1987.

6. Macintosh, D. J. and Conry, S. E. and Meyer, R. A.: *Distributed Automated Reasoning: Issues in Coordination, Cooperation, and Performance*, IEEE Transactions on Systems, Man and Cybernetics, Vol. 21, No. 6, 1991, pp. 1307-1316.

7. Maeda, S., Guan, C. and Sawamura, H. : *An Argument-based Agent System with the Contract Net Protocol*, Liu, J. and Zhong, N. (eds.): Intelligent Agent Technology: Systems, Methodologies, and Tools, The World Scientific Publication, pp. 99-103. 1999.

8. Nute, D.: *Defeasible Reasoning and Decision Support Systems*, Decision Support Systems, Vol. 4, pp. 97-110, 1988.

9. Parker, J. H.: *Social Logics: Their Nature and Uses in Social Research*, Cybernetica, Vol. 25, No. 4, pp. 287-308, 1982.

10. Pollock, J. L..: *Defeasible Reasoning*, Cognitive Science, Vol. 11, pp. 481-518, 1987.

11. Prakken, H. and Sartor, G.: *Argument-based Extended Logic Programming with Defeasible Priorities*, J. of Applied Non-Classical Logics, Vol. 7, No. 1-2, pp. 25-75, 1997.

12. Rescher, N.: Dialectics - a controversy-oriented approach to the theory of knowledge -, State University of New York Press, 1977.

13. Routley, R. and Meyer, R.: *Dialectical Logic, Classical Logic, and the Consistency of the World*, Studies in Soviet Thought, Vol. 16, pp. 1-25, 1976.

14. Sawamura, H. and Asanuma, D.: *Mechanizing Relevant Logics with HOL*, The 11th International Conference on Theorem Proving in Higher Order Logics (TPHOLs'98), Lecture Notes in Computer Science, Vol. 1479, Springer, pp. 443-460, 1998.

15. Sawamura, H., Umeda, Y. and Meyer, R. K.: *Computational Dialectics for Argument-based Agent Systems*, to be presented at the Fourth International Conference on MultiAgents Systems (ICMAS '2000), Boston, USA, 2000.

16. Sawamura, H. and Maeda, S.: *An Argumentation-Based Model of Multi-Agent Systems*, Proc of the 10th European-Japanese Conference on Information Modeling and Knowledge Bases, pp. 96-109, 2000.

17. Umeda, Y. and Sawamura, H.: *Towards an Argument-based Agent System*, 1999. Proc of 3rd Int. Conf. on Knowledge-Based Intelligent Information Engineering Systems, IEEE, 1999, pp. 30-33.

18. Yamashita, M., Inagaki, M., Umeda, Y. and Sawamura, H.: *Agents Meet Dialectics*, 2000. (unpublished manuscript)

Rationality Assumptions and Optimality of Co-learning

Ron Sun and Dehu Qi

CECS, University of Missouri
Columbia, MO 65211, USA
http://www.cecs.missouri.edu/~rsun

Abstract. This paper investigates the effect of different rationality assumptions on the performance of co-learning by multiple agents in extensive games. Extensive games involve sequences of steps and close interactions between agents, and are thus more difficult than more commonly investigated (one-step) strategic games. Rationality assumptions may thus have more complicated influences on learning, e.g., improving performance sometimes while hurting performance some other times. In testing different levels of rationality assumptions, a "double estimation" method for reinforcement learning suitable for extensive games is developed, whereby an agent learns not only its own value function but also those of other agents. Experiments based on such a reinforcement learning method are carried out using several typical examples of games. Our results indeed showed a complex pattern of effects resulting from (different levels of) rationality assumptions.

1 Introduction and Background

Assumptions that an agent makes about other agents may have significant impact on co-learning by multiple autonomous agents. This issue has not been investigated sufficiently in the past. In this paper, we will investigate the impact of such assumptions on co-learning performance in extensive games. Extensive games involve sequences of steps and close interactions between agents, and are thus more difficult than more commonly investigated (one-step) strategic games. This type of assumption may thus have more complicated influences on co-learning (e.g., improving performance sometimes while hurting performance some other times).

In order to test the effect of such assumptions, we will develop a "double estimation" method for reinforcement learning suitable for extensive games, whereby an agent learns not only its own value function but also those of other agents. We will then carry out experiments, using the method, on several typical examples of extensive games.

1.1 Extensive Games

Game theory studies decision making under the condition of interaction of multiple agents (Osborne and Rubinstein 1994). A *strategic* game is the one in which

C. Zhang and V.-W. Soo (Eds.): PRIMA 2000, LNAI 1881, pp. 61–75, 2000.

all agents choose their actions simultaneously and once for all. In contrast, in *an extensive* game, agents take turn in performing actions. Formally, an extensive game is a 4-tuple: (N, H, P, U), where N is a set of agents, H is a set of history (see Osborne and Rubinstein 1994 for further specifications), P is the player function such that $P(h)$ specifies the player after history h, U is the payoff function that maps each terminal history to a real value. Such a game is the one with perfect information – all the previous steps are observable. On the other hand, an extensive form without perfect information can be defined as a 5-tuple: (N, H, P, U, I), where N, H, P, U are defined as before, I is a set of partitions where for each agent $i \in N$, I_i is a partition of $h \in H : P(h) = i$ and $I_i^h \in I_i$ is an information set of agent i (i.e., what it can observe).

A *pure strategy* of an agent in an extensive game is defined as follows: it is a function of an agent that assigns an action (among all the possible actions) to each of its information sets. A *mixed strategy* is a probability measure over the set of an agent's pure strategies, which is used to randomly select a pure strategy to use in game playing. A *behavior strategy* is a set of probability measures, each of which is over the set of all the possible actions for an agent given an information set and is used to select stochastically actions when facing the information set.

1.2   Reinforcement Learning

Reinforcement learning (RL) (Watkins 1989, Bertsekas and Tsitsiklis 1996) is a general learning framework suitable for learning extensive games. There is a discrete-time system, the state transitions of which depend on actions performed by an agent. A Markovian process is in the working in determining a new state (from state transition) after an action is performed: $prob(s_{t+1}|s_t, a_t, s_{t-1}, a_{t-1}, \dots) = prob(s_{t+1}|s_t, a_t) = p_{s_t, s_{t+1}}(a_t)$, where a_t is determined based on a policy L (i.e., $a_t = L(s_t)$). In this process, costs (or rewards) can occur for certain states and/or actions. Normally the costs/rewards accumulate additively, with or without a discount factor $\gamma \in (0, 1]$.

The cumulative cost/reward estimate J that results from following an optimal policy of actions satisfies the Bellman optimality equation (Bellman 1957):

$$J(s_t) = \max_{a \in A} \sum_{s_{t+1} \in S} p_{s_t, s_{t+1}}(a)(r(s_t) + \gamma J(s_{t+1}))$$

where r denotes cost/reward, s_t is any state and s_{t+1} is the new state resulting from action a. Or, using the notation $Q(s_t, a_t)$ (where $\max_{a \in A} Q(s, a) = J(s)$), we have

$$Q(s_t, a_t) = \sum_{s_{t+1} \in S} p_{s_t, s_{t+1}}(a_t)(r(s_t) + \gamma \max_{a \in A} Q(s_{t+1}, a))$$

Based on the Bellman optimality equation, there are a number of on-line algorithms for learning Q or J functions. One is the Q-learning algorithm of Watkins (1989). The updating is done completely on-line, without explicitly using probability estimates:

$$Q(s_t, a_t) :=$$

$$(1 - \alpha)Q(s_t, a_t) + \alpha(r(s_t) + \gamma \max_{a_{t+1} \in A}(Q(s_{t+1}, a_{t+1})))$$

That is,

$$\Delta Q(s_t, a_t) = \alpha(r(s_t) + \gamma \max_{a_{t+1} \in A} Q(s_{t+1}, a_{t+1}) - Q(s_t, a_t))$$

where a_t is determined by an action policy: e.g., $prob(a_t) = \frac{e^{Q(s_t, a_t)/\tau}}{\sum_{a \in A} e^{Q(s_t, a)/\tau}}$, where τ is the temperature that determines the degree of randomness in action selection. The updating is done based on actual state transition instead of transition probabilities; that is, on-line "simulation" is performed. Such learning allows completely autonomous learning from scratch, without a priori domain knowledge. Singh et al (1994) showed that if transition probability and reward estimates satisfy some ergodic conditions, the on-line Q-learning will converge to Q values that satisfy the Bellman optimality equation involving true means of transition probabilities and rewards.

2   Levels of Rationality Assumptions

In using RL in game theoretical settings, there is an extra twist that we must consider. When a small set of agents (for example, two) is involved, it is advantageous to learn an (relatively) accurate estimate of the action propensities of other agents. Without such knowledge (and being blind to the choices made by other agents), it may not be possible to reach jointly optimal outcomes (in some sense), as demonstrated by early work in learning games, such as Shoham and Tennenholtz (1994) and Sen and Sekaran (1998). Shoham and Tennenholtz (1994) showed that simple learning rules could be very inefficient in cooperative games. Sen and Sekaran (1998) also attempted to learn to coordinate without explicit regard to other agents. They achieved limited success in small domains. Sen and Sekaran (1998), however, pointed out that such learning is problematic "when agent actions are strongly coupled, feedback is delayed, and there is one or a few optimal behavior combination". Claus and Boutilier (1998) dealt partially with such problems in reinforcement learning of strategic, cooperative games, and tried to encourage reinforcement learners to reach the optimal outcomes by incorporating the values of "optimal strategies" of other agents in updating value functions. [1]

The issue can be formulated as the levels of rationality assumptions: whether we assume that an agent makes the rationality assumption about its opponent (that is, whether it believes that its opponent will always choose the best action with respect to its own reward function), [2] and whether we assume that an agent assumes that its opponent makes the rationality assumption about it, and so on (cf. Hu and Wellman 1998 b). If an agent assumes that its opponent is rational (i.e., tends to select the best actions in various circumstances), we call

---

[1] See also Littman (1994) and Hu and Wellman (1998 a).

[2] Here the word "opponent" is simply used to denote the other agent in a game.

it the level-1 rationality assumption. If an agent assumes that its opponent in turn makes the same rationality assumption about it, this is a case of the level-2 rationality assumption. In the same vein, we term it level-0 rationality if an agent tends to choose best actions in given circumstances with no regard to its opponents.

We want to investigate how different levels of rationality assumptions affect learning of multiple interacting agents. Will deeper levels of rationality assumptions help to improve co-learning? Arguments can be made that the more information one gathers, the better one learns. Or will deeper levels of rationality assumptions hurt co-learning? Arguments can also be made that inaccurate, partial, or irrelevant information may prove to be harmful. Some empirical work showed that this may indeed be the case (e.g., in strategic games; Hu and Wellman 1998 b). We thus would like to better understand this issue by performing more extensive experiments.

3   "Double-Estimation" Reinforcement Learning

Our RL algorithms that incorporate rationality assumptions are based on "double estimation": An agent not only learns its own value function (which is dependent on other agents' value functions), but also learns others' value functions (and uses them in learning its own value function).

First is the case where only the level-0 rationality assumption is made. Assuming two agents are involved, we will deal with individual learning of these two agents, not social learning (of randomly paired agents). We assume that the two agents take action alternately, and the sequence is $a_1^0, a_2^1, a_1^1, a_2^2, a_1^2 \ldots\ldots$, where generally a_1 denotes actions of agent 1, a_2 denotes actions of agent 2, and superscripts denote time steps. The corresponding observed states at the time when each of these actions is taken are, respectively, s_2^0 (when a_1^0 is taken), s_1^1 (when a_2^1 is taken), s_2^1 (when a_1^1 is taken), s_1^2 (when a_2^2 is taken), s_2^2 (when a_1^2 is taken), $\ldots\ldots$ For the first part of the double estimation, self-estimation (i.e., updating the value function of agent 1) is as follows:

$$\Delta Q_1(s_1^1, a_2^1, a_1^1) = \alpha(r_1(s_1^2) + \gamma \max_{a_1^2 \in A_1} Q_1(s_1^2, a_2^2, a_1^2) - Q_1(s_1^1, a_2^1, a_1^1))$$

where Q_1 is the value function of agent 1, r_1 is the reward function for agent 1, [3] A_1 is the action set of agent 1, Note that the updating is done after action a_2^2 is completed (by agent 2 in state s_1^2). [4] This is appropriate because agent 2 may be using a stochastic policy (i.e., mixed or behavioral strategy in a game theoretic sense) and agent 1 has no a priori knowledge to determine whether this is the case or not. On the other hand, in referring to its own future action, agent 1 may reasonably assume that a greedy policy will be used and hence the MAX

---

[3]   In game learning, reward can only occur at the end when a terminal state is reached. Thus $r(s)$ is zero except in terminal states.

[4]   To get agent 2's actual action, agent 1 has to wait until agent 2 takes an action before it can learn.

operation (using the level-0 rationality assumption). (Alternatively, agent 1 may adopt a stochastic policy (mixed strategy), in which case the MAX operation should be replaced by the statistical average resulting from different possible actions.)

For the second part of the double estimation, updating the (estimated) value function of agent 2 by agent 1 (i.e., opponent-estimation) is as follows: [5]

$$\Delta Q_2(s_2^0, a_1^0, a_2^1) = \alpha(r_2(s_2^1) + \gamma Q_2(s_2^1, a_1^1, a_2^2) - Q_2(s_2^0, a_1^0, a_2^1))$$

Where Q_2 is the value function of agent 2 as estimated by agent 1, A_2 is the action set of agent 2, r_2 is the reward function for agent 2, This updating is done after action a_2^2. Here we do not take MAX in estimating future Q-values, because we try to avoid making any assumption about the actions of agent 2. [6]

The above formulation does not put the double estimation to use in learning "optimal" value functions (e.g., in the sense of encouraging convergence to optimal joint outcomes in some sense). Remedying this shortcoming, utilizing some further rationality assumptions (level-1 and level-2), we can have instead the following set of equations:

For self-estimation,

$$\Delta Q_1(s_1^1, a_2^1, a_1^1) = \alpha(r_1(s_1^2) + \gamma \max_{a_1^2 \in A_1} Q_1(s_1^2, a_2^{best}, a_1^2) - Q_1(s_1^1, a_2^1, a_1^1))$$

where $a_2^{best} = argmax_{a_2' \in A_2} Q_2(s_2^1, a_1^1, a_2')$. Here the assumption of rationality of one's opponent (hereby termed the level-1 assumption of rationality) is essential: Agent 1 assumes that agent 2 will (likely or eventually) choose the best action for its own sake (and hence the use of a_2^{best}). [7]

For opponent-estimation,

$$\Delta Q_2(s_2^0, a_1^0, a_2^1) = \alpha(r_2(s_2^1) + \gamma \max_{a_2^2 \in A_2} Q_2(s_2^1, a_1^{best}, a_2^2) - Q_2(s_2^0, a_1^0, a_2^1))$$

---

[5]   We generally assume that an agent can observe its opponent's payoffs.

[6]   (1) Note that in the above equations, we use different action orders for the two different estimations: from agent 2 to agent 1 (for learning Q_1), or from agent 1 to agent 2 (for learning Q_2). This is because it is easier to formulate value functions this way: the action of the other agent has already been performed at the time of the action for which the value function is being learned. (2) At the beginning of a game, the same updating equations may be used with dummy actions being padded at the beginning of a sequence (that is, turning $[a_1^0, a_2^0, a_1^1, a_2^1, ...]$ into $[...., a_1^{-1}, a_2^{-1}, a_1^0, a_2^0, a_1^1, a_2^1, ...]$). (3) Similarly, in case of termination without action by agent 2, we can assume agent 2 performs a pseudo-action "end".

[7]   We use a_2^{best} even though we know the actual action taken by agent 2. This is because we want to take into consideration what is the best for agents, even though they may be taking suboptimal actions occasionally for reasons of exploration or simply wandering around (in a way similar to the idea of "trembling hands"; Osborne and Rubinstein 1994).

Where $a_1^{best} = argmax_{a_1' \in A_1} Q_1(s_1^1, a_2^1, a_1')$. Here beside making the level-1 assumption in terms of taking the MAX when estimating future Q-values, we utilize also the level-2 assumption of rationality: Agent 1 assumes that agent 2 will assume that agent 1 will (likely or eventually) choose the best action (and hence the use of a_1^{best}). If we do not want to make the level-2 assumption, we can use instead the previous equation for opponent-estimation (while using the current equation for self-estimation if we stick to the level-1 assumption). [8]

The two different sets of learning equations for value functions may be combined. As suggested by Claus and Boutilier (1998), because one set encourages the adoption of optimal actions (which may lead to jointly optimal outcomes) and the other set learns on the basis of current action probabilities, the combination may tend to "steer" both agents toward jointly optimal outcomes (in some sense). To combine the two sets of equations, we use the following equation (cf. Claus and Boutilier 1998) for self-estimation,

$$Q_1^{(total)}(*, *, *) = \mu_1 Q_1^{(r)}(*, *, *) + (1 - \mu_1) Q_1^{(nr)}(*, *, *)$$

where (r) indicates the Q-values resulting from the second set of equations using double estimation with the level-1 and level-2 rationality assumptions, (nr) indicates the Q-values from the first set of equations without such assumptions, $(total)$ indicates the combined Q-values, μ_1 is the weighting factor that determines the relative contributions from the two sets of equations. Similarly, for opponent-estimation, we have

$$Q_2^{(total)}(*, *, *) = \mu_2 Q_2^{(r)}(*, *, *) + (1 - \mu_2) Q_2^{(nr)}(*, *, *)$$

where μ_2 is the weighting factor that determines the relative contributions from the two sets of equations in determining the values of opponent-estimation, which may or may not be the same as μ_1. (Note that this combination is different from Claus and Boutilier (1998), in that we do not need to compute the probabilities of opponent actions and their respective Q-values because we are dealing with extensive games in which actions are taken sequentially and alternately.)

Action selection in the course of a game is based on $Q_1^{(total)}$. Note that exactly the same equations may be applied for the other agent (agent 2), if we change the subscript 1 to 2 and vice versa.

4   Some Experiments

In this section, we will explore the effects of adding levels 1 and 2 rationality assumptions to the level-0 assumption. We need to compare different levels of rationality assumptions, in various game domains, through empirical means, in

---

[8] Level 0 and level 1 will not be the same. because the actual action by agent 2 involves random exploration or involves an entirely different learning algorithm (e.g., GA).

terms of (1) whether learning will converge, (2) the frequency of convergence and/or the rate at which it converges, (3) if it converges, what kind of attractor it converges to (e.g., in terms of Nash equilibria or Pareto efficiency). In the present paper, we focus mostly on optimality of joint or individual outcomes.

We experiment with a range of domains, which differ in terms of (1) different lengths (or depths, i.e., numbers of steps), (2) different numbers of action choices at each step (i.e., different widths), or (3) cooperativeness. Such variations are important, given the fact that learning methods may have widely varied performance when tested in different domains, "flavored" by the domain characteristics (see e.g. Shoham and Tenenholtz 1994 for instances).

Both agents will be learning on-line, together; i.e., both start out from scratch and learn while exploring. The best actions have also to be learned on-line, not estimated a priori. In experiments, we vary the following parameters associated with our RL algorithms: (1) learning rates and discount rates, (2) combination weights (for generating Q^{total}), to obtain the best performance possible for each algorithm. We also try different temperature parameters (i.e. τ) in the Boltzmann equation. However, we perform the periodic test of agents by choosing the best actions (according to Q-values), thereby generating learning curves.

Our results show that higher levels of rationality assumptions may have varied effects, depending on a large number of factors. They may help, hurt, make a difference that is neither, or make no difference at all, on the performance of learning.

4.1   The Left/Right (LR) Game

Three variations of this game are described by Figure 1. Let us analyze the three cases of this game, comparing the level-0 and level-1 assumption in terms of learning performance. Note that in this game, level 2 is meaningless due to short sequences (of 1 or 2 steps only). Note also that for agent 2, opponent-estimation, and thus level 1 or 2, is irrelevant, since there will be no more actions after its action.

– In case 1, we expect using level 1 will speed up convergence and help the performance of agent 1. This is because using a_2^{best} (that is, using level 1), agent 1 knows that it will receive a reward of 1 if it does r; using a_2 (level 0 alone), agent 1 will receive an average of 1 and 3 if it does r, which is the same as that resulting from its action l. So, with level 1, the action sequence should converge more quickly to $(l, \perp)$. However, even with level 0 alone, the best action for agent 1 should be l eventually (which is a Nash equilibrium). This is because eventually agent 2 will settle on l (in order to receive a payoff of 4 instead of 3), and consequently the difference for agent 1 is between a payoff of 2 and a payoff of 1 (resulting from its actions l and r respectively) and thus the better action should be chosen eventually.
In addition to speeding up convergence, using level 1 may also help to improve the performance of agent 1 by identifying the best action. Since the interests of agent 1 and 2 do not coincide in this case, helping the performance of agent 1 means hurting the performance of agent 2.

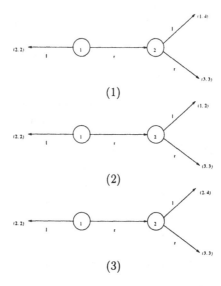

Fig. 1. Three cases of the Left/Right game. The numbers in circles indicate agents. l and r are two possible actions. The pair of numbers in parentheses indicate payoffs (where the first number is the payoff for agent 1 and the second for agent 2).

- In case 2, the use of level 1 should improve the speed of convergence as before. However, in this case, it also helps the performance of both, because in this case, the best action sequence is the same for both agents, or in other words, their interests coincide. The use of level 1 helps agent 1 to identify the best action for agent 2 being r (through opponent-estimation) and consequently the best action for agent 1 being r (through self-estimation), thus resulting in the action sequence (r, r), which is the best for both (and a Nash equilibrium). It thus improves the performance of both during learning and speeds up the convergence.

- In case 3, we expect that the use of level 1 does not have much effect on the speed of convergence because there is not much ambiguity in this situation. We also expect the level-1 curve of agent 1 to be somewhat worse, because, especially early on during learning, self-estimation based on a_2^{best} leads to a payoff of 2 for agent 1, but self-estimation based on a_2 leads to an average of 2 and 3 for agent 1. Therefore, the level-0 learner should be able to accrue more payoffs early on. However, eventually, agent 1 will receive a payoff of 2 regardless of its action (l or r) in the end, because agent 2 will settle on action l when action r is taken by agent 1 (because it leads to a payoff of 4, instead of 3). Both outcomes are Nash equilibria. In addition, when level 1 is used, agent 2 may be also worse off early on because it may be forced to receive a payoff of 2 due to the action l taken by agent 1, which may be more favored early on by agent 1 with the use of the level-1 assumption.

See the learning curves in Figures 2, 3, and 4, which fully confirmed our expectation. In the curves, we can compare level 0 and level 1 (with the combination of the two sets of equations). The figures contain learning curves averaged over 20 runs for each 10 iterations. That is, in the figures, the x axis is number of iterations (averaged over 20 runs) and the y axis is the performance measure (individual payoffs or total payoffs).

In the experiments, we randomly initialized the Q-values to some very small random positive values before the learning began, which represented initial (random) guesses. We did so for both agents and both levels. [9] We varied the combination weights. In the LR game, for agent 1, self-estimation was in the form of $Q_1(s, begin, a_1)$. Dummy actions ("begin") were padded at the beginning to make the equations work. The state s remained the same and was irrelevant in this game. The opponent-estimation was in the form of $Q_2(s, a_1, a_2)$, where a_1 was the action by agent 1 in the previous step and a_2 was the action by agent 2 in the current step. Payoffs were given at the end as indicated in the game trees (see Figure 1). For agent 2, opponent-estimation was irrelevant. For the self-estimation of agent 2, there was no need to consider actions by agent 1, because, for agent 2, actions by agent 1 were always r. The parameter settings were as follows: $\alpha = 0.05$, $\gamma = 0.8$, $\tau = 0.5$, and $\mu_1 = \mu_2 = 0.8$.

The results show that the level-1 assumption is beneficial, except in situations in which the agent fails to take into account randomness in the other agent.

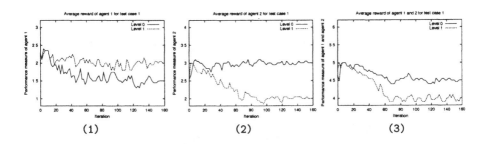

Fig. 2. The learning performance in case 1 of the left/right game. (1) The payoff of agent 1. (2) The payoff of agent 2. (3) The total payoff.

4.2   The Repeated Prisoner's Dilemma (RPD) Game

In this game (the repeated play of a strategic game – Prisoner's Dilemma), actions are organized into rounds. A "round" refers to a pair of actions by the two agents, which are simultaneous and not mutually observable at the time of

---

[9]   So initially, the best actions of agent 2 as seen by agent 1 can be totally off. Agent 1 will then learn the true best action for agent 2 through the (simultaneous) learning process.

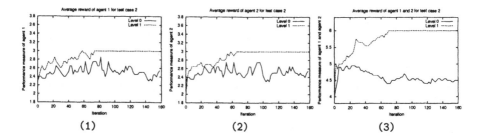

Fig. 3. The learning performance in case 2 of the left/right game. (1) The payoff of agent 1. (2) The payoff of agent 2. (3) The total payoff.

action. The action choices (C or D) and the payoff table are shown in figure 5. A fixed number of rounds is used, which is set at 8. The partial observability is captured through the use of information sets. An information set is implemented by a state that includes all the observable previous actions, up to a certain length (say, 1, 2, or 5).

In the RPD game, agent 1's self-estimation is in the form of $Q_1(s, a_2, a_1)$, in which a_2 is the action by agent 2 in the previous round (which is the immediately preceding *observable* action) and a_1 is the action by agent 1 in the current round. Likewise, the actions in s' needed for self-estimation (as in $Q(s', a'_2, a'_1)$) are the action by agent 2 in the current round and the action by agent 1 in the next round, respectively. The opponent-estimation is in the form of $Q_2(s, a_1, a_2)$, where a_1 is the action by agent 1 in the previous round (which is the immediately preceding *observable* action) and a_2 is the action by agent 2 in the current round. The next actions in s' needed for opponent-estimation (as in $Q(s', a'_1, a'_2)$) are the action by agent 1 in the current round and the action by agent 2 in the next round, respectively. State s consists of past sequences up to depth x (where x is 0 in our experiments because in this game such history is obvious from the previous action of the opponent). Dummy actions ("begin") were padded at the beginning to make the equations work. It is essentially the same for agent 2.

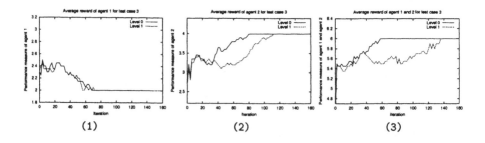

Fig. 4. The learning performance in case 3 of the left/right game. (1) The payoff of agent 1. (2) The payoff of agent 2. (3) The total payoff.

We compare here the case of learning with the level-1/2 rationality assumption and the case without. In a single-play PD game, the use of the level-1/2 assumption will not lead to a higher likelihood of jointly optimal outcomes, because mutual defection is the best (the most mutually rational) choice. [10] On the other hand, in the RPD game, an ideal outcome is as follows: If the opponent (agent 2) selects C the previous round, agent 1 would be better off selecting C, because in this case a_2^{best} is C and so the opponent will likely select C the next round, which leads to a high payoff (for both). (C is a_2^{best} under this circumstance because it is more likely to lead to further cooperation, which leads to higher payoffs.) Otherwise, if agent 1 selects D, then the opponent will likely select D the next round, which leads to worse payoffs for both. The use of the level-1/2 assumption can serve the purpose of encouraging agent 1 (and likewise agent 2) to play C, because, despite the actual action by agent 2, agent 1 "pretends" that the best action (i.e., C) is taken by agent 2 and is thus encouraged to take action C also. The learning curves are shown in Figure 6. The parameter settings are as follows: $\alpha = 0.05$, $\gamma = 0.8$, $\tau = 0.5$, and $\mu_1 = \mu_2 = 0.8$.

	C	D
C	3,3	0,5
D	5,0	1,1

Fig. 5. The game of prisoner's dilemma. Each row indicates a possible action by agent 1 (C or D). Each column indicates a possible action by agent 2 (C or D). In each pair, the first number indicates payoff for agent 1 and the second for agent 2.

However, we do not expect such improvement over level 0 to happen in every learning run and under every parameter setting, because alternative (worse) scenarios are also likely. Under different parameter settings (e.g., increasing the temperature to 0.7), we indeed obtained opposite results as well. [11]

4.3   The Poker (P) Game

In the poker game, there are two players: the gambler and the dealer. First the gambler has the choice of betting one dollar or passing. Then the dealer has the same choice. Finally the gambler has another chance of betting (if the gambler chose to pass previously and the dealer chose to bet). There are three cards: J, Q, and K, two of which will be dealt to the two agents. The agent who receives the higher card wins the pot.

---

[10] Shoham and Tennenholtz (1994) managed to reach a jointly optimal outcome, but through using a dumb learning rule which unnecessarily limits even the level-0 rationality of agents with no exploration and no sense of optimality.

[11] In future work, we shall extend the length of history, as contained in states, to see what effect it may bring.

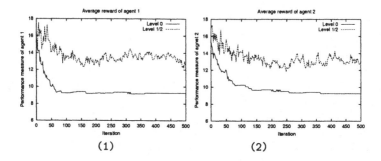

Fig. 6. The learning performance in the RPD game. (1) The payoff of agent 1. (2) The payoff of agent 2.

For agent 1 (the gambler), self-estimation is in the form of $Q_1(s, a_2, a_1)$, in which a_2 is the action by agent 2 (the dealer) in the immediately preceding step and a_1 is the action by agent 1 for the current step. The state s is the information about the card of agent 1 and the actions up to the point where these two actions (a_2 and a_1) are taken, up to a depth x (where $x = 0$ in our current experiments). The opponent-estimation is in the form of $Q_2(s, a_1, a_2)$, where a_1 is the action by agent 1 in the immediately preceding step (which may be empty, in which case a dummy action "begin" is added) and a_2 is the action by agent 2 for the current step.

There are some difficulties in this game. The previous actions and an agent's own card provide the only context for learning decision making. For example, the gambler knows only his own card (which is the state) and the dealer's action. The dealer knows his own card and the gambler's action. Each agent has to estimate its own move and the opponent's next move without the benefit of knowing the opponent's card, which determines its and the opponent's best actions. But in self-estimation, the gambler, for example, can learn its own action based on the eventual payoff. In opponent-estimation, the gambler can learn the dealer's action also based on the payoff it generates eventually. Of course the payoff will vary, depending on the card the opponent has, which the estimating agent has no knowledge of. But we believe that opponent-estimation can still be useful because it can capture some statistical regularities in the card distribution, and thus the statistical regularities in action selection, and it may lead to better average payoffs.

For each agent, we plot the cases of J, Q, and K in separate figures, with each figure containing multiple curves under different levels of rationality assumptions. We assume that there is a 60% probability that the dealer will receive K (and 20% receiving J and 20% receiving Q). We randomly assign a card to the gambler that is different from the one assigned to the dealer. The reason for doing this is that since it is much more likely that the dealer will receive K, the gambler's response will be more tailored to that setting. So we can study the dynamics of the interaction of the two agents in that setting. We compare curves (level 0 vs. level 1/2) under this condition, in terms of the performance of the gambler (since the performance of the dealer is simply the opposite). We tried the following combinations of temperatures: dealer-temp= 10 or 30, and gambler-temp = 0.5, 10, or 30. We also tested the following combinations of levels of rationality assumptions: dealer-level = 0 or 1, [12] and gambler-level = 0 or 1/2. [13] The performance of dealer-temp=10/dealer-level=0 and gambler-temp=30/gambler-level=0 vs. 1/2, which is fairly representative, is shown in Figure 7. The effect of the level-1/2 assumption is helpful sometimes: It helps the performance of the gambler when the gambler receives J or Q, which is the more common situation for the gambler to deal with (because the dealer receives K 60% of the time).

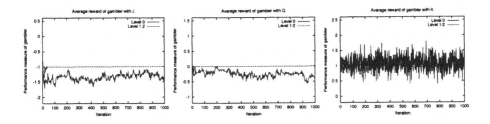

Fig. 7. The learning performance in the Poker game, in terms of the payoff of the gambler (three cases).

5   Discussions

The difference in the results of these three tasks may be attributed to the complexities of the tasks. The LR game is the simplest game we examined, and we can easily analyze the settings and anticipate the outcome. The Poker game is the most complex: Too many factors are involved in determining the learning process and as a result, we failed to clearly delineate the conditions under which the level-1/2 assumption is useful. Generally speaking, however, the more complex a task is, the more likely an agent is to assume something incorrect about its opponent during opponent-estimation (Hu and Wellman 1998 b). Thus, it is more likely to lead to worsened performance (as a result of wrong or incomplete information about opponents). The LR and RPD games also pointed to the fact that randomness (and other factors) that was not taken into account in level-1 or level-2 opponent-estimation led to worsened performance. In all, the three games point to the conclusion that the effect of higher levels of rationality

---

[12] The dealer's level-2 assumption is irrelevant, since there can only be one more step in an action sequence.

[13] $\alpha = 0.05$, $\gamma = 0.8$, and $\mu_1 = \mu_2 = 0.8$.

assumptions is not uniform: It may either help or hurt performance and needs to be understood on a case-by-case basis.

Judging from the results of the above experiments, the necessity of the benefit or the harm of higher levels of rationality assumptions on the part of an agent regarding opponents is unclear. In contrast to some previous results, we show here that such assumptions are not necessarily harmful, which seemed to be what was commonly perceived in the literature (e.g., with regard to auction games; Hu and Wellman 1998 b).

Some limitations and shortcomings of the present study include that it deals only with a fixed opponent: We assume that throughout a game, agents are fixed, not randomly drawn from a population. It is not clear how the results extend to cases of random encounters of samples out of a large population of opponents. Another shortcoming is the lack of deeper levels of rationality assumptions: We have not yet explored deeper levels of rationality assumptions beyond level 2. We may need longer chains of actions in order to test deeper levels. We also need to include longer history (information sets) in states.

Finally, it should be noted that our RL approach here is different from multi-agent RL that involves a central controller (such as Sun and Peterson 1999, Tham 1995) or cooperative game learning scenarios in which bidding and other cooperative mechanisms may be used (e.g., Sun and Sessions 1999). We do not assume here any explicit act of cooperation, or any central control that coordinates or even commands cooperation. The present approach is more generic.

References

R. Bellman, (1957). *Dynamic Programming*. Princeton University Press, Princeton, NJ.

D. Bertsekas and J. Tsitsiklis, (1996). *Neuro-Dynamic Programming*. Athena Scientific, Belmont, MA.

C. Claus and C. Boutilier, (1998). The dynamics of reinforcement learning in cooperative multiagent systems. *Proceedings of AAAI'98*. AAAI Press, San Mateo, CA.

D. Fudenberg and D. Levine, (1998). *The Theory of Learning in Games*. MIT Press, Cambridge, MA.

T. Haynes and S. Sen, (1996). Co-adaptation in a team. *International Journal of Computational Intelligence and Organizations*.

J. Hu and M. Wellman, (1998 a). Multiagent reinforcement learning: theoretical framework and an algorithm. *Proceedings of International Conference on Machine Learning*, 242-250. Morgan Kaufmann, San Francisco, CA.

J. Hu and M. Wellman, (1998 b). Online learning about other agents in a dynamic multiagent system. *Second International Conference on Autonomous Agents*. ACM Press, New York.

M. Littman, (1994). Markov games as a framework for multi-agent reinfocement learning. *Proc. of the 11th International conference on Machine Learning*, 157-163. Morgan Kaufmann, San Francisco, CA.

M. Osborne and A. Rubinstein, (1994). *A Course on Game Theory*. MIT Press, Cambridge, MA.

R. Salustowicz, M. Wiering, and J. Schmidhuber, (1998). Learning team strategies: soccer case studies. *Machine Learning*. 1998

S. Sen and M. Sekaran, (1998). Individual learning of coordination knowledge. *Journal of Experimental and Theoretical Artificial Intelligence*, 10, 333-356.

Y. Shoham and M. Tennenholtz, (1994). Co-learning and the evolution of social activity. Technical Report STAN-CS-TR-94-1511, Stanford University.

S. Singh, T. Jaakkola, and M. Jordan, (1994). Reinforcement learning with soft state aggregation. In: S.J. Hanson J. Cowan and C. L. Giles, eds. *Advances in Neural Information Processing Systems 7*. Morgan Kaufmann, San Mateo, CA.

R. Sun and T. Peterson, (1999). Multi-agent reinforcement learning: weighting and partitioning. *Neural Networks*, Vol.12, No.4-5. pp.127-153.

R. Sun and C. Sessions, (1999). Bidding in reinforcement learning: a paradigm for multi-agent systems. *Proc. of The Third International Conference on Autonomous Agents (AGENTS'99)*, Seattle, WA.

M. Tan, (1993). Multi-agent reinforcement learning: independent vs. cooperative agents. *Proceedings of Machine Learning Conference*. Morgan Kaufmann, San Francisco, CA.

C. Tham, (1995). Reinforcement learning of multiple tasks using a hierarchical CMAC architecture. *Robotics and Autonomous Systems*. 15, 247-274.

M. Vidal and E.H. Durfee, (1998). Learning nested models in an information economy. *Journal of Experimental and Theoretical Artificial Intelligence*, 10 (3), 291-308.

C. Watkins, (1989). *Learning with Delayed Rewards*. Ph.D Thesis, Cambridge University, Cambridge, UK.

G. Weiss, (1995). Distributed reinforcement learning. *Robotics and Autonomous Systems*, 15, 135-142.

Experiences in the Development of an Agent Architecture

Geoff Bush, Martin Purvis, and Stephen Cranefield

Department of Information Science, University of Otago,
P.O. Box 56, Dunedin, New Zealand
email: {gbush,mpurvis,scranefield}@infoscience.otago.ac.nz

Abstract. The current interest in agent-based software development has increased the demand for agent architectures upon which to build agent-based systems. While several agent architectures have been made publicly available, work in this area is not by any means finished—there are still many reasons to research new agent architectures. Although development of an agent architecture has been identified as a difficult process, little has been written about the issues involved—this contributes to the difficulty of the process. It is important for future agent architecture development that such issues be identified and widely discussed so that common pitfalls are not repeatedly encountered. This paper outlines the development of a new agent architecture and discusses experiences gained while using it to develop a prototype for the New Zealand Distributed Information Systems project. It is found that a useful agent architecture requires far more than a string-based peer-to-peer messaging platform to support effective agent-based software development.

1 Introduction

The current interest in agent-based software development has increased the demand for agent architectures[1] upon which to build agent-based systems. Agent architectures provide the low level machinery needed to enable agent-based development, allowing development effort to focus on the application specific parts of a project rather than infrastructure. Several agent architectures have been made publicly available [2,7], offering off-the-shelf tools for agent-based development. However there are still many valid reasons for developing new agent architectures, such as research interest or commercial gain. Agent architecture development has been identified as a difficult process [13], however little has been written about the issues involved. It is important for the future development for agent architectures that such issues be identified and widely discussed. This paper outlines the development of a new agent architecture and discusses

---

[1] The use of the term "agent architecture" refers to a software package that provides an agent platform, agent framework and associated agent-oriented tools for developing agent-based systems. This is not to be confused with an agent's internal architecture which is a model of the internal components of an agent, for example the BDI architecture.

C. Zhang and V.-W. Soo (Eds.): PRIMA 2000, LNAI 1881, pp. 76–87, 2000.

experiences gained while using it to develop a prototype for the New Zealand Distributed Information System (NZDIS) [8,10] project.

The rest of this paper is structured as follows. Section 2 provides background to the NZDIS project and rationale for the development of a new agent architecture, Sect. 3 describes the initial agent architecture, Sect. 4 discusses problems encountered while using this architecture to build a prototype of the NZDIS system, Sect. 5 discusses how these observations relate to future development of agent architectures and Sect. 6 provides some concluding remarks.

2   Background

The NZDIS project seeks to provide a framework for integrating heterogeneous information sources. The project employs a software architecture based on a loosely coupled collection of distributed software agents following in the tradition of agent-based software interoperability [6]. For the purposes of this project, agents are thought of as encapsulated, coarse-grained software components that are capable of flexible, autonomous interaction with other agents in order to meet their design objectives. Each agent is presumed to be a specialist for a particular task and the expectation is that complex tasks will be undertaken by a group of agents, none of which are capable of completing the tasks alone.

It was decided to embark upon constructing an in-house agent architecture compatible with Foundation for Intelligent Physical Agents (FIPA) specifications [1]. This approach was taken because of interest in agent architecture research and also because at the time there were no suitable agent architectures publicly available. This agent architecture makes novel use of object-oriented ontologies for specifying the semantics of message content [3], and employs the robust communication infrastructure provided by commercial Common Object Request Broker Architecture (CORBA) implementations and in particular allows the use of CORBA to transfer large datasets. This architecture is further discussed in Sect. 3 and its use in building the NZDIS prototype system is discussed in Sect. 4.

While this paper discusses the building of a new agent architecture, it does not intend to defend the decision to build an agent architecture from a commercial software production perspective—the NZDIS project is not a commercial software production project, but rather a research project conducted within a University. The authors believe that the research in agent architecture building is by no means complete, agent-oriented software engineering is still in its infancy and much work is still needed to move agent technology from research labs to common use in industry. Discussing the issues involved in building agent architectures is important for continued work in this area. Were the NZDIS project to have chosen a publicly available agent architecture it might be completed in a shorter time, but this would come at the expense of several of our research goals. Reasons for deciding to build our own architecture include:

- Most publicly available agent architectures are research software, which is often not robust, not well documented nor well supported.

- We required full knowledge and control of the critical lower level components of our system.
- We sought a robust communication layer such as that provided by a commercial CORBA implementation.
- We were interested in investigating and supporting object-oriented representation of ontologies.

3   The Initial Architecture

The requirement of the initial agent architecture was to provide support for string-based peer-to-peer agent messaging using the Java programming language. A secondary goal was to enable interoperation with similar FIPA-based agent architectures. This was thought to be a sufficient baseline for implementing the NZDIS prototype system. It was intended that other more advanced features would be added once the prototype system had been developed.

An architecture was built where agents were created by extending a certain abstract base class. This base class provided the mechanisms for sending agent messages and specifying how to handle incoming messages. Agents sent messages to other agents using a well known string-based syntax specified by the FIPA Agent Communication Language (ACL) [1]. This provides a framework for specifying message parameters such as a communicative act, a receiver and a sender, as well as the message content for each agent message (see Fig. 1, left). In this architecture the string-based syntax was used for the transport of messages between agents but enabled developers to view messages as objects with fields corresponding to the FIPA ACL fields (see Fig. 1, right).

```
( <communicative-act>              public class Message {
   :sender <sender>                    private String performative;
   :receiver <receiver>                private Address sender;
   :ontology <ontology>                private Address receiver;
   :language <language>                private String ontology;
   :content <content>                  private String language;
   :conversation-id <conv-id>          private String content;
   etc                                 private String conv_id;
)                                   etc
                                    }
```

Fig. 1. FIPA ACL string format (left). Object-oriented abstraction (right).

The simple agent-based scenario used to test this agent architecture included an agent with the capability of adding two numbers (the *adding* agent) and another agent which needed to use this capability (the *client* agent). The client agent sent a 'request' message with the content containing an arithmetic expression such as (2+3) and the adding agent performed the requested operation and sent an 'inform' message containing the result to the client agent. The agent architecture described thus far provided a suitable tool for building this scenario, so the larger project of building the prototype NZDIS system was enthusiastically embarked upon.

4   Lessons Learned

The architecture was used to build a prototype of the NZDIS system. The process uncovered several problems with the architecture that were not initially apparent. The simple provision of peer-to-peer messaging was found to be an insufficiently powerful tool for developing an agent-based system. More tools were needed for controlling, monitoring and organising agents (Sect. 4.1), the message content language needed to be better matched to the internal knowledge storage format (Sect. 4.2) and tools were needed for grouping related agent messages into logical conversations (Sect. 4.3).

While few of these ideas are particularly novel, in the authors' experience it is all too easy to regard these tools as advanced features that can be added in later, rather than as essential elements of an agent architecture.

4.1   Control, Monitoring, and Organisation Tools

The agents in the system ran as separate processes using only agent messaging to communicate. This was difficult to manage because there was no single point of control in the system. While having no single point of control is an important feature of agent systems, in practice this made the prototype system difficult to control and monitor. To run the prototype NZDIS system several agents had to be started up manually (See Fig. 2).

This was merely tedious when running the small number of agents used in the prototype NZDIS system at one location; however distributing the system across several computers was difficult, this approach would not have scaled for a system including a large number of agents. For example a current prototype scenario of the NZDIS system involves ten agents distributed in four geographical locations. Running all these agents individually would involve, at best, several telnet sessions and at worst several humans coordinating the launching of agents by telephone or email.

This problem demonstrates the need for a tool to be provided to control an agent-based system centrally as part of an agent architecture. Such a tool would allow an agent-based system to be run from a single point of control, eliminating the task of switching between windows or communicating between geographically separated locations. However, such a tool needs to be carefully designed so as

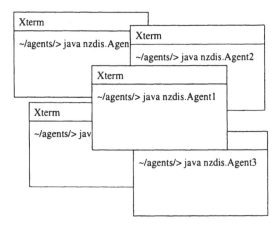

Fig. 2. Running several agents.

not to diminish the distributed, autonomous properties of agent-based systems. If the system were somehow restricted to communicating only with agents that were launched using this tool, it would preclude interoperation with other agent architectures. Such a tool needs to be provided as a *system utility*, not as the only method of using the system — other agents should not be excluded from participating in the system (See Fig. 3).

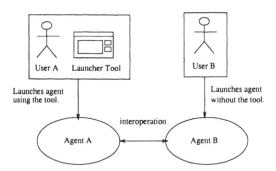

Fig. 3. The launcher would be a utility.

Another problem encountered while running the system was that of obtaining an overall view of the system behaviour. This made debugging and demonstrating the system difficult. The only information made available by the system was text output generated by each process for debugging and, if a query was successfully executed, feedback through the user interface. Developers found the debugging output difficult to follow as output from the the agent architecture was intermingled with output from the application level code, and this debugging output certainly offered no enlightenment to the casual observer. Ideally the utility described above would be capable of monitoring the messages sent between agents and would provide a useful summary of what the system was doing. This would provide a central place where the agent-level behaviour of the system could be examined for debugging or demonstration purposes. Again this would need to be seen as a *utility* so as not to break agent autonomy.

The third difficulty encountered was getting the various agents in the system to know what other agents they could communicate with. In the prototype NZ-DIS system this was achieved by always running each agent at a fixed location (eg, on the same TCP/IP port and host) and statically specifying each agent's address. It became tedious to respecify the agent addresses each time the system needed to be run using a different configuration of agents.

Statically specifying agent addresses also did not allow several agents of one type to exist simultaneously, perhaps for parallel processing of different queries. If an agent wanted to find another agent offering some particular service type it had no choice but to contact the one agent pointed to by the statically specified address. These problems show the need for some agent directory facility that agents can dynamically interrogate to locate other agents to collaborate with. While this is not a new concept [6] it has been found to be an essential part of an agent architecture, even for the initial stages of development and for use with a relatively small test application.

4.2   Matching Message Content to Internal Storage

While FIPA ACL provides a structured form for most parts of the agent messages, the language for the message content is left up to the implementation. The initial intention was that the agents built using this architecture would communicate using Knowledge Interchange Format (KIF) sentences [6]. This language is designed for agent messaging, supporting the declarative interchange of knowledge.

Unfortunately it was later discovered that KIF was ill-matched to the internal knowledge storage of the system (See Fig. 4). A fundamental goal of this agent architecture was to investigate the use of the object-oriented modelling paradigm for representing agents' domains of discourse (or ontologies) [4], in particular using the industry standard Unified Modelling Language (UML) [12]. Therefore the natural approach for storing knowledge about the problem domain in the object-oriented application level was to use objects[2], whereas KIF is oriented towards logic-based storage of knowledge. There was no formal way to map between the object-oriented internal knowledge storage and fact-based KIF sentences and so the content of the agent messages degenerated into ad hoc s-expressions used to transfer data structures (see Fig. 4, right).

---

[2] Objects were used as data-structures to represent knowledge. These are strongly typed objects, with structure corresponding to some ontology in UML [4,5]. This

```
public class DataSourceInformation {        (DataSourceInformation
    private String name;                        (name ...)
    private Adress address;                     (address (host ...)
    private String ontology;                             (port ...))
    private String metadata;                    (ontology ...)
                                                (metadata ...)
    (etc ...)                               )
}
         Internal Representation            S-Expression Encoding
```

Fig. 4. Conflicting paradigms.

To create and interpret these ad hoc s-expressions for message content much work was performed marshalling objects to s-expressions and unmarshalling s-expres-sions back to objects. This turned out to be a time-consuming task that created many program bugs. Figure 5 shows an example of unmarshalling a simple two-field s-expression[3]. Even though a KIF pattern matcher is being used here, the developer still has to use some low-level string manipulation. For example the string returned on the line labelled (A) still requires processing by the trimString function.

```
    // Specify a pattern of interest
    String pattern =
      "(register (iiop :iiop) (ontology :ontology))";
    // Invoke KIF pattern matcher
    Vector v = matchKif(messageContent, pattern);
    // Vector v now contains a Hashtable for each
    // match with the String pattern.
    Enumeration enum = v.elements();
    while(enum.hasMoreElements()){
      Hashtable h = (Hashtable)enum.nextElement();
      // Extract the address
(A)   String iiop =
        trimString(h.get("iiop").toString()); // has to be in quotes
      // Extract the ontology name
      String ontology =
        h.get("ontology").toString().trim(); // should be no quotes
      // Add record to internal data structure.
      dataSources.add(new DataSourceInfo(ontology, iiop));
    }
```

Fig. 5. Example Java code for unmarshalling an s-expression.

---

is quite different to the behaviour rich, but semantically under-specified types of objects supported by mobile agent frameworks.

[3] This s-expression is a simpler version of the s-expression in Fig. 4.

It was soon decided that it would be far more efficient just to send knowledge using the existing object-oriented data structures. However the idea of sending objects (for example, by using Java RMI) breaks the declarative agent messaging paradigm, as it is impossible to understand the serialised objects sent between agents without reference to details about an agent's internal structure. Sending objects also breaks the ability of this agent architecture to interoperate with other FIPA ACL-based agent architectures. Other architectures may well be able to parse the strings sent by this architecture, but it is unlikely that they would have any idea how to process a serialised object.

For these reasons the idea of sending objects was nearly discarded, until it became apparent that some layer of abstraction could be provided to allow the developers to view the content as objects but keep the low-level string based encoding. The actual transport level encoding of the message content is not of concern to developers if there is a sufficient abstraction layer to shield them from it.

The agent architecture needed to provide some way of interfacing between declarative string-based agent message content and the internal object-oriented knowledge storage. A standard mapping from an object-oriented data structure to a string-based representation and tools for performing this translation are needed. One such standard mapping is that offered by the Extensible Markup Language (XML) Data Binding facility for Java [11]. This forthcoming technology will provide generic mechanisms to marshall and unmarshall information between XML and in-memory networks of objects that are defined in the XML document's schema[4]. This would free agent system developers from having to implement language-specific parsers and should make it easier to achieve interoperability between different agent architectures [4,5].

However the ability to send arbitrary objects, no matter what their transport encoding, still breaks the declarative nature of agent messaging. It should be possible for a human to read the message content, and with reference to an *ontology* understand the meaning of the message. The sending of arbitrary objects should not be the goal of providing this additional layer of abstraction, but rather sending objects that have semantics specified in some ontology.

4.3   Supporting Agent Conversations

The initial agent architecture provided support for single messages between agents. In practice agents do not send messages in isolation, but rather as part of conversations involving several messages and two or more agents (see Fig. 6). As the agent architecture did not provide any support for this beyond the simple ability to specify a conversation identifier in each message, the work of reasoning about conversations was left to the application level. Because of this lack of support, the most advanced "conversation" that was used was simply recognizing that one received message was in fact a reply to a previously sent

---

[4] Unfortunately there is not yet a published technology for generating an XML schema for a particular UML model, although this is anticipated to be available soon.

message. This simple request-reply interaction is insufficient to permit the rich interaction modelling capabilities of the agent messaging paradigm, for example the FIPA-request, FIPA-query and FIPA-contract-net protocols [1] would be difficult to implement without further tools. Some generic method of working with conversations is required.

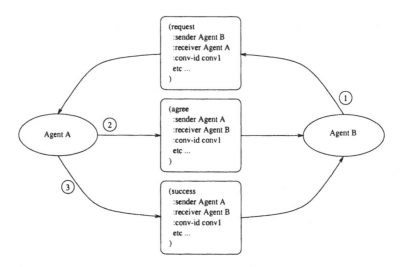

Fig. 6. A conversation between agents.

FIPA specifies several conversation protocols, such as the FIPA Request protocol (See Fig. 7). These can be modelled as finite state machines, where the transitions between states are triggered by sending or receiving certain messages. Another alternative is to model protocols in an agent-oriented modelling language, such as AUML [9].

It would be useful for this architecture to support some method of representing conversation protocols and map this representation to an object that automatically performs the reasoning about the state of the conversation. This object would provide a mechanism for an application to specify the actions to take for each step of the conversation and provide support for sending the correct responses to messages that require certain replies. This would help the agents that are built using this architecture to engage in the rich interactions promised by the agent messaging paradigm.

5   Recommendations for Further Work

Having a suitable agent architecture is essential to the success of agent-based software engineering projects. However implementing a bespoke agent architecture may, in many cases, not be the best choice. Building an agent architecture

Sent by:

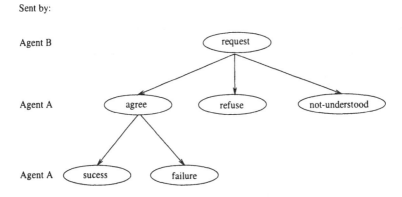

Fig. 7. FIPA request conversation protocol.

has been identified as a difficult task, it has even been claimed that "designing an agent architecture from scratch ... is usually a mistake" [13]. There are many agent architectures that are currently available, and it may be more appropriate to use an off-the-shelf package. Two such off-the-shelf agent architectures have been investigated as alternatives to the agent architecture discussed in this paper for the NZDIS prototype system. These are the Java Agent Template Lite (JATLite) [7] and the ZEUS agent building toolkit [2].

JATLite offers a Java based toolkit for sending and receiving Knowledge Query and Manipulation Language (KQML) [6] messages and an agent router that performs message routing and acts as a directory service. This tool offers only slightly more functionality than the agent architecture discussed in this paper. It is however an open-source project and may provide a useful starting point for new agent architecture projects.

In contrast the ZEUS agent building toolkit offers a rich set of tools that cover many of the deficiencies discussed in this paper. It comes with a built-in agent name server and facilitator agent and includes a set of utility agents, including a Reports Tool, Agent Viewer and Control Tool. Using this toolkit may have avoided some of the problems discussed in this paper[5]. ZEUS appears to be a useful agent architecture for new agent-based software development projects.

However despite the existence of these and other agent architectures there are still many reasons for developing new agent architectures. Some such reasons are:

– Developing novel agent architectures as part of ongoing agent research[6].
– Developing agent architectures for commercial gain.

---

[5] ZEUS was not released at the time the decision to build the NZDIS agent architecture was made.
[6] For example, the use of object-oriented UML ontologies, and CORBA-based communication in the architecture discussed in this paper.

- Simply preferring to use an agent architecture developed in-house so as to avoid dependence on other people's software.

Anyone embarking on a project to build an agent architecture needs to be aware of the extent of the requirements for producing a useful architecture. As learnt in the NZDIS project the provision of string-based peer-to-peer messaging is not sufficient; agent architectures require several other tools to support agent-oriented development.

6   Conclusions

The experience gained by using the agent architecture described in Sec. 3 to implement the prototype NZDIS system has uncovered many shortcomings of the agent architecture. It is clear that simply providing peer-to-peer string-based messaging is an insufficient tool-set on which to develop a complex agent-based system. Tools to control and monitor agents and a directory service are essential for working with many agents even in the early stages of development. A sufficient level of abstraction between the message content language and internal knowledge storage is needed to avoid much unnecessary work. The grouping of messages into logical conversations provides a much better abstraction for the agent messaging paradigm.

Thus several tools that were initially regarded as advanced features turned out to be essential elements of a useful agent architecture. An agent architecture needs to provide a significant level of supporting tools to make the agent messaging component usable.

It is important that problems encountered in developing agent architectures are identified, discussed and circulated among the research and commercial community. By learning from these experiences future projects that seek to build agent architectures can avoid common pitfalls.

Acknowledgments. The work discussed in this paper was funded by the New Zealand government's Public Good Science Fund. The agent architecture and prototype NZDIS system discussed here was the work of the NZDIS team, consisting of Geoff Bush, Dan Carter, Bryce McKinlay, Mariusz Nowostawski, and Roy Ward, under the guidance of Martin Purvis and Stephen Cranefield.

References

[1] Foundation For Intelligent Physical Agents. FIPA specification. Located at http://www.fipa.org/, 2000.

[2] J C Collis, D T Ndumu, H S Nwana, and L C Lee. The ZEUS agent building toolkit. *BT Technology Journal*, 16(3), July 1998.

[3] S. Cranefield and M. Purvis. UML as an ontology modelling language. In *Proceedings of the Workshop on Intelligent Information Integration, 16th International Joint Conference on Artificial Intelligence (IJCAI-99)*, 1999. http://sunsite.informatik.rwth-aachen.de/Publications/CEUR-WS/Vol-23/cranefield-ijcai99-iii.pdf.

[4] S. Cranefield and M. Purvis. Extending agent messaging to enable OO information exchange. In R. Trappl, editor, *Proceedings of the 2nd International Symposium "From Agent Theory to Agent Implementation" (AT2AI-2) at the 5th European Meeting on Cybernetics and Systems Research (EMCSR 2000)*, pages 573–578, Vienna, April 2000. Austrian Society for Cybernetic Studies. Published under the title "Cybernetics and Systems 2000".

[5] Stephen Cranefield, Martin Purvis, and Mariusz Nowostawski. Is it an ontology, a meta-model or an abstract syntax? Modelling FIPA agent communication. In *Proceedings of the Workshop on Applications of Ontologies and Problem Solving Methods, 14th European Conference on Artificial Intelligence*, pages 16.1–16.4, 2000.

[6] Michael R. Genesereth and Steven P. Ketchpel. Software agents. *Communications of the ACM*, 37(7):48–53, July 1994.

[7] JATLite Web site. Located at http://java.stanford.edu/.

[8] New Zealand Distributed Information Systems Project Web site. Located at: http://nzdis.otago.ac.nz/.

[9] James Odell, H. Van Dyke Parunak, and Bernhard Bauer. Representing agent interaction protocols in UML. Paper submitted to AAAI Agents 2000 conference.

[10] Martin Purvis, Stephen Cranefield, Geoff Bush, Daniel Carter, Bryce McKinlay, Mariusz Nowostawski, and Roy Ward. The NZDIS Project: an Agent-based Distributed Information Systems Architecture. In R.H. Sprague Jr., editor, *CDROM Proceedings of the Hawaii International Conference on System Sciences (HICSS-33)*. IEEE Computer Society Press, 2000.

[11] M Reinhold. XML data binding specification, Java Specification Request JSR-000031. Sun Microsystems, 1999. http://java.sun.com/aboutJava/communityprocess/jsr/jsr_031_xmld.html.

[12] James Rumbaugh, Ivar Jacobson, and Grady Booch. *The Unified Modeling Language Reference Manual*. Addison-Wesley, 1998.

[13] Michael Wooldridge and Nicholas R. Jennings. Pitfalls of agent-oriented development. In *Proceedings of the 2nd International Conference on Autonomous Agents*, pages 385–391, 1998.

Building a Network Community Support System on the Multi-agent Platform **Shine**

Sen Yoshida, Koji Kamei, Takeshi Ohguro, Kazuhiro Kuwabara, and
Kaname Funakoshi

NTT Communication Science Laboratories
{yoshida,kamei,ohguro,kuwabara,kf}@cslab.kecl.ntt.co.jp

Abstract. An increasing number of applications have been developed
for supporting network communities. The authors have developed *Community Organizer*, which supports people in forming new network communities by providing places where people sharing interests and concerns
can meet and communicate. The authors are also developing a platform
named Shine to reduce the tasks needed to implement a variety of network community support systems such as Community Organizer. Shine
has a multi-agent architecture because it is effective for network community support systems that have to adapt to dynamic changes in community organizations. This paper explains both Community Organizer and
Shine, and then gives a description of building Community Organizer on
top of Shine.

1 Introduction

With the advance of public communication networks such as the Internet, a
new type of community, called a network community or a virtual community
[18], is beginning to emerge on the networks. Members in a network community
actively and intimately communicate with each other by using e-mail, electronic
chat rooms, bulletin board systems, and so on. Furthermore, a multitude of
projects are devoted to developing systems to support communications especially
in network communities [7]. These systems are called *socialware* [5].

The authors have developed *Community Organizer* to support people in forming new network communities by providing places where people sharing interests and concerns can meet and communicate.

The authors are also developing a platform named Shine [23] to reduce the
tasks needed to implement a variety of socialware application programs such as
Community Organizer. Shine has a multi-agent architecture because it is effective
for socialware that has to adapt to dynamic changes in community organizations.

We explain Community Organizer in Section 2 and Shine in Section 3. We
then give a description of building Community Organizer on top of Shine in
Section 4.

C. Zhang and V.-W. Soo (Eds.): PRIMA 2000, LNAI 1881, pp. 88–100, 2000.

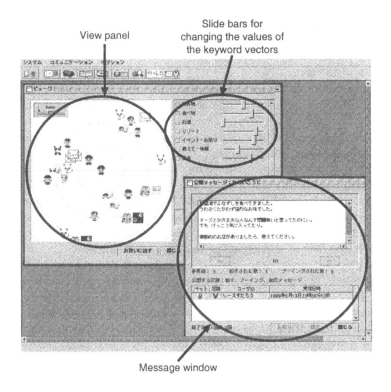

Fig. 1. Sample screenshot of Community Organizer (Japanese version)

2   Community Organizer

Unlike traditional communities where geographical and institutional properties define the boundary of the community, most network communities are *communities of interest* [6], which consist of people who share common interests. Considering this characteristic of network communities, Community Organizer regards people sharing interests as members of a potential community and provides them with a place where they can meet and communicate.

Figure 1 is a sample screenshot of Community Organizer. Community Organizer displays representations of potential community members and communications among them.

Community Organizer has as its main feature a view panel that visualizes the relationships among users in real-time [5,22]. A user is represented as an icon in the view panel. Its placement in relation to others reflects the closeness of users' interests. A user's interest is represented as a keyword vector, which is a set of pairs of a keyword (e.g., 'travel' or 'foods') and a numerical value (i.e., the degree of his/her interest in the keyword). The system calculates the degree of closeness for each pair of keyword vectors from the cosine measure

[19] and places icons on the view panel using a physically-based model adopted from Ref. [1]. As a result, icons with similar keyword vectors are placed closer to each other. By observing how icons are distributed, a user can envision potential communities of interest.

The center point of the view can be set by the user. The center point has its keyword vector too, and the user can determine its values by adjusting the slide bars next to the view panel. The placement of the icons will change according to the positions of the slide bars. This function enables users to look around the display to find potential communities.

In addition, a user can easily express his/her interest to other users by placing a new icon representing the user in the center of the view panel. The newly placed icon has the same keyword vector as that of the center point. Consequently, it will appear on the display of other users whose slide bars' positions are similar to those of the placing user. A user can place multiple icons on different positions, which allows him/her to participate in multiple communities.

Community Organizer integrates a communication function with this visualization function. This is done by providing an interface that allows a user to attach his/her message to an icon. Other users can read the message by clicking the icon, and reply to it by placing a new icon on a closer position and attaching a reply message to it. This integration of the visualization function and the communication function produces a utility that is quite suitable for members of a community of interest.

We have conducted a psychological experiment to explore the effect of Community Organizer's spatial representation [8]. The results indicate that this two-dimensional representation enhances community feelings of the users more than one-dimensional representation that simply displays a list of users in decreasing order of the closeness.

3 Shine: A Multi-agent Platform for Network Community Support Systems

In this section, we explain Shine, a multi-agent platform for network community support systems that the authors are developing [23].

It is easy to think of many applications for supporting network communities. There are applications that support exploitation of the merits of forming communities. Such applications include:

- Circulation of information via word-of-mouth human networks, such as recommendations and collaborative filtering [20];
- Arrangement of informal, suggestive or creative conversations, such as brainstorming sessions [4,11];
- Establishment of efficient collaborations for developing resources such as open source software or databases; and
- Arrangement of localized and informal economic activities like auctions [10] and flea markets.

There are also applications that support community formation, maintenance, and evolution. For example:

- Arrangement of effective encounters and support for becoming aware of potential communities [15,22];
- Maintenance of intimacy and community feelings [17];
- Coordination of conversations [12,13] and collaborations; and
- Planning for the establishment of individual identities in communities.

While we can think of a variety of network community applications, certain functions are commonly required by these applications. These functions include:

- Dynamic adaptation to acquaintance relations or group formation;
- Analysis of each person's features, role, and situation within a community;
- Analysis of a community's comprehensive features;
- An interface that links a user's community feeling to a system's logical information; and
- Flexible communication utilities.

At present, however, there is no platform that can provide these common functions. Consequently, most network community support systems are developed as independent systems. Therefore, there is no cooperation among application programs or sharing and reuse of program components. For this motivation, we are developing a platform named Shine as a common base for various network community applications.

In the following subsections, we examine the design of the platform's architecture.

3.1 Multi-agents for Network Community Applications

A network community has the advantage of providing communication capabilities to an actual community that are open and free from geographical or temporal constraints. However, this openness brings the difficulty of gate keeping. Because people are unable to deal with too much information or too many other humans, they tend to lose the proper perspective for acting or hesitate to act and end up isolated in a huge mass of strangers.

Unfortunately, most of the network community support systems available today do not attempt to tackle this gate keeping problem. They were designed as client-server (CS) systems, which assume that a single host machine serves thousands or millions of clients accessing from anywhere on the Internet. In this architecture, the server program holds a huge database, in which the personal information of all users is stored and from which it is retrieved. The quantity of such a system's users group is beyond the human capability to develop community feeling. Or otherwise, in case there were a lot of sites that serves small number of people, each user's chance to enlarge his/her acquaintance relation is restricted.

In real society, people meet unknown others by mediating or introducing themselves. Consequently, they flexibly change their acquaintance relations and

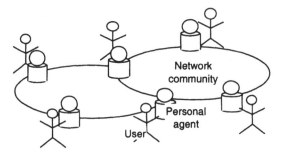

Fig. 2. Personal agents

reorganize their communities. Humans do these tasks of gate keeping in a quite decentralized and cooperative way. This decentralized gate keeping mechanism used in real society can also work efficiently in network communities. Therefore, in Shine, we adopt a multi-agent architecture.

In our approach, the control mechanisms and data for human relations are distributed to each person. Namely, the Shine system provides each user an agent that is dedicated to the person's social interactions as shown in Fig 2. A Shine agent exchanges personal information with other agents, and they all collaboratively perform the necessary actions such as mediation or self-introduction to dynamically change community formation.

When we introduce mediation mechanism to Shine, we must consider privacy control mechanism. For example, when agent a tells a private issue to agent b, and a wants b not to tell the issue to anyone else, it must be forbidden for b to tell it to anyone. Shine will provide this kind of privacy control mechanism in future.

3.2   Internal Structure of a Shine Agent

Figure 3 shows an overview of a Shine agent's internal structure. In a Shine agent, there are several modules, i.e., Person Database, Planner, Post, and the user interfaces of application programs.

Person Database. The Person Database holds data on others and the user whom the agent is associated with. These data are appropriately circulated via communication among agents.

To analyze a person's features, role, or situation in a community systematically, a network community application has to adopt a kind of user model. By following a specific user model, the application can store data on the attributes and status of a person into a database and then use the data for analysis.

One of a number of user models can be used depending on how it regards a human. For example, when a user model considers a human to be a knowledge source, it can describe the person in a knowledge representation language [16].

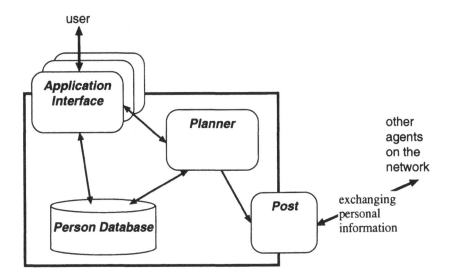

Fig. 3. Internal structure of Shine agent

To roughly represent a person's interests, keyword vectors of the vector space model are suitable [22]. In addition, there is a method that describes communication entities as state transition systems to model each person's situation and conversation flow [21].

Each current network community support system uses a suitable user model. For Shine to achieve cooperation among application programs and the sharing of software components in application development, it has a generic architecture that can process various user models in a unified way. Moreover, it can handle multiple user models simultaneously. An application programmer makes his/her own user model in a style that Shine accepts and installs it in the Shine system. Shine also provides a library of popular user models such as the vector space model.

Practically speaking, Person Database is an object-oriented relational database (Fig. 4). Persons are stored in a table, which has a number of attributes concerning the user models used. For example, 'agent id,' 'name,' 'birth date,' 'interest,' etc. are thought of. Each line of the table represents a person and the agent that the person is associated with.

Some attributes of the table are *key* attributes used for identifying a person from a value. For instance, 'agent id' is a key attribute, and its values are used as the addresses for inter-agent communication.

We adopt an object-oriented database so that we can store not only simple strings or numeric values but also structured objects into a table. For example, we can make an 'interest' attribute whose data are keyword vectors, i.e., sets of pairs of a keyword string and a numeric value. We can also make a 'mailbox' attribute, whose data are collections of mails received from corresponding persons.

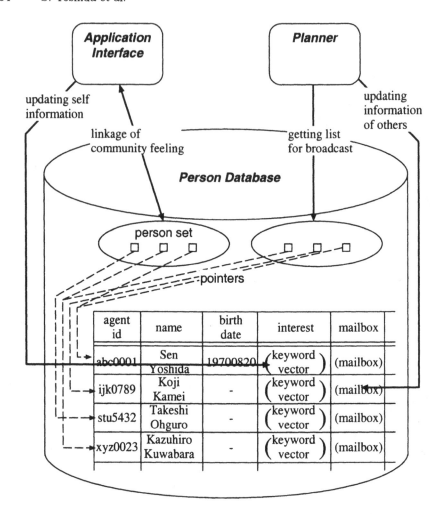

Fig. 4. Person Database

Person Database has an event generation function. When an attribute value of a person is added, changed, or removed, an event occurs. Other modules such as Planner observe occurrences of these events, and do appropriate actions in response to them. This event notification mechanism enables cooperation among multiple modules and federation of multiple applications.

In most multi-agent systems, although an agent holds and handles information on other agents, it isn't conscious that a set of agents, or people whom the personal agents are associated with, comprise a community. A network community support system, however, always uses information on the community. Therefore, a Shine agent needs a flexible framework for dealing with information on not only each agent but also a community of agents.

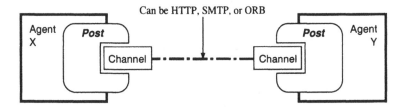

Fig. 5. Channel

To handle communities, a Shine agent defines for each community a *person set*, and provides operations for dealing with a set of personal information. A person set observes each member's data stored in the table for adjusting to dynamic changes in the organization of the real community.

When we use a network community support system to determine whom to communicate with, especially when we want to broadcast a message to the members of the community, it is essential that the communications adapt to all dynamic changes in the community formation and be linked to the community feelings of users. Shine can provide a function that can flexibly determine the range of group communication because it uses person sets of Person Database as destination lists for broadcasting.

Post. The Post module exchanges messages with other agents. It abstracts lower-level communication procedures as an internal channel submodule (Fig. 5). Specifically, it encodes and decodes messages to adjust the lower-level communication protocol, e.g., HTTP, SMTP, or ORB. The channel submodule is hidden from other modules or application programmers.

The format of the messages is similar to KQML [2] or other agent communication languages. Each message has a message type, a user model indication, and contents described following the indicated user model. A user model in Shine corresponds to an ontology in KQML.

Planner. The Planner decides the action of the agent. Figure 6 shows the structure of the Planner. The agent acts in response to external events such as messages received from other agents, inputs from the user, and changes of values stored in the Person Database.

Each application has one or more plans, and the Planner executes them concurrently. There are also plans provided by Shine that do fundamental or common tasks. The Planner contains a message dispatcher, which dispatches each incoming message to appropriate plans according to message type. Plans can cooperate via Person Database: When a plan changes an attribute value of a person, another plan can perceive the change by catching the event occurred according to it.

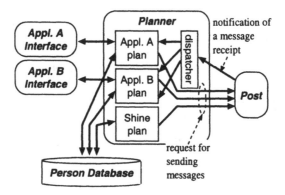

Fig. 6. Planner

Application Interface. The application interface connects the user with the Person Database and the Planner. There can exist multiple applications on one Shine agent, and each application has its own interface module.

A network community support system needs a user interface that allows users to relate their feelings about acquaintances or communities to the system and to understand intuitively the meaning of the logical information stored in the Database in accordance with a user model. Therefore, Shine not only provides popular user models but also interface libraries for those models. Such interface libraries of user models include visualization mechanisms and other mechanisms that use available human-computer interaction media.

The application interface also helps interactions between the user and the Planner by providing dialogue messages and other aids.

3.3   Comparisons with Other Multi-agent Platforms

MINDS [14] is a multi-agent system for collaborative document retrieval. In this system, each personal agent knows documents stored in its user's workstation, and also has metaknowledge about who possibly owns documents about what topic. When a user asks his/her agent for retrieving documents about a topic, the agent intelligently submits queries to other agents using this metaknowledge. MINDS is one of pioneers in collaborative personal agents, but it's domain is limited to information retrieval.

KQML [2] specifies a message format and a set of message handling protocols that are suitable for knowledge sharing among agents. There are a number multi-agent platforms that implement this specification. KQML can transfer various kinds of knowledges because it provides a function to select an ontology based on the domain of each knowledge. However, in KQML framework, agents don't have capabilities to dynamically reorganize their social relation, for example by mediation. To perform such a dynamic reorganization, an agent has to be able to exchange not only knowledge about the application domain but also information about the agent itself or its acquaintances. Furthermore, this reorganization must be linked to the change of the user's community feeling. Therefore, Shine includes human-computer interface libraries besides knowledge exchange functions.

The ADIPS Framework [9] is a platform for flexible distributed systems. Several network applications such as a flexible video conference system, a flexible asynchronous messaging system, and a system named CyberOffice have been developed on top of the ADIPS Framework. The main feature of the ADIPS Framework is that each node of an ADIPS application system can be flexibly and dynamically reconfigured to adapt to changes in its environment such as QoS or the user's preference. To achieve this adaptability, each module of an ADIPS system's node is agentified.

The difference between ADIPS and Shine is the policy of agentification. The ADIPS system agentifies the modules in a node to obtain adaptability to their environment. On the other hand, we call a node of Shine an agent because it is personalized and communicates with other personal agents to adapt to changes in the user's social situation.

4   Community Organizer on **Shine**

This section gives a description of revising Community Organizer by porting it to the Shine platform. This revision brings certain advantages to Community Organizer.

- The implementation of Community Organizer can make use of the libraries of program components included in the Shine package. What we need to make for Shine-based Community Organizer are only a plan installed to the Planner, a user interface, and some additional attributes for the Person Database.
- The architecture of the system changes from the conventional client/server architecture to a more flexible multi-agent architecture.
- It is possible to integrate Community Organizer with other network community applications by sharing data on people with those applications.

In the Community Organizer, each icon's feature is represented as a keyword vector. In other words, the Community Organizer adopts the vector space model of an information retrieval technique as the user model. Because Shine provides a library for this model, the program of the Community Organizer can make use of prepared methods such as the cosine measure [19]. Furthermore, the user interface of the Community Organizer can choose its visualization mechanism from Shine's community visualization library, which includes not only the physically-based model but also other mechanisms such as the dual-scaling method [11].

As described in Sec. 3.1, Shine adopts a flexible multi-agent architecture. When Community Organizer is ported to Shine, each client program is agentified. Such an agent exchanges personal information with other agents, and they all collaboratively perform mediation or self-introduction to find potential communities. The architecture of the Shine-based Community Organizer is shown in Fig. 7.

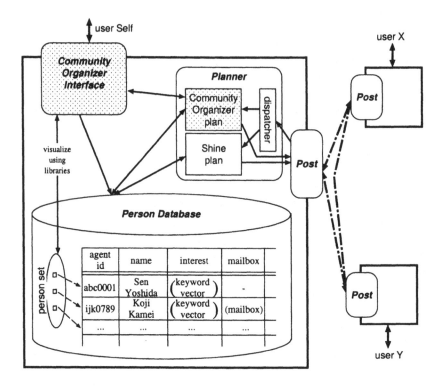

Fig. 7. Shine-based Community Organizer

In the current client/server version of Community Organizer, all data are stored in one database of the server. A client program sends the center point's keyword vector reflecting the slide bars' positions as a query. After receiving the query keyword vector, the server program searches its database for other keyword vectors close to the query's one, and then responds to the query with the found keyword vectors with corresponding icon images. Finally, the client program places these icons on the view panel.

In contrast, the Shine-based Community Organizer has no central database server. The queries are broadcasted to other personal agents. When an agent receives a query, it seeks icons whose keyword vectors are closer to the query's one from the icons of the user who owns the agent and then responds to the query with the found icons. Therefore, the computation of query processing is distributed.

5 Conclusions

In this paper, we explained both Community Organizer and Shineand then described how we built Community Organizer on top of Shine.

Much work remains to be done, however. We are going to study the architecture of Shine in more detail. We will also provide an implementation of Shine as a Java class library. We plan to do this work in parallel with the development of several network community support systems such as Community Organizer and Gleams of People [17]. There are also various other matters to deal with, including a privacy control mechanism.

Acknowledgments. We thank Advanced Business Works at NTT Communications for the implementation of Community Organizer.

References

[1] Matthew Chalmers and Paul Chitson. Bead: Explorations in information visualization. In Nicholas Belkin, Peter Ingwersen, and Annelise Mark Pejtersen, editors, *Proceedings of the Fifteenth Annual International ACM SIGIR Conference on Research and Development in Information Retrieval*, SIGIR Forum, pages 330–337. ACM Press, 1992.

[2] Tim Finin, Rich Fritzson, Don McKay, and Robin McEntire. KQML — a language and protocol for knowledge and information exchange. In Fuchi and Yokoi [3].

[3] Kazuhiro Fuchi and Toshio Yokoi, editors. *Knowledge Building and Knowledge Sharing*. Ohmsha and IOS Press, 1994.

[4] Kunihiko Fujita and Susumu Kunifuji. A realization of a reflection of personal information on distributed brainstorming environment. In Takashi Masuda, Yoshifumi Masunaga, and Michiharu Tsukamoto, editors, *Proceedings of the International Conference on Worldwide Computing and Its Applications '97*, volume 1274 of *Lecture Notes in Computer Science*, pages 166–181. Springer-Verlag, 1997.

[5] Fumio Hattori, Takeshi Ohguro, Makoto Yokoo, Shigeo Matsubara, and Sen Yoshida. Socialware: Multiagent systems for supporting network communities. *Communications of the ACM*, 42(3):55–61, 1999.

[6] John Hagel III and Arther Armstrong. The real value of ON-LINE communities. *Harvard Business Review*, 5–6 1996.

[7] Toru Ishida, editor. *Community Computing — Collaboration over Global Information Networks*. John Wiley & Sons, 1998.

[8] Koji Kamei, Eva Jettmar, Kunihiko Fujita, Sen Yoshida, and Kazuhiro Kuwabara. Community organizer: supporting the formation of network communities through spatial representation. Submitted to the 2001 Symposium on Applications and the Internet.

[9] Tetsuo Kinoshita and Kenji Suganuma. ADIPS framework for flexible distributed systems. In *Proceedings of the First Pacific Rim International Workshop on Multi-Agents (PRIMA '98)*, volume 1599 of *Lecture Notes in Artificial Intelligence*, pages 18–32. Springer-Verlag, 1998.

[10] Stefan Klein. Introduction to electronic auctions. *International Journal of Electronic Markets*, 7(4):3–6, 1997.

[11] Kenji Mase, Yasuyuki Sumi, and Kazushi Nishimoto. Informal conversation environment for collaborative concept formation. In Ishida [7], chapter 6, pages 165–205.

[12] Shigeo Matsubara, Takeshi Ohguro, and Fumio Hattori. CommunityBoard: Social meeting system able to visualize the structure of discussions. In *Proceedings of the Second International Conference on Knowledge-based Intelligent Electronic Systems (KES'98)*, pages 423–428. IEEE, 1998.

[13] Shigeo Matsubara, Takeshi Ohguro, and Fumio Hattori. CommunityBoard 2: Mediating between speakers and an audience in computer network discussions. In Oren Etzioni, Jörg P. Müller, and Jeffrey M. Bradshaw, editors, *Proceedings of the Third Annual Conference on Autonomous Agents*, pages 370–371. ACM Press, 1999.

[14] Uttam Mukhopadhyay, Larry Stephens, Michael Huhns, and Ronald Bonnell. An intelligent system for document retrieval in distributed office environments. *Journal of the American Society for Information Science*, 37:123–135, 1987.

[15] Yoshiyasu Nishibe, Ichiro Morihara, Fumio Hattori, Toshikazu Nishimura, Hirofumi Yamaki, Toru Ishida, Harumi Maeda, and Toyoaki Nishida. Mobile digital assistants for international conferences. In Ishida [7], chapter 8, pages 245–284.

[16] Toyoaki Nishida and Hideaki Takeda. Towards the knowledgeable community. In Fuchi and Yokoi [3].

[17] Takeshi Ohguro, Sen Yoshida, and Kazuhiro Kuwabara. Gleams of People: Monitoring the presence of people with multi-agent architecture. In Nideyuki Nakashima and Chengqi Zhang, editors, *Approaches to Intelligent Agents — Proceedings of the Second Pacific Rim International Workshop on Multi-Agents*, volume 1733 of *Lecture Notes in Artificial Intelligence*, pages 170–182. Springer-Verlag, 1999.

[18] Howard Rheingold. *The Virtual Community: Homesteading on the Electronic Frontier*. Addison-Wesley, 1993.

[19] G. Salton and M. J. McGill. *Introduction to Modern Information Retrieval*. McGraw-Hill, 1983.

[20] Upendra Shardanand and Pattie Maes. Social information filtering: Algorithms for automating "word of mouth". In *CHI '95 Proceedings: Conference on Human Factors in Computing Systems: Mosaic of Creativity*, pages 210–217. ACM SIGCHI, 1995.

[21] Terry Winograd and Fernando Flores. *Understanding Computers and Cognition: A New Foundation for Design*. Ablex, 1986.

[22] Sen Yoshida, Koji Kamei, Makoto Yokoo, Takeshi Ohguro, Kaname Funakoshi, and Fumio Hattori. Community visualizing agent. In *Proceedings of the Third International Conference and Exhibition on The Practical Application of Intelligent Agents and Multi-Agent Technology (PAAM 98)*, pages 643–644. The Practical Application Co. Ltd., 1998.

[23] Sen Yoshida, Takeshi Ohguro, Koji Kamei, Kaname Funakoshi, and Kazuhiro Kuwabara. Shine: a cyber-community application platform — a proposal —. In *Short Papers Proceedings of the Second Pacific Rim International Workshop on Multi-Agents*, pages 31–40, 1999.

A Secure Route Structure for Information Gathering Agent

Tieyan Li, Chuk-Yang Seng, and Kwok-Yan Lam

Centre for Systems Security
School of Computing
National University of Singapore
{litieyan, sengcy, lamky}@comp.nus.edu.sg

Abstract. Mobile agents are more likely to be launched over the Internet to collect information. However, an autonomous agent running on a host may suffer attacks if the host is malicious. Possible targets of attacks include: the collected information or the agent itself, including its route. In this paper, we propose a new secure route structure, which provides enhanced security and robust solution to protect an agent's route. Besides security and robustness, the solution also offers features such as: flexibility in routing and high performance. In addition, we highlight areas where we can apply agents to collect information, with the use of the secure route structure: electronic commerce and intrusion detection system.

1 Introduction

The proliferation of the Internet results in a new medium for accessing information. With information scattered across the Internet, gathering information becomes a problem. Search engine is a useful tool to search for information. However, some efforts may be required to identify the real gems among the pile of results returned by the search engine.

The above problem may be solved by using an Information Gathering Agent (IGA). An IGA can be informally described as an agent that performs the task of collecting and filtering information. Although there is no universally accepted definition for an agent, Wooldridge and Jennings's "weak notion of agency" [1] illustrates key properties that an IGA should possess:

1. Autonomy
2. Social ability
3. Reactivity
4. Pro-activeness.

In addition, an IGA is required to move from host to host to collect information. By doing so, the user's computer can free the resources for other applications while the agent is roaming the Internet. Moreover, the user can even go offline during this period of time. This feature is essential if the user is

C. Zhang and V.-W. Soo (Eds.): PRIMA 2000, LNAI 1881, pp. 101–114, 2000.

using a mobile device, which is constrained by limited battery life or expensive connection charges. Therefore, an addition property of mobility is required for an IGA.

The use of mobile agents faces 2 general classes of security issues:

1. Protection of hosts from malicious agents
2. Protection of agents from malicious hosts.

The first issue can be dealt with in the context of operating systems, which provides some levels of protections for process execution. The second problem is more challenging because for an agent to be executed, it needs the resources of the host, such as the run time environment or the memory. Thus the host has the ability to browse the code and information, and in the worst scenario, tampers with the agent's code or information. Many researchers have been working on this problem and many of their works can be found in [2].

In this paper, we shall address an important problem of protecting an agent's route. The problem of protecting an agent's route is slightly different from the problem of protecting an agent from a malicious host. This will be addressed in Sect. 2. Section 3 introduces a solution to the problem. In Sect. 4, we will propose a secure route structure, which is a further refinement to the solution in Sect. 3. This will be followed by 2 examples of applications in Sect. 5, which illustrates how our route structure can be used.

2   Protecting an Agent's Route

The concept of an agent's route has been described in [3]. In this paper, we shall define route formally as:

Definition 1. *An agent's route is defined as a sequence of* $[c_0, c_1, \ldots, c_n]$*. Each* c_i*, for* $0 \le i \le n$*, represents the IP address of a host. The route indicates the itinerary of an agent, who will visit each host in the same order as the sequence.*

Definition 2. *A route structure is a data structure used to store the route of an agent.*

An IGA carries its route structure when it roams the Internet to gather information. This route will help the IGA to determine the sequence of host to visit. However, knowledge of the IGA's route allows a host to have a peek of the information gathered, even though the information may be hidden by cryptographic means. To illustrate, considering an IGA on a mission to collect information on the prices of a particular book from various online bookstores. Lets assume that host X views the route structure of agent A and finds out that the agent has visited hosts V and W. Since A is likely to make the same request from all hosts visited, X can deduced that A has collected information on the price of that book. By doing some market research, X can guess the price offered by V and W.

In addition, by allowing X to have an estimation of information gathered earlier, it would be possible for X to offer a higher or lower price instead of the real price of the book to gain patronization of A or to maximize profits.

Thirdly, a malicious host is able to tamper with the route structure. With reference to the previous example, X finds out that the next destination is host Y. However, X knows that Y offers a better price for the book. Therefore, X modifies the route structure so that the next destination becomes Z, which offers a higher price than X.

From the above example, we can see that it is necessary to protect the route of an IGA. Although we can apply cryptographic techniques to hide the information gathered from the current host, hiding the route has a slight complication. While we do not wish the current host to know where the IGA has visited or will visit, it is necessary for the current host to know at least the next destination so that it can send the IGA to the next host. Thus, what we want is not to hide the route information from the current host, but to restrict the current host's knowledge of the route information.

In [4], Westhoff et al proposed a method to protect a mobile agent's route structure. The route structure, r, can be represented by (1):

$$r = E_{c_1}[ip_{c_2}, S_h(ip_h, ip_{c_1}, ip_{c_2}, t)]\|$$

$$\vdots$$

$$E_{c_{n-1}}[ip_{c_n}, S_h(ip_{c_{n-2}}, ip_{c_{n-1}}, ip_{c_n}, t)]\|$$
$$E_{c_n}[EoR, S_h(ip_{c_{n-1}}, ip_{c_n}, EoR, t)] \ . \tag{1}$$

In (1), E_x represents a public-key encryption method with the public key of x, while S represents the signing method and h represents the home server where the agent originates. Since $E_{c_i}[ip_{c_{i+1}}, S_h(ip_{c_{i-1}}, ip_{c_i}, ip_{c_{i+1}}, t)]$ is encrypted with host c_i's public key, only host c_i can obtain this information by decrypting it with its secret key and thus, obtain the ip address of the next host (which is ip_{c+1}).

The digital signature signed by the home server proves to c_i that the route entry has not been modified. In addition, the address of the previous host in the signature helps to ensure that the agent is following its route. This will also prevent an agent from being intercepted and replayed by some malicious host. The trip market, t, is unique for each journey. It uniquely identifies an agent's journey and prevents replay attacks. EoR represents the end of journey and the agent can return to the home server. For more details of this mechanism, readers are referred to [4].

While the above method is effective in limiting the current host's knowledge of the agent's route, it is not robust. Should any host be unreachable, the agent is unable to skip over such host. In this case, the agent either has to wait in the current host until the next host is reachable, or to abort the journey and return to the home server. Thus the performance of the system is affected.

3   A Simple Route Structure

The above method can protect the route information by giving the host only the information it requires. However, this compromises on the robustness of the system. Thus, we shall attempt to modify the previous method by improving on the robustness. In our approach, our route r', can be defined as follows:

$$r' = E_{c_1}[ip_{c_2}, ip_{c_3}, S_{ASC}(ip_{ASC}, ip_{c_1}, ip_{c_2}, ip_{c_3}, t)]\|$$
$$\vdots$$
$$E_{c_{i-1}}[ip_{c_i}, ip_{c_{i+1}}, S_{ASC}(ip_{c_{i-2}}, ip_{c_{i-1}}, ip_{c_i}, ip_{c_{i+1}}, t)]\|$$
$$\vdots$$
$$E_{c_{n-1}}[ip_{c_n}, EoR, S_{ASC}(ip_{c_{n-2}}, ip_{c_{n-1}}, ip_{c_n}, EoR, t)]\|$$
$$E_{c_n}[EoR, S_{ASC}(ip_{c_{n-1}}, ip_{c_n}, EoR, t)] \ . \tag{2}$$

Equation (2) is similar to (1), except that the current host has a second option, should the next host be unreachable. Based on [5], the probability of failures in 2 consecutive hosts is very low. Thus the robustness of the system has improved.

In addition, we name the home server of an agent as Agent Service Center (ASC). An ASC's main role is to create agents to service the requests of users. It is also the launching and ending point of an agent during a journey.

Recall that the receiving host can verify if the agent is following its route. However, when an agent skips over a host due to some failures, the receiving host will have difficulty in determining whether the agent is following its route. For example, when a host, c_i receives the agent, it can check that the sending host is indeed c_{i-1} as indicated in the route structure. When c_{i-1} is unreachable, the agent will move from c_{i-2} to c_i. However, based on its limited knowledge of the route structure, c_i has no knowledge of the host before c_{i-1}. In this situation, c_i can verify that c_{i-2} is the correct sending host by issuing a challenge to c_{i-2}. To respond to this challenge, c_{i-2} will reveal a shared secret between c_{i-2} and c_i. This piece of shared secret is the identity of c_{i-1}. If the response is incorrect, the agent can be rejected and returned to the source.

The agent's route can be described by Fig. 1:

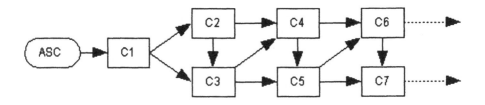

Fig. 1. A diagrammatic description of an agent's route

Unfortunately, this solution is not without any problem. Security flaws exist if the hosts are in some form of competition. We shall use an example to describe these flaws.

Suppose that an IGA is tasked to roam the Internet to collect information on prices of air ticket for a trip from country X and Y for a user. Host c_i is aware of the IGA's next 2 destinations. Suppose that through its own market research, c_i knows that c_{i+1} is able to provide a better offer than what c_i can offer, and c_i is confident that it can give a better offer than c_{i+2}. Since these 3 hosts are competing parties, c_i may deceive the IGA that c_{i+1} is unreachable and sends the IGA to c_{i+2}. Thus the IGA will miss the opportunity of collecting information of a good offer.

Another flaw occurs if some hosts collude to compete against others. For example, c_i and c_{i+2} may be from a business alliance. Therefore, c_i may pass the IGA to c_{i+2} instead of c_{i+1}.

4   A Secure and Robust Route Structure

Equation (2) gives us a route structure that is more robust than (1). Unfortunately, it is only secure if the hosts involve do not compete against one another. At this point, it seems that there is a tradeoff between robustness and security. When we secure the route information in (1), robustness is affected and improving the robustness compromises the security in (2). Fortunately, this problem can be overcome by using multi-agents. In this Sect., we introduce an improved route structure that is robust and secure.

4.1   Cooperative Protection of Agent's Route - Basic Model

In this basic model, 2 agents cooperate to protect each other's route. Let $C = [c_o, c_1, \ldots, c_n]$ be the set of hosts that are to be visited. Divide C into C_1 and C_2 such that: $C_1 = [c_0, c_1, \ldots, c_{\lfloor \frac{n}{2} \rfloor}]$ and $C_2 = [c_{\lfloor \frac{n}{2} \rfloor+1}, c_{\lfloor \frac{n}{2} \rfloor+2}, \ldots, c_n]$. Next, assign 2 IGAs, A_1 and A_2 to gather the same information that the user has requested. C_1 and C_2 will be the route for A_1 and A_2 respectively. Let r_1'' and r_2'' be the route structures of A_1 and A_2 respectively.

$$r_1'' = E_{c_1}[ip_{c_2}, E_{A_2}(ip_{c_3}), S_{ASC}(ip_{ASC}, ip_{c_1}, ip_{c_2}, E_{A_2}(ip_{c_3}), t)]||$$

$$\vdots$$

$$E_{c_{\lfloor \frac{n}{2} \rfloor-1}}[ip_{c_{\lfloor \frac{n}{2} \rfloor}}, E_{A_2}(EoR), S_{ASC}(ip_{c_{\lfloor \frac{n}{2} \rfloor-2}}, ip_{c_{\lfloor \frac{n}{2} \rfloor-1}}, ip_{c_{\lfloor \frac{n}{2} \rfloor}}, E_{A_2}(EoR), t)]||$$

$$E_{c_{\lfloor \frac{n}{2} \rfloor}}[EoR, S_{ASC}(ip_{c_{\lfloor \frac{n}{2} \rfloor-1}}, ip_{c_{\lfloor \frac{n}{2} \rfloor}}, EoR, t)] \ . \tag{3}$$

$$r_2'' = E_{c_{\lfloor \frac{n}{2} \rfloor+1}}[ip_{c_{\lfloor \frac{n}{2} \rfloor+2}}, E_{A_1}(ip_{c_{\lfloor \frac{n}{2} \rfloor+3}}),$$
$$S_{ASC}(ip_{ASC}, ip_{c_{\lfloor \frac{n}{2} \rfloor+1}}, ip_{c_{\lfloor \frac{n}{2} \rfloor+2}}, E_{A_1}(ip_{c_{\lfloor \frac{n}{2} \rfloor+3}}), t)]||$$

$$\vdots$$

$$E_{c_{i-1}}[ip_{c_i}, E_{A_1}(ip_{c_{i+1}}), S_{ASC}(ip_{c_{i-2}}, ip_{c_{i-1}}, ip_{c_i}, E_{A_1}(ip_{c_{i+1}}), t)]||$$

$$\vdots$$

$$E_{c_{n-1}}[ip_{c_n}, E_{A_1}(EoR), S_{ASC}(ip_{c_{n-2}}, ip_{c_{n-1}}, ip_{c_n}, E_{A_1}(EoR), t)]||$$

$$E_{c_n}[EoR, S_{ASC}(ip_{c_{n-1}}, ip_{c_n}, EoR, t)] . \tag{4}$$

The 2 cooperating agents' routes can be described diagrammatically by Fig. 2. In this approach, each agent's route structure is similar to that in (2). The main difference is that the host will only know the next host to send the agent to under normal circumstances. Should the next destination be unreachable, an alternative host will then be revealed. From (3), we can see that the location of such host is being encrypted by A_2's key $(E_{A_2}(ip_{c_3}))$. This is a symmetric key, which can be used to decrypt the ciphered information and this can only be performed by A_2 who is carrying the key.

Compared to previous methods, we have 2 agents cooperating to provide security to each other's route structures, as well as enhancing the robustness of the system. Although we can make use of the ASC to reveal the alternative host, we prefer to distribute this job to another agent, as the ASC may have many information gathering requests to attend to.

In addition, by employing 2 agents, we can distribute the task of information gathering to 2 agents to perform in parallel. However, the parallelism achieved does not necessary translate to better overall performance. This is due to overheads incurred by the additional encryptions required. The rational behind the employment of multiple agents is not so much of achieving parallelism, but to allow cooperation in order to prevent tampering by malicious hosts. Future research can be conducted to investigate various strategies to reduce the overheads and to improve the overall performance.

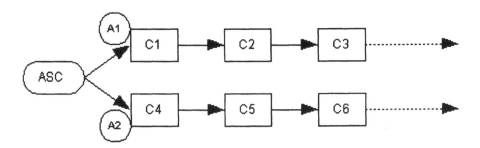

Fig. 2. A diagrammatic description of 2 cooperating agents' routes.

4.2 Protocol to Obtain the Location of the Alternative Host

Step 1 When a host, c_i discovers that the next host, c_{i+1} is unreachable, it informs the agent, say A_1.

Step 2 A_1 will locate A_2. Methods to locate an agent are discussed in [6], [7] and [8].

Step 3 After locating A_2, A_1 will send $[MSG, Cert_{ci}, ip_{c_{i+1}}, E_{A_2}(ip_{c_{i+2}})]$.
$E_{A_2}(ip_{c_{i+2}})$ is the information to be decrypted (the location of the alternative host). MSG is the message to indicate that host $ip_{c_{i+1}}$ is unreachable. $Cert_{c_i}$, is the certificate of host c_i. We assume the use of X.509 Authentication Framework [9], whereby the public key of c_i is contained in its certificate, $Cert_{c_i}$.

Step 4 A_2 will verify that $ip_{c_{i+1}}$ is indeed unreachable. A_2 will also record such requests and their possible outcomes. When the agents return to the ASC, such records can be checked to discover any cheating attempt by any hosts.

Step 5 Once it is confirmed that $ip_{c_{i+1}}$ is unreachable, A_2 will reply with $[E_{c_i}(D_{A_2}(E_{A_2}(ip_{c_{i+2}})))]$, where D is the decryption function.

Step 6 (optional) If $ip_{c_{i+1}}$ is reachable, then A_2 will respond with:
$[E_{c_i}(Reachable, ip_{c_{i+1}})]$.

4.3 Security Issues

There are a few security issues that need to be addressed in the above scheme. The first is the management of the symmetric key of an agent while the second deals with replay attack and the third addresses the possibility of collusion between hosts.

Key Management. The symmetric key carried by the IGA can be obtained by the host, which provides an execution environment to the IGA. The host can locate the host where the other IGA is in, and pass the knowledge of the key to that host. Since we are assuming that both hosts are competing against one another, it is unlikely for one host to pass the knowledge of the key to another, except for collusion situation. We shall address this problem in the later stage.

In addition, since the host knows the key the agent is carrying, this key is only valid for the current information gathering trip. Another key has to be generated for the next trip. It is also important that the keys generated are not predictable. This means that knowledge of the current key should not lead to knowledge of the keys used in future sessions.

Observation of the messages reveals that there is a possibility for a malicious host to tamper with messages 5 and 6 so as to send the other IGA to another unintended destination. Fortunately, the damaging effects are limited. Should an IGA be sent to an unintended host, it is highly likely to be unable to proceed to the next destination, as such unintended host cannot access the information in the route structure. The IGA will then be sent back to the previous host. The agent will then try to determine its next destination again.

However, if by coincidence, such host is included to the agent's route, verification described in Sect. 2.1 will reveal that the visiting sequence is wrong. The agent will then be sent back to the previous host to obtain the correct location of the next destination.

Replay Attack. The message sent in step 3 can be replayed by a malicious host by locating agent A_2 and sending $[MSG, Cert_{c_i}, ip_x, E_{A_2}(ip_{c_{i+2}})]$, where ip_x is the location of a host that is known to be unreachable. Thus the encrypted content will be revealed to the malicious host.

However, for a malicious host where the agent is not occupying it, such attempt is meaningless as it is unable to control the movement of the agent. For a host where the agent is residing in it, the host is able to choose the next destination. However, since requests for decryption are recorded by the agent holding the key, the host faces the risk of being detected and possible prosecution. Thus the payoff for such actions is negative.

Collusion Attack. In a collusion attack scenario, a malicious host will attempt to locate the other agent. It will then contact the opposite host and offer to share information on the agents' keys. However, when a host approaches another to offer to share information, it faces the risk of being reported by the other host and it may face prosecution. Moreover, if both parties are competitors, the risk of such action being reported is higher. Therefore, the payoff is negative for such hosts, making it unlikely for such attacks to take place.

However should such scenario occurs, the 2 hosts that collude are able to send their respective agents to hosts that are less likely to threaten their business interest. However, this requires both agents to be in each corresponding host at the same time. This is not likely to happen since the movement of each agent is independent of one another. Moreover, even if such situation occurs, the ASC can still find out about it. If one agent did not visit a host and the other agent does not record the incident of that particular host being unreachable, the ASC will be able to know the culprit and can then take action against it.

4.4   An Extension to the Basic Model

We have described a basic model to protect an agent's route based on cooperation between 2 agents. The model is also robust in the sense that if the next destination is unreachable, an alternative destination is revealed. However, what happens if both destinations are unreachable? Although we have previously assumed that the probability of such occurrence is low, we can extend the basic model to remedy such situation.

Our approach is to employ 3 agents, A_1, A_2 and A_3. r''' is the route structure of A_1, where:

$$r''' = E_{c_1}[ip_{c_2}, E_{A_2}(ip_{c_3}), E_{A_2}(E_{A_3}(ip_{c_4})),$$
$$S_{ASC}(ip_{ASC}, ip_{c_1}, ip_{c_2}, E_{A_2}(ip_{c_3}), E_{A_2}(E_{A_3}(ip_{c_4})), t)]\|\|$$

$$\vdots$$

$$E_{c_{i-1}}[ip_{c_i}, E_{A_2}(ip_{c_{i+1}}), E_{A_2}(E_{A_3}(ip_{c_{i+2}})),$$
$$S_{ASC}(ip_{c_{i-2}}, ip_{c_{i-1}}, ip_{c_i}, E_{A_2}(ip_{c_{i+1}}), E_{A_2}(E_{A_3}(ip_{c_{i+2}}))t)]||$$

$$\vdots$$

$$E_{c_{\lfloor \frac{n}{3} \rfloor - 1}}[ip_{c_{\lfloor \frac{n}{3} \rfloor}}, E_{A_2}(EoR), S_{ASC}(ip_{c_{\lfloor \frac{n}{3} \rfloor - 2}}, ip_{c_{\lfloor \frac{n}{3} \rfloor - 1}}, ip_{c_{\lfloor \frac{n}{3} \rfloor}}, E_{A_2}(EoR), t)]||$$
$$E_{c_{\lfloor \frac{n}{3} \rfloor}}[EoR, S_{ASC}(ip_{c_{\lfloor \frac{n}{3} \rfloor - 1}}, ip_{c_{\lfloor \frac{n}{3} \rfloor}}, EoR, t)] \ . \tag{5}$$

The route structures for the other 2 agents are similar to (5). This equation is similar to (3) or (4) except that there is an additional host, whose location is encrypted using the keys of the other 2 agents.

Consider the case for agent A_1 at c_i. When the next host, c_{i+1} is unreachable, the protocol in 3.2 will be used to obtain the location of the alternative host, c_{i+2}. Till this point, things work exactly as described above. However, if the alternative choice is also unreachable, then there is another option for the agent to go to. To obtain the location, the protocol is used to request for agent A_2 to decrypt the information. This results in obtaining $E_{A_3}(ip_{c_{i+3}})$. The protocol will then be used again to request for A_3 to decrypt the information.

The reason for using 2 keys to encrypt the last information is for additional reliability. Recall that 2 hosts can collude to obtain the contents of the encrypted information. Since it is unlikely for 2 consecutive host to be unreachable, the suspicion of collusion is higher. Thus we required the involvement of the third agent to decrypt the last information. This makes collusion difficult as it now requires the cooperation of 3 hosts.

The above approach can also be used to cater to deal with situations when i consecutive hosts are unreachable. Suppose there are n hosts to visit, these hosts will be divided among $i+1$ agents. The jth (for $1 \le j \le \lfloor \frac{n}{i+1} \rfloor$) entry in the route structure of agent A_i would be:

$$E_{c_j}[X, S_{ASC}(ip_{c_{j-1}}), ip_{c_j}, X), t] \ . \tag{6}$$

where:

$$X = [ip_{c_{j+1}}, E_{A_1}(ip_{c_{j+2}}), E_{A_1}(E_{A_2}(ip_{c_{j+3}})), \ldots,$$
$$E_{A_1}(E_{A_2}(\ldots E_{A_{j-1}}(ip_{c_{2j}}) \ldots)), E_{A_1}(E_{A_2}(\ldots E_{A_{j-1}}(E_{A_{j+1}}(ip_{c_{2j+1}})) \ldots)), \ldots,$$
$$E_{A_1}(E_{A_2}(\ldots E_{A_{i+1}}(ip_{c_{j+I+1}})) \ldots))] \ .$$

Figure 3 illustrates such arrangement.

Since $max(i) = n$, when $i = n$, this implies that there will be n agents being sent out to collect information and each agent will only visit one host. In this situation, the route structure of the agent will simply store the address of the location to move to and the agent will return to the ASC without going anywhere. This arrangement is shown in Fig. 4.

When such situation occurs, the route structure of the agent is very simple. It simply stores:

$$r'''' = E_{c_i}[EoR, S_{ASC}(ip_{ASC}, ip_{c_i}, EoR), t] \tag{7}$$

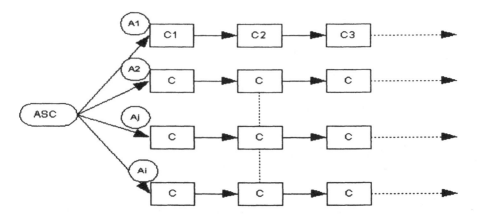

Fig. 3. Scenario of i agents gathering information

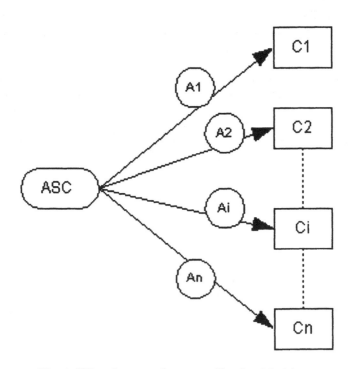

Fig. 4. When i = n, each agent will only visit 1 host.

With this extension, an *ASC* can now vary the i value according to its assessment of the network. It can be seen that as i increases, it is harder for hosts to collude and thus more secure. In fact, when $i = n$, it is impossible for the hosts to collude as there are no information hidden from them, and the agent has no other hosts to visit, except returning to the *ASC*.

However the performance suffers as i increases. Firstly, the information stored in the route structure becomes larger. Secondly, the *ASC* will be loaded with tasks to prepare the route structures, as encryptions require a large amount of system resources. In addition, it is also inefficient to run protocol in 3.2 many times to request for other agents to decrypt and such decryptions will add load to the host concern. Fortunately, this rarely happens, as it is not likely for many consecutive to be unreachable at the same time.

It is also interesting to note that when $i = n$, the *ASC* does not need to perform encryptions when preparing the route structures. Instead, it creates n agent, instructs each of them and concatenates all the information brought back by them. Intuitively, without incurring the overhead of performing numerous encryptions, the load in this situation is lighter than when i equals to other values, such as $i = n\text{-}1$. Future research and experiment can be carried out to compare the load, when $i = n$, with the loads for other values of i.

5   Application Scenario

In this Sect., we shall discuss a few applications where IGA with secure route structure can be used to gather information.

5.1   Electronic Commerce

Information gathering is an important part of an electronic commerce system. IGA can be used to gather information about the goods that the user is interested to buy. This set of information gathered is critical to the decision making process and thus data collected has to be protected, as well as the route structure.

An IGA for electronic commerce has been proposed in [10]. We shall give a brief description of this system. Interested readers are referred to the actual work itself.

In this work, an agent consists of static and dynamic components. Static components include the code and static data. The *ASC* signs on the static component. This will allow a host to verify whether the code and static data has been tampered with or not.

The dynamic component consists of data collected and the route structure (or routing table in the context of the mentioned work). To secure the information base, detection object (DO) is introduced. A DO is a string of random bytes. Before sending the IGA out to the Internet, the ASC generates a DO and put it into IGA's information base. During the information gathering process, any new information gathered will be encapsulated with DO as follows:

$$DO_n = E_{ASC}(I_n, E_{ASC}(I_{n-1}, \ldots, (E_{ASC}(I_1, DO))\ldots)), \qquad (8)$$

where I_n is the information provided by the nth host.

The host that is sending the IGA to the next destination will also append $Cert_{send}$ and $Sign_{send}$, which is the certificate and signature respectively, of the sending host. The signature is signed on the message digest of the agent. This will allow the receiving host to verify that the agent has not been tampered during the transportation process. All hosts are also required to maintain some information on the state of the agent when they entered and after they left the host. This will help the ASC to investigate and detect any tampering attempts when its suspicions are aroused.

Although this is useful in protecting the information and code of an IGA, the route structure is not protected and the IGA is thus vulnerable to the attacks mentioned previously. Even though the ASC can detect any tampering on the route structure, this is not practical as investigation involves a significant amount of work, which involves tracing the activities of the agent throughout the entire shopping process. Therefore, incorporating our route structure to this system would enhance it. Moreover, to detect any tampering of the route structure, our method do not require tracing of the activities. Instead, the ASC only needs to discover the missing host based on the information collected and check if there are any incident reports on that host being unreachable. If such report does not exist, then the culprit can be identified, which is the host before the missing one.

5.2   Intrusion Detection

A trend in the intrusion detection system (IDS) recently is to use agents to collect data or to analyze system behavior, as described in [11]. As agents are independently running entities, they can be added, removed or reconfigured from a system without altering other components or without having to restart the IDS. In addition, agents can be tested on their own before introducing them into a more complex environment. An agent may also be part of a group of agents that perform different simple functions. These agents can exchange information and derive more complex results than any one of them may be able to obtain on their own.

Mobile agents are used to collect data in a "Secure Domain Agent-based Intrusion Detection System" (SedaIDs). SedaIDs uses mobile agent to do different simple tasks. The mobile agent can roam around the dynamic domains to collect the UNIX host logs or network packets, or even network management information. It then transfers the data to another agent, which roams around the domain named analysis agent. From here, the data is analyzed based on the anomaly pattern. The anomaly message alarm will be passed to the upper layer for reporting.

Since the roaming agent will take the sensitive data collected from the network and host, we must hide the information together with the route structure from the malicious host. The above mentioned route structure and agent structure can be used to secure the agents. As the research for SedaIDs is currently in progress, we shall report our research findings in the future.

6   Future Works

Here are some of the specific areas we have identified for future development:

1. Improve on the overall performance by identifying the overheads and formulating strategies to reduce them.
2. Investigate the performance of the protocol for various values of i to find the balance between security, roubstness and performance.
3. Enhance system reliability and fault tolerance.
4. Fast location of an agent to improve the inter-agent communication.
5. Incorporate automatic configuration of agents, negotiation and payment protocols into agent prototypes for our electronic commerce and intrusion detection systems.

7   Conclusion

In this paper, we emphasize on the importance of protecting an agent's route. We have introduced various methods of protecting an agent's route. The first is based on [4] . However, this approach is not robust to react to failure of hosts. Next we modify the first approach to improve on the robustness. Unfortunately, this introduces security problems when hosts collude and is useful only when there is no competition between the hosts. Therefore, we proceed to introduce a third method, which provides us with both security and robustness. In addition, we have also extend the idea to allow stricter security and more robustness, but at the cost of performance.

References

1. M. Wooldridge and N.R Jennings. *Intelligent Agents: Theory and Practice*. Knowledge Engineering Review 10(2), 1995.
2. G.Vigna (Ed.). *Mobile Agents and Security*. Springer Verlag, LNCS 1419, 1998.
3. K. Rothermel and M. Strasser. *A Fault-tolerant Protocol for Providing the Exactly-once Property of Mobile Agents*. Proceedings of the Seventeenth IEEE Symposium on Reliable Distributed Systems, 1998.
4. D. Westhoff, M. Schneider, C. Unger and F. Kenderali. *Methods for Protecting a Mobile Agent's Route*. Proceedings of the Second International Information Security Workshop, (ISW'99), 1999. Springer Verlag, LNCS 1729, 1999.
5. M. Dalmeijer, E. Rietjens, D. Hammer, A. Aerts and M. Soede. *A Reliable Mobile Agents Architecture*. Proceedings of the First International Symposium on Object-Oriented Real-time Distributed Computing, (ISORC 98), 1998.
6. H. Maass. *Location-aware Mobile Applications Based on Directory Services*. Mobile Networks and Applications 3(1998), Baltzer Science Publishers BV, 1998.
7. W. Van Belle, K. Verelst and T. D'Hondt. *Location Transparent Routing in Mobile Agent Systems Merging Name Lookups with Routing*. Proceedings of the Seventh IEEE Workshop on Future Trends of Distributed Computing Systems, 1999.

8. S. Lazar, I. Weerakoon and D. Sidhu. *A Scalable Location Tracking and Message Delivery Scheme for Mobile Agents*. Proceedings of the Seventh IEEE International Workshops on Enabling Technologies: Infrastructure for Collaborative Enterprises, (WET ICE '98), 1998.

9. CCITT, Recommendation X.509-1989. *The Directory - Authentication Framework*. Consultation Committee, International Telephone and Telegraph, International Telecommunications Union, Geneva, 1989.

10. X.F. Wang, X. Yi, K.Y. Lam and E.Okamoto. *Secure Information Gathering Agent for Internet Trading*. Proceedings of the Eleventh Australian Joint Conference on Artificial Intelligence, Brisbane, Australia, 13 July 1998. Springer Verlag, LNAI 1544, 1998.

11. J.S. Balasubramaniyan, J.O. Garcia-Fernandez, D. Isacoff, E. Spafford and D. Zamboni. *An Architecture for Intrusion Detection Using Autonomous Agents*. Proceedings of the Fourteenth Annual Computer Security Applications Conference, 1998.

An Approach to Specifying Coordinated Agent Behaviour

Kenichi Yoshimura[1], Ralph Rönnquist[2], and Liz Sonenberg[3]

[1] Department of Computer Science and Software Engineering
The University of Melbourne
Melbourne, Australia
kyosh@cs.mu.oz.au

[2] Agent Oriented Software Pty. Ltd
207 Bouverie St. Carlton 3053
Melbourne, Australia
www.agent-software.com.au
ralph@agent-software.com.au

[3] Department of Information Systems
The University of Melbourne
Melbourne, Australia
l.sonenberg@dis.unimelb.edu.au

Abstract. 'Team oriented programming' indicates a number of different approaches to the formation of teams of agents and their coordination in order to achieve specified goals. This paper describes a framework, called SimpleTeam, aimed at team oriented programming. SimpleTeam supports the writing of team plans that represent the activity of a group of agents or sub-teams in order to achieve a team goal, and provides a set of primitives to control concurrency, exception handling and so on. An example application is presented, with discussion of how the approach can help to simplify the design of coordinated behaviour in multi-agent systems.

Keywords: multi-agent collaboration, teamwork

1 Introduction

'Team Oriented Programming' is a nuance of Agent Oriented Programming wherein agent collaboration is specified from the abstract view-point of the group as a whole. The concept behind this approach is that coordinated behavior is specified from a high-level ('bird's-eye') perspective and that the underlying machinery maps such specifications into the required individual activities of the agents (or sub-teams) concerned (Kinny et al, 1992, Tambe 2000, Tidhar, 1993).

Theoretical analyses of teamwork over the past decade, e.g. (Cohen and Levesque, 1991; Grosz and Kraus 1996; Tambe, 1997; Tidhar, 1999) have lead to a variety of practical approaches to facilitating the implementation of coordinated agent activity, e.g. (Grosz and Hunsberger, 1999; Haddadi, 1996; Hodgson et al, 1999; Lesser, 1998; Tambe, 2000; Tidhar, 1999). Agent coordination has been characterised as "the selection, ordering, and communication of the results of agent activities so that an agent works effectively in a group setting" (Lesser, 1998, pg 89). It is recognised that organising agents in terms of roles and responsibilities can significantly decrease the computational burden of coordinating their activities by limiting both the information that needs to be acquired and the scope of the

C. Zhang and V.-W. Soo (Eds.): PRIMA 2000, LNAI 1881, pp. 115-127, 2000.

decision process (Dignum et al, 2000; Lesser, 1998), and aspects of this have been well illustrated in Tambe's empirical work, eg (Tambe 1997; Tambe 2000). Although there is a growing body of work in this area, identifying appropriate frameworks that support coordinated activity but that do not add unreasonable performance or design overheads, is still a valuable area for research. In this paper we report on work that starts at the pragmatic end of exploring frameworks for specifying coordinated behaviour. This work stands in contrast to the above referenced research that seeks to stay within theoretical frameworks such as Cohen and Levesque's *Joint Intentions* approach, and Grosz's *SharedPlans* approach with various colleagues. Here we focus on a programmer's perspective – looking at the features provided in one programming framework currently under development. The key objective is to provide a lightweight agent programming environment that will enable robust development of (the coordination aspects of) multi-agent systems, i.e. here we are more interested in improving the 'design performance' of the system designer, rather than the run-time performance of the individual agents.

JACK Intelligent Agents™ is a Java-based multi-agent framework developed by Agent Oriented Software Pty. Ltd. JACK enables the development of complex agents in Java and supports the Belief-Desire-Intention (BDI) architecture (Rao & Georgeff 1992). It is further designed to allow extensions that implement new or extended agent models. The BDI architecture has been used in a wide range of applications and can be extended to introduce teamwork concepts, e.g. (Tidhar et al, 1999). Here we discuss modeling principles regarding specifications of teams and schemes for centrally specifying multi agent dialogs/protocols can be introduced. We believe that such abstractions are valuable for developing complex systems involving many collaborating agents.

Two key abstractions facilitating design are embodied in the current version of SimpleTeam – (a) support for separating coordination specification from other sub-team tasks (c.f. Figure 1), and (b) support for team/sub-team hierarchies, more elaborate than requiring all teams to be comprised just of individual agents (sec 2.2).

In this paper we present key concepts of the SimpleTeam framework and use an example of team-based programming to illustrate specification of coordinated agent behaviour within this framework. We discuss how SimpleTeam addresses various issues of the multi-agent system development and conclude with a discussion of aspects to be addressed in order to improve the robustness and comprehensiveness of the framework.

2   The SimpleTeam Programming Framework

Among the goals we set out to achieve, two are worth mentioning before introducing the software architecture.

The first is to reduce the inherent complexity in design, computation and communications that arises from attempting to implement fully distributed control of coordinated behavior. A simple example is addressing when sending a message to a team as a whole instead of a specific agent; for instance, in a military situation, a commander may wish a command to include the entire platoon, without needing to send individual messages to each soldier.

The second goal relates to a specific domain of application; that is, simulation of social entities (for example, military organizations such as platoon, brigades, and armies). Very often, a coarse-grained view of the social organisation is sufficient for the level of fidelity required, whereas the effort required for simulation in terms of the single entities composing a team (soldiers and commanders in the example above) may be excessive. For instance, it may be sufficient to know that a platoon moved from one location to another and that it suffered a certain percentage of losses during the manoeuver, without requiring that the fate of individual soldiers be traceable. For system development, however we want to be able to use only one language for specifying the coordinated behavior of a team, no matter how this may be simulated: and perhaps simulation at different granularities might be available: by any number of agents; by one per member of the team; or by a single entity.

We have chosen to achieve these goals by the introduction of a new software entity, a 'team instance'. A *team instance* is the software representative for a team, and it exists to coordinate the behavior and facilitate the communications of zero, one or more agents; or, recursively, other team instances, each representing single elements or further aggregations within the team. In software terms, a team is viewed as having a centralized ('star') organization with the team instance at the centre, independent of the structuring and internal dynamics of the social organization being represented. All communication and decision-making related to coordinated behavior happens by means of the team instance. Teams can be created dynamically during execution; moreover, agents and teams can be part of multiple teams at the same time.

Team instances can be compared with the so-called facilitators which are commonly used in multi-agent systems (see, for instance, Open Agent Architecture (Cohen 1994)). However, while facilitators normally provide only a communications and brokering facility, team instances actually perform all reasoning related to coordination and distribution of activity among members.

The TEAMCORE project (Tambe, et al 2000) focuses on supporting formation of individual agents into individual teams, without providing a notion of team type. SimpleTeam, in contrast, offers team modeling in an object-oriented setting. This means in particular that team definitions are type definitions rather than specifications of individuals. An individual team is an instance of a defined team type. As mentioned previously, teams are explicit BDI reasoning entities in SimpleTeam separate from the entities constituting the team members. This may be contrasted with "implicit team" approaches, where team activity arises by agents acting in concert, but where there is no explicit team entity as such. Tambe et al have studied this approach in STEAM, and with TEAMCORE, they show how to separate out coordination activity of team members into a replicable module that can be the same for all team members.

2.1 The Team Construct

The team construct is designed to:

- specify what a team is capable of doing (i.e., what roles it can fulfill);
- specify which components are needed to form a particular type of team;
- specify the coordinated behavior among the team members; and
- specify some team knowledge.

The team specification determines what each team member does, and it also handles failure of members to achieve their goals. Team members act in coordination by being given goals according to the specification, and they are themselves responsible for determining how to satisfy those goals. Following the JACK paradigm, team concepts are part of a strictly typed language. This is an accepted practice within Software Engineering, as it allows early detection of inconsistencies during the compilation and initialization process.

Team knowledge is not an implementation of mutual beliefs (Grosz and Kraus, 1996; Kinny et al, 1994; Tambe 1997), but is rather a practical way to keep state information about the team and its activity. In other words, the team members do not have mutual beliefs, but the framework includes a place for shared knowledge in connection with the team specification. Team members can then access this information through standard messaging.

A team is a class level construct which brings together the various components that form that type of team. It appears as follows:

```
team SearchTargetTeam extends SimpleTeam {
        // Team declarations
}
```

In essence, a team class is an extension to agent taking responsibility for managing the coordination of team member activity and holding the team's knowledge base.

A key element of a team definition is the declaration of which roles this team can play as member of other teams. The JACK statement #performs role is used for this, as illustrated by the following example.

```
#performs role NorthAgent;
#performs role SouthAgent;
```

Each #performs role statement is a declaration that the type of team can perform the role.

The members of a team are declared through role requirements rather than explicit sub-team type requirements. This can be compared with the use of interfaces in Java; it expresses the functional requirements for the members rather than restricting to particular team types. Team member declarations are as follows:

```
#requires role NorthAgent north_agent;
#requires role SouthAgent south_agent;
```

Statements like these describe the team in terms of the roles of the sub-teams. Role entries are filled during team formation. The team is then allowed to choose from the set of available team instances that are 'willing' to take on the roles: the actual team formation is done by handling a TeamFormationEvent in the team. There is a range of control primitives to use in the TeamFormationEvent handling, but these will not be discussed further here.

2.2 The Role Construct

The role construct is used to specify abstract capability; that is, it is an interface definition, which declares the goals a team must be able to handle to be a performer of the role. This is specified in terms of events handled and posted by the subteam that is to fill a role.

Role definitions can be compared to the use of interfaces in Java. Its purpose is simply to declare the interface between team and subteam, so it falls within the strong typing paradigm while separating the needs of the team from the ways in which subteams fill them. For instance, an application may include subteam definitions based on different modelling fidelity; the same role would be performed by the one subteam in a complex way that provides a high level of fidelity in the modelling, and by another subteam in a simple way that operates without sub-dividing the role tasks further.

A role definition has two parts: a 'downwards' interface that declares the events a subteam must handle to take on the role, and an 'upwards' interface that declares the events the team entity needs to handle when having a team member of the role. The following is an outline of a role definition:

```
role NorthAgent extends Role {
    // the downwards interface
    #handles event ....
    // the upwards interface
    #posts event ....
}
```

Note that both 'downwards' and 'upwards' events are sub-tasked by means of @team_achieve statements. The 'downwards' events are subtasked by the team as goals that the subteams achieve, and conversely, the 'upwards' events are subtasked by subteams requesting counter services as subgoals performed by the team.

Roles are used within teams to define how the structure of teams and subteams looks in terms of which goals the teams and subteams expect and require of each other. The ability to perform a role is declared with a #performs role statement, and the need of a role filler is declared with a #requires role statement. The #requires role statements also introduce symbolic references, i.e., variables, that are used in team plans referring to the role fillers. Team plans are written referring to any subteams involved symbolically via the role filling, allowing the choice of which team that fills a role be postponed until run-time.

The #requires role statement is presently limited to a form where every role position is identified individually. This means that role filling in effect is strictly tied to skill as well as capability. Team plans commit not only to the requirements of the various roles, but directly to which particular role position performs which task. In other words, when a subteam takes an a role x of type Y, it is automatically elected to perform the x tasks of the team plans. In particular, even if the team has another role z of the same type, Y, the team plans have already committed to use the x subteam for certain tasks, without concern that the z subteam, which is of the same role type, technically is able to perform the x tasks.

2.3 Coordinating Sub-team Activity

The underlying notion of a team plan is important in the SimpleTeam approach, and is somewhat different from a notion of the same name used elsewhere (Kinny et al, 1994; Tidhar, 1999). Here, a team plan is a sequence of activities provided by the system designer that describes the coordination behaviour among team roles. We briefly present key constructs available – just enough to follow the example below.

SimpleTeam includes a designator, @team_achieve(subteam, goal), through which a team issues goals for subteams, and a statement form, @parallel(...) for expressing parallel activity. The @team_achieve statement is similar to a synchronous sub-task which succeeds or fails with the processing of the goal. That processing, however, is carried out by the designated team member rather than by the team entity itself.

The @parallel statement is a block statement whose sub-statements are performed in parallel rather than sequentially. The execution processes the sub-statements a parallel task, which adhere to the statement atomicity principle of JACK. That is, although the tasks are executed in parallel, it is a controlled execution that ensures computations to never be interrupted in the midst of a volatile region.

A @parallel statement also takes control arguments relating sub-statement success and failure to overall success and failure. This includes firstly the choice of whether success for the parallel statement as a whole requires all or only some sub-statements to succeed. Secondly, the programmer chooses whether the parallel statement should complete immediately when its success or failure can be determined, or whether all the parallel tasks should be executed exhaustively regardless of the overall success or failure. Further, the control arguments allows specification of a termination condition and which exception to use to signal premature termination.

3 Example

This section illustrates the use of the team modeling concepts by means of an example. The example domain we have chosen is a kind of pursuit game (Grinton et al, 1997), where groups of predators try to capture targets that appears at random locations. The environment is highly parameterized (allows for different setting of experiments to be conducted) and communicates with agents through the sockets. The separation of agents from the environment allows for evaluations of various agent-oriented-frameworks/programming languages. The motivation behind the development of the environment was to develop a testbed to study various aspects of multi-agent systems. An interface between the environment and agents are kept simple to allow rapid implementation of agents, while the environment is kept reasonably complex (E.g. involves uncertainties arising from limited sensory range of agents) to accommodate "interesting" experiments. The team of agents for the simulation has been implemented using JACK with SimpleTeam extension and elsewhere we will present results relating to exploration of alternate strategies within the game. Here we focus on design implications of working with and without the design support offered by SimpleTeam.

Although the problem is somewhat artificial, as the domain involves potentially many teamwork activities including dynamic team formation and cooperation of team members' activities, we see it as a realistic testbed for exploring ideas of teamwork. Arguably, a more realistic domain would be the newly emerging RoboCup Rescue domain (Kitano et al, 1999), introduced to encourage research of various agent technologies that were not well covered with RoboCup soccer simulation (Kitano et al, 1997). The domain is a simulation of disaster rescue (earthquake). Research problems that can be studied in more detail within this domain include multi-agent planning, execution monitoring, resource-bounded planning and teamwork of heterogeneous agents.

Compared to RoboCup, our pursuit domain has the advantage of potentially more variability in team member's capabilities and availabilities, and much less opportunity for pre-defined strategies (Stone and Veloso, 1999). Further, dynamic team (re)formation is a more ambitious task here. Compared to our pursuit game, the RoboCup Rescue simulation involves a greater number of agents. Moreover, an individual agent's skills vary more dramatically from one agent to another. Both domains require coordination of heterogeneous agents and heterogeneous teams must be formed dynamically as required.

An implementation of agent teams for the pursuit game is a useful starting point to evaluate the SimpleTeam framework. Below we explain the implementation of our agents for the pursuit game and later we hope to demonstrate features of SimpleTeam that are useful to apply in more realistic domains.

The rules of the game are simple. An agent searches for a potential target to capture. Upon the identification of a target, the agent tries to identify potential team members, which are situated within a sensory range of the agent (a team is formed dynamically as required). In order to capture a target, four agents of different capabilities must coordinate. That is, a target must be surrounded from four directions (north, south, east and west). Once all team members are positioned correctly, the team sends a command to the simulator to capture the target.

In SimpleTeam, every agent is defined by inheriting from SimpleTeam's base class called SimpleTeam. A team with no subteam is a definition/specification of an agent where as a team that requires subteam is a definition of team behavior.

With our implementation, two different types of teams are defined. The first team is called SearcherTeam. We will refer this as an agent because it basically is a specification of individual agent (i.e. no subteam required). The main purpose of the SearcherTeam is to identify a target and capture it while forming a team appropriately. The definition of SearcherTeam is as follow.

```
team SearcherTeam extends SimpleTeam{
    #performs role NorthAgent north_agent;
    #performs role SouthAgent south_agent;
    #performs role EastAgent east_agent;
    #performs role WestAgent west_agent;

    #uses plan IdentifyTargetPlan;
    #uses plan IdentifyPotentialTeamMembersPlan;
    #uses plan FormCaptureTargetTeamPlan;
}
```

The definition of SearchTeam above defines a set of role that this team can take and a set of plans that speficifies behaviour of the agent.

The second team type is called CaptureTargetTeam. Upon an identification of a target by SearcherTeam/agent, the agent creates an instance of CaptureTargetTeam. The associated plans of CaptureTargetTeam define a set of team activities/behaviors. It is interesting to note, that the instances of SearcherTeam are actual agents that appear in the simulated environment, while instances of CaptureTargetTeam are objects within the SimpleTeam framework that reason about coordination of team members. Our definition of CaptureTargetTeam is as follow.

```
team CaptureTargetTeam extends SimpleTeam{
    #requires role NorthAgent north_agent;
    #requires role SouthAgent south_agent;
    #requires role EastAgent east_agent;
    #requires role WestAgent west_agent;

    #uses plan CaptureTargetTeamFormationPlan;
    #uses plan CaptureTargetPlan;
}
```

The plans, CaptureTargetTeamFormationPlan and CaptureTargetPlan, are different from 'ordinary' BDI plans in that they define the coordination activity of the team members rather than (merely) the actions of the team. As mentioned before, a team to capture a target (CaptureTargetTeam) is formed dynamically as required and is not statically defined by a programmer at the development of the system. CaptureTargetTeamFormationPlan is then a plan for assigning individual subteams to roles as required by CaptureTargetTeam. In our example, the agent causing the team to be formed also decides which partners to it requires, and the team formation plan, shown below, is merely a matter of performing the assignments.

```
teamplan CaptureTargetTeamFormationPlan
    extends TeamPlan{
    #uses interface CaptureTargetTeam ctt;
    #handles event TeamFormationEvent ev;

    body(){
            ctt.north_agent.attach(ctt.partner_names.north);
            ctt.south_agent.attach(ctt.partner_names.south);
            ctt.east_agent.attach(ctt.partner_names.east);
            ctt.west_agent.attach(ctt.partner_names.west);
    }
}
```

The TeamFormationEvent is posted to the team instance by the SimpleTeam kernel when it is created. As mentioned before, an instance of team is an explicit BDI entity that can perform any amount of reasoning to determine its behaviour. By handling the TeamFormationEvent (that is, including a plan that handles that event type in CaptureTargetTeam's plan library), any instance of CaptureTargetTeam, when created, will assign desired team members dynamically. It is the agent that proposes that a CaptureTargetTeam is formed that decides which its partners need to be, and it passes this information to the team instance as construction argument. The partner names are stored in a structure, partner_names, in the CaptureTargetTeam instance, and are used by the CaptureTargetTeamFormationPlan plan to assign team members.

CaptureTargetPlan is a TeamPlan that is unique to the SimpleTeam framework. It provides general-purpose framework to specify coordination among teams/subteams.

As can be seen from the example below, coordination among team members can be specified using TeamPlan statements. Firstly, by using @parallel statements, we can specify concurrent executions of various activities. All statements in the body of an @parallel statement are executed concurrently. In this example, each subteam tries to move to their specified locations in parallel. Upon successfully exiting from parallel statement, the programmer can assume that all actions are taken successfully by individual subteams.

Secondly, by using @team_achieve statements, we can specify the activity of team members as goals for them to achieve, while the team plan suspends and waits for the team to complete. In this way sequencing of coordinated actions is obtained. For instance, all team members must be positioned correctly before NorthAgent can send the command to capture the target. The team members can move in parallel, and the target can be captured only when all the team members are positioned.

```
teamplan CaptureTargetPlan extends TeamPlan{
    #handles event InitiateCaptureEvent ice;

    #uses role NorthAgent north_agent;
    #uses role SouthAgent south_agent;
    #uses role EastAgent east_agent;
    #uses role WestAgent west_agent;

    body(){

            @parallel(){
            @team_achieve(north_agent,
north_agent.pne.position_north_event());
            @team_achieve(south_agent,
south_agent.pse.position_south_event());
            @team_achieve(east_agent,
east_agent.pee.position_east_event());
            @team_achieve(west_agent,
                west_agent.pwe.position_west_event());
            };

            @team_achieve(north_agent,
                north_agent.rfce.ready_for_capturing());
    }
```

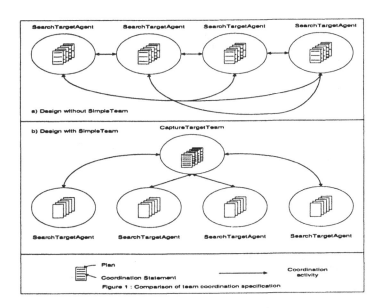

Figure 1 : Comparison of team coordination specification

Figure 1 shows a comparison of team coordination specifications using SimpleTeam extension and without the extension. Without the SimpleTeam extension, the specification of team coordination must be embodied in many plans of the agents. The resulting plans/program will be more difficult to modify and maintain. For example, if a team coordination strategy must be modified (e.g. the environment requires a team to behave differently to capture a target) a programmer (potentially) needs to make modifications to many plans of the system.

As it is shown in the figure, the agent must coordinate with all the agents in a team. In order to interact with another agent, the agent must keep track of current state of negotiation to perform team activities. Such book keeping can easily lead to errors especially when a team involves many team members (E.g. a team in RoboCup rescue simulation).

In contrast, a design approach with SimpleTeam extension provides an abstraction that separates specification of team coordination (CaptureTargetTeam) and specification of individual agent's activities (SearcherTeam). To make modification to team behaviors specification, a programmer only need to make modification to TeamPlan that belongs to CaptureTargetTeam. For example, if the environment requires different team coordination to capture a target, a programmer only needs to modify CaptureTargetPlan. Similarly, to make modifications to an individual agent's behaviors, a programmer can do so by modifying a set of plans of the agent without impacting on team coordination.

4   Discussion

We have demonstrated that the SimpleTeam framework can provide a plausible framework to specify coordination of agents' activities. Such a general-purpose framework avoids rewriting domain specific coordination plans that are required to implement agent teams. In this way SimpleTeam provides robust, lightweight support for the specification of coordinated agent activity. However, the framework lacks certain features that can be argued to be desirable if rich agent interactions are to be supported without imposing an enormous burden on the programmer. Here we briefly discuss three such features.

Automated Team Formation

In SimpleTeam framework, writing necessary plans for team formation is left for programmers to implement. A process of team formation requires a number of steps, which are essentially the same across many different domains. A team formation typically requires the following steps.

1. Identification of available agents.
2. Identification of agents' skills/capabilities.
3. Role assignment to relevant agent for each role required within a team.

Writing plans to implement such steps are labor intensive and repetitive exercise. A framework of general team formation is more desirable to reduce the engineering complexity of building an agent team, eg (Tidhar et al, 1996).

Failure Detection and Recovery

A plan to specify team coordination behavior may fails because a team member(s) is not able to fulfil requirements to take on a role required by the team. Defaulting team commitment by a sub-team can occur in many different situations. Firstly, in the context of BDI agents, the agent/sub-team may decide to drop the current team commitment because it has discovered that it does not have any applicable plans to handle given event after considering the current context of the situation. Secondly, and more importantly, the agent reconcile their intention to newly raised opportunity, which are more attractive (or higher priority) than current team commitment.

Working with a team in dynamic and complex environment such as disaster rescue simulation, there are many situations where complete team cannot be formed due to unavailability of team members. For example, a team of firemen and life saving crew with an ambulance(s) must cooperate in order to rescue civilians from a building that is on fire. Arguably, in such situations, a team of firemen must proceed without life saving crew if they are not available at the creation of the team.

Such failures of a sub-team to achieve team goal require reformation of the team (in worst case, total failure of team plan, and not being able to achieve the goal). The programmer must provide a team with a set of plans to recover from such failures. But in highly dynamic and complex environment, it is time consuming to write such failure recovery plans for every possible scenario. We plan to borrow from the ideas of Tambe who has demonstrated that certain types of failures can be dealt with in a domain independent manner (Tambe, 2000)

Specification of Agents' Influences

In SimpleTeam, a team's capability is described by Role constructs. A role construct is used as an interface of Java programming language, where is defines a set of events that team must handle in order to take on a role within a team. To allow the framework to support reasoning about team formation, more extensive and comprehensive definition of role encompassing broad social issues such as authority dependencies and delegation power should be considered, e.g. (Dignum et al, 2000).

5 Conclusion

We have presented an introduction to team modeling concepts using the SimpleTeam extension of an available agent framework. It is a scheme for specifying and implementing coordinated distributed behavior in a manner that maintains type-safeness and generally follows the Java paradigm.

Our implementation of a team for the pursuit game has shown various constructs that are available in the SimpleTeam framework. We believe that our example is a useful starting point to apply SimpleTeam concepts to the more realistic domains, such as RoboCup rescue, where the environment requires coordination of heterogeneous agents.

Through our example, we have demonstrated the useful abstraction provided by SimpleTeam, in that it separates specifications of individual agent behavior from specifications of team activities that require coordination. We have identified various problems and limitations with the current implementation of SimpleTeam.

Acknowledgements. The authors are grateful for lively discussions with many colleagues on the topics of this paper. In particular we acknowledge the work of Gil Tidhar. A preliminary version of some of this work was presented elsewhere (Hodgson et al, 1999).

References

Cohen, P.R. & Levesque, H. (1991) 'Teamwork', Nous. *Special Issue on Cognitive Science and Artificial Intelligence*, 35(4):487—512.

Cohen, P.R., Cheyer, A., Wang, M. & Baeg, S.C. (1994) 'An open agent architecture', *Proceedings of the AAAI Spring Simposium on Software Agents*, AAAI Press, pp 1-8.

Dignum, F, Morley, D, Sonenberg, E and Cavedon, L (2000) `Towards socially sophisticated BDI agents', in *Proceedings of the 2000 Int'l Conf. on Multi-Agent Systems, ICMAS00*

Grinton, C, Sonenberg, E and Sterling L (1997) 'Exploring agent cooperation : studies with a simple pursuit game", in *Proceedings of the 1997 Australian AI Conference*

Grosz, B and Kraus, S. (1996) `Collaborative Plans for Complex Group Activity,' *Artificial Intelligence* 86, pp 269-357.

Grosz, B, and Hunsberger, L. (1999) `Planning and Acting Together,' AI Magazine, Special Issue on Distributed Continual Planning.

Haddadi, A. (1996) 'Communication and Cooperation in Agent Systems: A Pragmatic Theory', Number 1056 in *LNCS*. Springer Verlag.

Hodgson, A., Rönnquist, R., Busetta, P., (1999) 'Specification of Coordinated Agent Behaviour (The SimpleTeam Approach)', *Proceedings of the IJCAI-99 Workshop on Team Modelling and Plan Recognition.*

Kinny, D, Ljungberg, M, Rao, A, Sonenberg, E, Tidher, G and Werner E. (1994) `Planned Team Activity,' in *Artificial Social Systems*, (eds) C Castelfranchi and E Werner, Springer Lecture Notes in Computer Science, vol 830, pages 227-256.

Kitano, H, et al. (1997) 'RoboCup: A Challenge AI Problem", *AI Magazine, spring 1997.*

Kitano, H, et al. (1999) 'RoboCup-Rescue: Search and Rescue for Large Scale Disasters as a Domain for Autonomous Agents Research', *Proceedings of IEEE Conference on Man, Systems, and Cybernetics(SMC-99).*

Lesser, V.R. (1998) `Reflections on the nature of multi-agent coordination and its implications for an agent architecture,' *Autonomous Agents and Multi-Agent Systems*, 1, pages 89-111.

Rao, A.S. & Georgeff M.P. (1992) 'An abstract architecture for rational agents', *Proceedings of the Third Int'l Conf. on Principles of Knowledge Representation and Reasoning (KR'92)* C. Rich, W. Swartout & B. Nebel, editors, Morgan Kaufmann Publishers.

Stone, P and Veloso, M. (1999) 'Task Decomposition, Dynamic Role Assignment, and Low-Bandwidth Communication for Real-Time Strategic Teamwork.' *Artificial Intelligence*, vol. 100, , June 1999.

Tambe, M. (1997) 'Towards flexible teamwork', *Journal of Artificial Intelligence Research*, 7:83—124.

Tambe, M, Pynadath, D & Chauvat N. (2000) 'Building Dynamic Agent Organizations in Cyberspace', *IEEE Internet Computing (to appear)*.

Tidhar, G. (1993) 'Team Oriented Programming: Preliminary Report,' Technical Report 37, Australian Artificial Intelligence Institute.

Tidhar, G. (1999) 'Organization-Oriented Systems: Theory and Practice,' PhD Thesis, The University of Melbourne.

Tidhar, G., Sonenberg L. and Rao, A. (1999), 'A Framework for BDI Teams,' Technical Report 99/12, Department of Computer Science and Software Engineering, The University of Melbourne, 1999.

Tidhar, G. and Sonenberg, L. (2000) 'Organised Distributed Systems,' to appear, Proceedings of the Fifth IFCIS International Conference on Cooperative Information Systems (CoopIS 2000), Israel, September 2000.

Tidhar, G, Rao, A.S. & Sonenberg, L. (1996) 'Guided Team Selection' *Proceedings of the 1996 Int'l Conf. on Multi-Agent Systems ICMAS96* Japan M. Tokoro, editor, pp 369-376.

Specifying Agent Behaviour with Use Cases

Clinton Heinze, Michael Papasimeon, and Simon Goss

Air Operations Division - Aeronautical and Maritime Research Laboratory
Defence Science and Technology Organisation
Victoria, Australia
firstname.lastname@dsto.defence.gov.au

Abstract. The software engineering of multi-agent systems demands specification of the required agent behaviours to provide documented requirements for the design and implementation phases. A methodology for the analysis and specification of agent behaviours is proposed, which arises from a lengthy experience in the construction of multi-agent simulations for military operations research. The methodology builds upon the existing use case modelling techniques provided by the Unified Modeling Language (UML) and is in keeping with the agent extensions to the UML proposed elsewhere. A case-study from a specific multi-agent air combat simulation accompanies the elaboration of the methodology.

1 Introduction

The construction of agent systems requires associated software engineering techniques. This paper proposes a methodological approach for a use case oriented specification of the requirements of a system that may include intelligent agents, and details a case-study. By focussing on *scenarios* to constrain the scope of the development it differs from other modelling methodologies that stem from a domain focussed view [5]. The methodology suggested in this paper makes use of extensions to the Unified Modeling Language (UML) [6]. This paper meshes neatly with work by Odell, Parunak, and Bauer, [7,8] and Burmeister [9] in that it presents a view of agent oriented development that allies closely with the experiences of object oriented development. The development of Agent UML (AUML) [7,10] proposes to extend the UML for agents but concentrates on the documentation of the interactions between agents. This paper proposes to extend the UML for use case analysis. Future papers will address specific issues related to UML extensions for the design and implementation of specific classes of agents. For example the beliefs-desires-intentions (BDI) agents [11].

Broadly speaking there are two emerging classes of agent oriented software engineering. That are those interested in building software systems (that may or may not include intelligent agents in the finished product) and regard agents as a useful abstraction tool for the specification, design and documentation of those systems. And those concerned with software engineering technologies for building multi-agent systems (which may or may not use the abstract properties of agency as the means for specifying and designing those systems). There is

C. Zhang and V.-W. Soo (Eds.): PRIMA 2000, LNAI 1881, pp. 128–142, 2000.
© Springer-Verlag Berlin Heidelberg 2000

an overlap between the two groups and this paper presents a view of software development that subscribes to both views. That is that the agent metaphor is a useful one for the specification of the behaviour of a complex system and that agent technologies are useful for implementing those systems.

The Defence Science and Technology Organisation (DSTO) provides advice to the Australian Defence Force. Operations research studies form the basis of this advice. Typical studies will compare potential hardware upgrades to an aircraft— perhaps a new missile or a modification to the radar [1]. On occasion the acquisition of a new aircraft will dictate the evaluation of candidates. Comparisons of tactical decision making can also be made resulting in the provision of advice to the ADF about the adoption of standard operating procedures and tactics [2]. Studies are conducted using constructive simulations of air combat. The complexity of the domain presents a number of modelling challenges. The physical systems - aircraft, missiles, radars - are sophisticated, highly dynamic, and must be modelled to a sufficient level of fidelity. Traditional structured analysis and object oriented analysis techniques have been used with success to define the modelling requirements of these physical systems. The human operators of those systems—fighter pilots, fighter controllers, mission commanders—must also be modelled. Intelligent agents are used as the computational models of human decision making within these simulations [3,4]. Specifying the behavioural requirements of these agents has proved more challenging. This paper addresses the issue by proposing extensions to the UML to allow standard OO techniques to be used for agent development.

2   Use Case Analysis for Requirements Specification

A number of analysis techniques are used in software engineering for specifying requirements. These range from natural language software requirements specifications to formal methods using mathematical languages such as Z [12]. Use case analysis is one particular technique that has shown value for specifying requirements for many different types of systems. Use case analysis has gained prominence due to its inclusion in the Unified Modeling Language (UML) and therefore has gained popularity in the construction of object oriented systems. Benefits of a use case driven approach include:

1. A use case is a view of system functionality from the user's perspective.
2. A use case can be considered as a collection of scenarios about system use— developers and users often use scenarios to help them understand requirements.
3. Software can be developed using an iterative and incremental approach with one or more use cases defining the subset of functionality for the user which will be implemented in a given iteration.
4. Requirements can be specified in non-technical terms that a user can understand without needing to be a software engineer.
5. Traceability of requirements through the design, implementation and testing phases of a project is improved.

2.1   Use Cases for Non Agent Applications

A use case can be loosely defined as a typical interaction between a user and a software system. For example in a paint program, some example use cases may be *rotate an image* and *convert image to JPEG*. Although use cases can vary in size, their most important characteristic is that in some way each use case specifies some functionality which the software provides to the user, allowing the user to achieve some discrete goal. More precisely, a use case can be defined as follows: A use case is a scenario about system usage, which is described by a sequence of events. Each sequence is initiated by entities known as actors that may be a person, another system or the passage of time. The result of the sequence of events must be of use to the actor initiating the sequence or another actor. A use case model provides the information that would be expected in a traditional software requirements specification. For example, the actors are commonly the users of the system being specified, and the use cases provide the functional requirements of the users. The UML supports a standard notation for use cases and actors as shown in Figure 1. Participation in a particular use case by an actor is shown by a line between the actor, in this case an artist, and the use case. The notation allows for requirements to be abstracted and encapsulated in a structure that is logical and concise.

A use case can use or extend the functionality provided by another use case. In the UML stereotypes <<uses>> and <<extends>> define these specific associations. Figure 1 shows an example of <<uses>> and <<extends>> using some functionality from a simple paint program. An artist can *Convert Image to JPEG* which uses the *Save Image* use case and they can *Rotate Image* which extends the general use case *Transform Image*. The box surrounding all the use cases defines the system boundary of the paint program, with the artist actor being external to the system. It is possible to have multiple actors in use case diagrams. For example we might have an *Image Analyst* or a hardware device such as a *Printer* as actors interacting with the paint program.

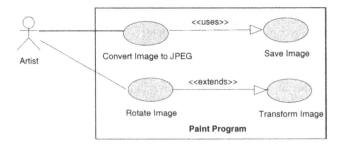

Fig. 1. Part of a use case model for a simple paint program

One or more use case diagrams is not usually enough to fully specify the requirements for a system. Each use case in the diagram needs to be fully documented and specified. The amount and type of documentation needed for each use case varies depending on the type of system being specified. It can range from a text description to including different types of UML diagrams. Common approaches to documenting uses cases for object oriented systems can be found in [13,14].

2.2   Use Cases for Agent Applications

Use case analysis has proved to be useful and successful for requirements specification of object oriented systems. It is proposed that with some modification and extension, use case analysis can become a useful tool for single and multi-agent requirement and behaviour specification. Wooldridge and Jennings [15], characterise agents as entities that are situated in an environment in which they can perceive and act. They exhibit autonomy, social ability, and act in reactive and goal directed ways. For the purposes of specification agents are elements of the software systems that exhibit these types of properties. Whether or not they are implemented as agents is a design time decision.

Agents are differentiated from the traditional use case view of actors by being internal to the system. Actors are external entities (humans or other systems), that interact with a particular software system. Agents, on the other hand are complex software components that are internal to the system but interact with the system in ways that are consistent with accepted notions of agency and function, at least conceptually, with the notion of an actor.

Agents are often ascribed qualities and capabilities normally associated with human actors. For some systems which have entities that can be ascribed with notions of agency (such as non player characters in video games), it often helps in the specification of behaviours if we treat these entities as real humans. Given that use case analysis has proved successful in specifying requirements of systems for human actors, it is proposed that the same techniques (with some modifications) could be applied to agent oriented systems. Using the UML's extension mechanism of stereotyping, two extensions for use in the requirements specification of agent oriented systems are proposed.

agent : An <<agent>> is an <<actor>> that is part of a software system, and has behaviours defined by agent use cases in the context of the system. In a use case diagram an agent is confined inside the system boundary. An agent can interact with other agents or other actors through agent use cases. The notation for an <<agent>> is the same as for an <<actor>>.

agent use case : An <<agent use case>> is a collection of scenarios about the agent's interaction with a system. Each scenario describes a sequence of events which the agent initiates. The result of the sequence of events has to be something of use to the initiating agent, to another agent, or to any other actor. The diagrammatic notation for an <<agent use case>> is the same as for a standard UML use case.

The two stereotypes defined above complement the UML's existing use case notation and methodology. Many multi-agent software systems are hybrid systems where multiple agents can interact with multiple actors. For example, consider many types of video games where human players (often in teams) compete against enemy opponents which may be considered as agents in a synthetic environment. Such a system is a hybrid multi-actor and multi-agent system where standard use case analysis, and the agent oriented extensions defined above can be combined to specify requirements of all the entities both human and artificial. This paper argues that the anthropomorphism that is often stated as an explicit benefit of agents provides the opportunity for them to assume the role of actors within the traditionally accepted usage of the UML. So whilst recognising that there is a difference between agents and actors—the former is internal to the system and the latter external to the system—from the perspective of the UML the treatment of agents and actors can be viewed in a similar way. The fact that agents are internal to the system places them within the scope of the software engineering design task and future work will explore techniques for *designing* agents. In this sense they are actors over which the designer has control. Interestingly this has parallels with recent notions of system design that include the human user as a internal to the system the purposes of design [18].

3   Methodology for Specifying Agent Systems

A methodology for specifying agent systems using use cases is required. We suggest a three step process which involves: identifying the agents and actors; identifying use cases for the agents and actors; and documenting the use cases.

3.1   Identify Agents and Actors

The analyst first decides what actors and what agents are going to be involved in the software system being specified. To identify the actors in a system, the analyst must determine who will be the users of the system, and with what external systems the software will be interacting. Identifying the agents in a system is a bit more difficult. In a military simulation this involves deciding what human operators to model. In a video game the agents are likely to be all non-player characters and in an information retrieval system the agent may be a web crawler.

3.2   Identify Use Cases for Agents and Actors

For each actor in the system the use cases are specified by drawing a use case diagram with a number of ellipses joined by lines to the actor. Each ellipse signifies a use case or some functionality provided by the system to the actor. The same approach can be applied to determining agent use cases for agents. However, instead of considering functionality for an agent use case, the types of behaviours an agent exhibits in the context of an environment should be considered. Therefore for each agent:

1. Decide on the behaviours that need to be exhibited by each agent - each type of behaviour becomes an agent use case.
2. Decide on the types of actor-agent and multi-agent interactions there will be in the system. Each interaction becomes an agent use case.
3. Refine the use case model by adding lower level functionality for actors and lower level behaviours for agents, making use of the <<uses>> and <<extends>> associations to show the relationships between use cases.

3.3   Document Each Use Case

Once an overall picture emerges of the functionality provided to actors and the general behaviours of agents, it is time to document the use cases. Use case documentation for actors in object oriented systems is described elsewhere [13]. For agent oriented specification of use cases, the following structure has proved to adequately capture the required behaviours for the projects on which use case analysis has been used.

1. Use Case Name - The name of the use case.
2. Descriptive Text - One or two paragraph description of what the use case involves, describing the agent behaviour in the context of the agent's environment (ie interaction with other objects), and interaction with other agents and actors.
3. Agents - A list of agents involved in this use case.
4. Actors - A list of actors involved in this use case.
5. Use Case Associations - A list of other use cases associated with this use case. This includes use cases which this use case <<uses>> and <<extends>>.
6. Environment - A description of the environment and the objects in the environment that the agent interacts with in this use case. A UML class diagram is often useful in this section to show how the agent fits into the environment.
7. Pre-Conditions - A list of all conditions that must hold to be true before the agent can initiate this use case.
8. Post-Conditions - A list of all conditions that must hold to be true after the agent has completed a behaviour defined by this use case.
9. Flow of Events - A numbered list of activities or events which the agent initiates which defines the behaviour of the agent in this use case. This section should also include a UML activity diagram which depicts the flow of events. The use of swim lanes shows interactions in the flow events with other agents. The use of UML sequence and collaboration diagrams can also be used to visualise the interaction of the agent with the entities or objects in the environment in a fashion similar to that suggested by Odell et al. [9].
10. Alternative Flows - A numbered list of activities or events which the agents performs in anomalous, or exceptional circumstances. An alternative flow describes agent behaviour in this use case not handled by the main flow of events. It is possible to have more that one alternative flow in a use case. This section should also include relevant activity, sequence and collaboration diagrams.

4   Case Study

This section describes a case study of the application of the proposed methodology. The system under consideration is a military simulation of air combat.

4.1   Domain Description

The BattleModel is one of the large simulation environments in use by DSTO. It provides an object oriented framework for simulation and is equipped with models of the required physical systems. Intelligent agents are used to provide the models of the human operators. Analysing, designing, testing and implementing the agents for a particular study is a common and ongoing task. There is the capacity to reuse existing agents, if not in their entirety then at least in part, but it is common to require new agent functionality. In either case, it is necessary to specify requirements so that decisions about reuse or development can be made.

Air Combat. The complexity of the air combat domain necessitates a certain amount of background information to clarify the roles and capabilities of the parties involved. The following definitions may assist in understanding the case study. DCA: Defensive Counter Air; an aircraft with the responsibility for defence of an area or an asset. This is achieved by flying a Combat Air Patrol (CAP). Fighter aircraft operate in pairs, as a leader and a wingman. Typically the leader is the more experienced pilot and is generally responsible for the tactical control of the mission. Strike: A role that involves attacking a surface target. Strike aircraft are less capable of defending themselves than fighter aircraft sometimes necessitating that they be accompanied by a fighter escort. Escort:A fighter aircraft that flies close to the strike aircraft in order to protect it from hostile threats. AEWC: Airborne Early Warning and Control; an aircraft equipped with highly capable radars and other sensors. These aircraft have a surveillance role and, because of their significant ability to detect and track targets, also provide advice to fighter aircraft concerning tactics to adopt. A crew of more than six is normal. They will fill a variety of roles: pilot, mission commander, fighter controller, and sensor manager.

Operational Scenario. The case study presented in this paper will focus on the specification of behaviours of the agents for the studying of tactics for defending a ground target against an air attack. The details of the study have been fabricated to avoid security related concerns but the methodological approach presented is that used in the construction of current agent systems. The scenario is presented below in Figure 2. This type of layout is an abbreviated form of the scenarios provided by air-force personnel to AOD for operations research purposes. In addition, analysts have access to standard operating procedures, tactical manuals, their own domain knowledge and experience, and clarifying interviews with pilots and controllers.

STUDY PURPOSE: Examine the impact of the presence of a fighter control capability in opposing a strike mission.

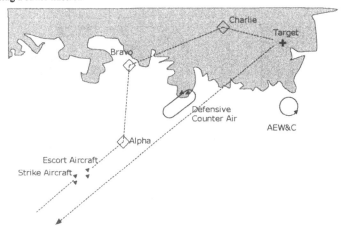

Red Side:
The pair of escort aircraft will accompany the pair of strike aircraft. At waypoint alpha the aircraft will descend to 500 feet and increase speed to 560 knots. At waypoint Charlie the strikers will split from the escort, reduce altitude to 250 feet and commence a bombing run into the target. If the escorts encounter opposition fighters they will intercept and kill or divert them. The escorts should attempt, where possible to remain in contact with the strikers to provide as much protection as possible.

Blue Side
An AEWC aircraft is airborne to provide surveillance coverage. In the event of an attack, the AEWC will vector fighters from their airborne combat air patrol (CAP) toward the attackers providing tactical control. A pair of fighters in a defensive counter air role is on a CAP covering the expected route of the attackers. Upon a radar detection or a command from the AEWC these fighters will attempt to intercept the attackers. The fighter controller on-board the AEWC aircraft will provide varying levels of control ranging from: no advice; to advice about the position of any hostile aircraft; to advice about the tactics to adopt.

Fig. 2. Schematic of Operational Scenario

4.2   Identifying Actors

A simple assumption in identifying the agents in this system is that an agent will be substituted for every human in the real scenario. This leads to the identification of the actors and agents (see Figure 3). This assumption can be revisited as the analysis proceeds.

The roles, responsibilities, and a brief description of the command control and communication relationships are included for each of these actors. Five of these brief descriptions are shown below in Table 1.

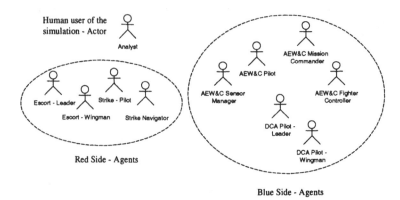

Fig. 3. Actors and Agents - First Iteration

Table 1. Actors and Agents - Description

Agent/Actor	Description
Analyst	Actor: The person who will use the finished system for operations research studies. Specifies the starting conditions, the data to be recorded, and other parameters associated with the conduct of the study.
Fighter Controller	Agent: The crew member(s) on board the AEWC aircraft responsible for scrambling, vectoring, and controlling fighter aircraft. DCA
Leader	Agent: The fighter pilot responsible for patrolling a region. Conducts mission in conjunction with the wingman. Commands the pair of aircaft and makes all high level decisions. Under certain circumstances will be controlled by advice from the AEWC.
Strike Pilot	Agent: The strike aircraft crew member (this particular aircraft has a crew of two) responsible for flying the aircraft and ensuring the safe conduct of the mission.
Strike Navigator	Agent: The strike aircraft crew member responsible for navigation, monitoring many of the on-board systems, and for weapons. The navigator and pilot have a close working relationship coordinating and communicating activities.

4.3   Identifying Use Cases

Primary Scenarios. The first step in identifying the use cases to be included in the use case diagrams is the preparation of primary scenarios. Primary scenarios can now be assembled from an inspection of the operational scenario. A primary scenario is prepared for each actor. Some examples of these scenarios are provided below.

Primary Scenarios High Level Scenarios for Selected Agents

Fighter controller :
1. Monitors radar for detection of tracks
2. Identifies tracks
3. Vectors fighters toward enemy aircraft
4. Provides advice about the position and action of the enemy aircraft
5. Vectors the fighters home after enemy aircraft have been successfully intercepted DCA

Leader :
1. Flies a combat air patrol (CAP) searching for enemy aircraft
2. Upon detecting an enemy aircraft (or upon advice from the AEWC) will vector toward the enemy aircraft
3. Conducts an intercept of the aircraft
4. Returns to base

A review of the actors was made and a decision to aggregate the Strike Pilot and Strike Navigator into a single agent (Striker) was taken. This change creates an agent that subsumes the functionality of the pilot and the navigator. This decision was taken because of the close linking between the two agents and because of the relative inactivity of the navigator. For functional specification it is reasonable to treat them as a single agent. The initial assumption of one actor/agent for each human has been revisited and modified. Further modifications to the numbers and types of agents will be made during the design of the system. Decisions taken at analysis time are to provide for a useful set of agents for specifying the required functionality. The implemented system need not implement this. From these primary scenarios an initial iteration of the use case diagrams is conducted. Use case diagrams are developed in a rather adhoc fashion. Actors are placed on the diagrams and functionality associated with them is added. Where agents cooperate, communicate, or in some way interact to provide a particular functionality two or more agents share a single diagram. The use case diagram shown in Figure 4 is for the fighter controller and the DCA leader that results from an analysis of the primary scenarios. This is may not be the only diagram that features these agents but it a useful one for indicating a certain set of functionality. As many diagrams as are necessary to specify the high level behaviours in a useful way should be developed. This initial use case diagram is only the first iteration and will be extended and detailed greatly when the secondary scenarios are considered.

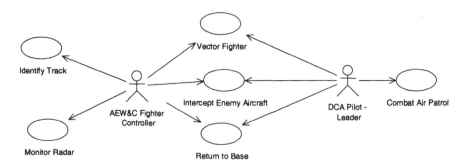

Fig. 4. Fighter Controller and DCA Pilot Use Case Diagram

Secondary Scenarios. Secondary scenarios allow for the consideration of possible eventualities that exist outside of the "everything goes right" scenario. If everything goes "as planned" in an air combat scenario there may be very little cooperation or interaction between agents. The mission unfolds with pre-briefed tactics being followed to achieve the mission goal. When unexpected events necessitate dynamic replanning and coordinated action the scenarios will tend to involve more agents. The secondary scenarios typically capture more of these multi-agent interactions. The scenario below illustrates this with an example that necessitates close cooperation between the fighter controller and the lead fighter pilot.

During the intercept of the enemy aircraft by the DCA the enemy escorts obtain the advantage and acquire a radar lock upon the DCA and launch missiles. This eventuality requires a radar-lock/missile evasion manoeuvre that can be assisted by the fighter controller.

1. DCA leader reports that s/he is locked by radar "DCA LEADER SPIKED"
2. Fighter controller advises a heading to fly to break the radar lock "Break left, heading 230".
3. The DCA leader commences a high g turn to the left to come around to heading 230.
4. The DCA leader loses contact with the wingman and the enemy aircraft.
5. The DCA leader successfully defeats the missile.
6. The fighter controller advises about the position of the wingman, the position of the enemy fighters and the vector to fly to rejoin the combat.

4.4   Documenting Use Cases

Once the use case diagrams have been completed with the input from the secondary scenarios the individual use cases can be documented. Section 3.3 described the range of techniques available for documenting use cases. The documentation for one of the use cases, defeat radar, is shown in table.

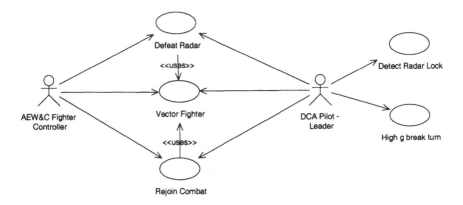

Fig. 5. Use Case Diagram From Secondary Scenario

Use Case Name : Defeat Radar

Description : When an aircraft launches a radar guided missile the launch aircraft's radar must lock to the target. The pilot of the target aircraft - in conjunction with advice from a fighter controller - can perform a series of manoeuvres designed to defeat the radar and the missile.

Agents : Pilot, Fighter Controller

Actors : None

Use Case Associations : uses "Vector Fighter"

Environment : Fighter aircraft, radios, missile, radar, radar-warning-receiver, AEWC

Pre-condition : An enemy has a radar lock on an aircraft

Flow of events :
1. The aircraft pilot informs the AEWC fighter controller that a radar is locked on.
2. The fighter pilot commences a high g turn. During this turn the fighter will lose contact with the enemy aircraft and will have no radar track information about the enemy aircraft action.
3. The fighter controller calculates a heading for the fighter to fly and provides updates to the fighter pilot about the location of the enemy aircraft.
4. The fighter pilot makes heading adjustments based on advice from the fighter controller
5. The radar lock is lost

Alternative Flow 1 :
1. If a missile is known to have been launched and the missile has had time to get close to its target missile evasion manoeuvre is commenced.

Post condition : The enemy radar has lost lock and the missile is defeated.

Additional information can be provided in the form of an activity diagram (see Figure 6). In the activity diagram below agent interactions are represented across the swim-lane in a manner similar to that proposed by Odell et al. [8].

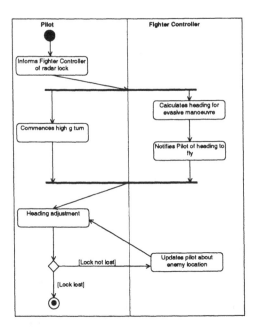

Fig. 6. Activity Diagram with "Swim Lanes" for Defeat Radar Use Case

5   Discussion and Future Work

5.1   Note about the BDI Agent Model

The beliefs-desires-intentions (BDI) rational agent [11] is the model of choice for
all of our agent systems development. This model is computationally implemented by languages such as dMARS [16] and JACK [17]. A detailed account of the
syntax of these languages is beyond the scope of this paper but both have language constructs that closely map to standard documentation fields of a use case.
By adding UML stereotypes such as <<plan>>, <<database>>, <<belief>>,
<<goal>>, <<event>>, <<capability>>, and others, it is possible to document
the design of a BDI agent within the UML. The <<capability>> stereotype is
used to document JACK capabilities. JACK capabilities are a collection of plans,
events, and databases, that provide the agent with some high level functionality.
The notion of capabilities in JACK aligns quite closely with the conceptual basis
of use cases. Thus high level use cases can map directly to JACK capabilities.
Details of the utility of these language properties in relation to UML and use
case analysis will be addressed in a future paper.

5.2   Human-in-the-loop Variant

Research into the interaction of humans and agents as team-members required
the construction a human-in-the-loop variant of the described system. This version required an interface to allow a human operator to play the part of a fighter

controller. Conceptually the new system was simply the changing of the fighter controller from an agent to an actor. The underlying use case analysis and documentation remained unchanged and was used to specify the requirements for the GUI for the human fighter controller.

5.3 More Complex Systems

The examples provided in this paper present a methodology that was successfully applied to the development of a system. The team structures in this system were relatively simple—no team had more than two members. This allowed for reasoning about role allocation, dynamic team restructuring, and complex coordination to be ignored. The behaviour required from the agents was more reactive than proactive. Although the agents are largely goal-directed there was no requirement to juggle many competing goals. More complex scenarios may have required a fundamental shift in the software engineering methodolgies applied. Possibilities include the work of Kinny [5] and Jennings and Wooldridge [19,20].

5.4 Conclusions

The utilisation of a use-case analysis for the specification of functional requirements for a multi-agent system, has been discussed. Future papers will document further extensions to the UML for the design and implementation of a BDI multi-agent system. The case-study presented here is not a complex one by AOD's standards. There are fairly few agents and the scenarios require minimal cooperation. Furthermore, the agents themselves do not exhibit the complexity of reasoning of other AOD systems. Not all agent development within AOD makes use of a use case analysis documented with UML. Several techniques have been tried and tested. The use case and UML approach presented here has been successful on small projects. At present a capacity exists to use the UML to capture and document the requirements of a multi-agent system. Work is progressing toward the addition of stereotypes that allow for the architectural and detail design of an agent system. Two larger multi-agent systems are presently being implemented using these techniques and will test the concepts presented in this paper still further.

Acknowledgments. The authors would like to thank Martin Cross, Graeme Murray, Dr. Gary Kemister, Ian Lloyd, and Dr. Sam Waugh from DSTO for their advice and feedback. The comments from attendees at a workshop on the engineering of agent systems held in Melbourne, Australia in 1999 was particularly valuable with specific thanks to Dr. Tim Menzies, Dr Adrian Pearce, Dr Ralph Ronnquist, Mario Selvestrel, Professor Liz Soneneberg, Professor Leon Sterling, Dr Gil Tidhar, and Dr Peter Wallis for their insights into the relative strengths and weaknesses of this work and for their encouragement to continue.

References

1. McIlroy, D., B. Smith, M. Turner, and C. Heinze. Air Defence Operational Analysis Using the SWARMM Model. In Proceedings of the Asia Pacific Operations Research Symposium, 1997.
2. Heinze, C., B. Smith, and M. Cross. Thinking Quickly: Agents for Modeling Air Warfare. In Proceedings of the Australian Joint Conference on Artificial Intelligence AI '98. Brisbane, Australia, 1998.
3. Tidhar, G., C. Heinze, and M. Selvestrel. Flying Together: Modelling Air Mission Teams. Applied Intelligence, 8(3): p. 195-218, 1998.
4. Tidhar, G., C. Heinze, S. Goss, G. Murray, D. Appla, and I. Lloyd. Using Intelligent Agents in Military Simulation or Using Agents Intelligently. In Eleventh Innovative Applications of Artificial Intelligence Conference, IAAI99. Deployed Application Case Study Paper, Orlando, Florida, 1999.
5. Kinny, D., and M. Georgeff. Modelling and Design of Multi-Agent Systems. In J. P. Mueller, M. Wooldridge and N. Jennings, editors, Intelligent Agents III (LNAI Volume 1193), 1-20, Springer Verlag 1997.
6. Fowler, M., UML Distilled - Applying the Standard Object Modeling Language. Object Technology Series, ed. J. Booch, Rumbaugh: Addison Wesley, 1998.
7. Odell, J. Engineering Artifacts for Multi-Agent Systems. Technical Report, ERIM CEC, 1999.
8. Odell, J. Representing Agent Interaction Protocols in UML. In Proceedings of the AAAI Agents Conference, 2000.
9. Burmeister, B. Models and Methodology for Agent-Oriented Analysis and Design. In proceedings of the Workshop on Agent-oriented Programming and Distributed Systems at the Twentieth German Annual Conference on Artificial Intelligence (KI'96), Dresden, Germany, 1996.
10. Bauer, B. Extending UML for the Specification of Interaction Protocols. Submitted to the 6th call for Proposal of FIPA, 1999.
11. Rao, A.S. and M.P. Georgeff. Modeling rational agents within a bdi-architecture. Australian Artificial Intelligence Institute: Melbourne, Australia, 1991.
12. Woodcock, J. and J. Davies. Using Z. Prentice Hall, 1996.
13. Schneider, G. and J. Winters, Applying Use Cases - A Practical Guide. Object Technology Series, ed. J. Booch, Rumbaugh. Addison Wesley, 1998.
14. Rosenberg, D. and K. Scott, Use Case Driven Object Modeling with UML. Object Technology Series, ed. J. Booch, Rumbaugh. Addison Wesley, 1999.
15. Wooldridge, M. and N. Jennings, Agent Theories, Architectures, and Languages: a Survey, in Intelligent Agents, W.a. Jennings, Editor. Springer Verlag, pp1-22, 1995.
16. d'Inverno, M., et al. A formal specification of dMARS. in Fourth International Workshop on Agent Theories, Architectures and Languages (ATAL '98), Springer Verlag, 1998.
17. Busetta, P., et al. JACK Intelligent Agents - Components for Intelligent Agents in JAVA, in Agent Link Newsletter. 1999.
18. Rasmussen, J., A. M. Pejtersen, and L. P. Goodstein. Cognitive Systems Engineering. Wiley Series in Systems Engineering. Andrew P. Sage, Series Editor. John Wiley and Sons, 1994.
19. Jennings, N. On agent-based software engineering. Journal of Artificial Intelligence Volume 117 (2000) pp277-296, 2000.
20. Jennings, N. and M. Wooldridge. Agent oriented software engineering. In J. Bradshaw (Ed.), Handbook of Agent Technology, AAI/MIT Press, 2000, (to appear).

Market-Based Network Resource Allocation with Non-tâtonnement Process

Kosuke Nakatsuka, Hirofumi Yamaki, and Toru Ishida

Department of Social Informatics, Kyoto University,
Kyoto 606-8501, Japan
{nakatuka,yamaki,ishida}@kuis.kyoto-u.ac.jp

Abstract. There are two types of market mechanism that can be used to allocate network resources efficiently based on users' preference. One, mainly considered in previous works, is the Tâtonnement process; the allocation is not changed until the price reaches equilibrium. When the user preference changes dynamically, the resource allocation derived by the Tâtonnement process may not reflect the curent preference.
The other is the Non-Tâtonnement process, where the allocation is changed dynamically even while the allocation is being calculated. Consequently, it suits resource allocation in dynamic environments. However, the property of this process in terms of the time needed to complete all calculations has not been studied sufficiently.
As a first step,this paper compares the quality of the results derived by the Non-Tâtonnement process to that by the Tâtonnement process for dynamic network resource allocation. We find that the Non-Tâtonnement process works better in rapidly changing environments and that the Tâtonnement process offers superior results when there is enough time for the market to converge to equilibrium.

1 Introduction

Today, many application programs involve communication over networks, which is usually performed in a best-effort fashion. In some cases, where the value of the communication links varies, this approach leads to an inefficient usage of network resources, which are of course limited, and thus some kinds of resource control is required. To provide such environments, many network architectures provide QoS control mechanisms. Such mechanisms require the network administrators to establish a network allocation policy, which is often extremely complex in large networks and heterogeneous users. To deal with this issue, we applied a market-based approach [7], where the pricing mechanism of a market is utilized to allocate network resources efficiently based on users' preferences.

Previous market-based approaches [2,6,7] mainly apply the process called Tâtonnement, the properties of which are summarized as follows:

- Agents do not barter resource until the price reaches equilibrium.
- After the completion of market calculation, all the transferred resource is consumed (No storage), and thus resale does not occur.

C. Zhang and V.-W. Soo (Eds.): PRIMA 2000, LNAI 1881, pp. 143–155, 2000.

The calculation process of Tâtonnement is given as follows.

1. Calculation begins.
2. Consumer agents get price vectors from an auctioneer. They calculate demand and bid them.
3. The auctioneer renews price to resolve the difference between demand and supply.
4. The market repeats 2. and 3. until the price reaches equilibrium.

It is known that the allocation is feasible and Pareto optimal when the price reaches equilibrium.

In the above process, we assume that the environment, i.e. users' preference and the network, remains constant. However, this process requires time and the environment changes dynamically. If the environment changes, the allocation given by the process is Pareto optimal only for the old environment and does not match the new environment.

To solve this problem, the approach where by the calculation closes before the allocation is made obsolete by environmental change has been proposed [8]. It can resist environment change with some loss. However, to assure feasibility, it needs centralized calculation.

In this paper, we adopt the approach called Non-Tâtonnement process. It has the following characteristics [3].

- The allocation can be changed during calculation. This allocation is feasible in each of the iteration.
- Consumer agents change the allocation by the *transaction rule* based on barter manner. The transaction rule prevents speculation and the quality of allocation is improving during calculation.
- Pareto optimality can be assured if the transaction rule is set appropriately.

From the above, the Non-Tâtonnement process is superior to Tâtonnement process in that:

- Each agent can change its allocation in accordance with the dynamic environment.
- Some transaction rules enable distributed resource allocation.

One of the methods based on the Non-Tâtonnement process is the *resource-directed approach* [2,9]. In it, each agent computes the parameter of marginal utility and reallocates resources accordingly.

However, the mechanism of the resource-directed approach is complex, and the characteristics of the process have not been studied enough.

The contribution of this paper is its introduction of resource allocation based on the Non-Tâtonnement process to dynamic network resource allocation with multiagent systems. In this paper, we clarify the characteristics of network resource allocation based on the Non-Tâtonnement process in the initial stage of allocation, and we conclude that the approach based on the Non-Tâtonnement process adapts to environmental change at the beginning of the calculation while the allocation provided by the approach based on the Tâtonnement process is efficient in a static environment.

2   An Approach Based on Non-tâtonnement Process

2.1   Formalization of Non-tâtonnement Process

The Non-Tâtonnement process was studied by Negishi[3]. It consists of:

- Consumer agents barter endowment without assuming any equilibrium.
- Commodities stores.

In this paper, commodities means resouce. As a consequence of the first property, the resource is always allfocated feasibly in process and agents can improve their utility by exchanging the resource while calculating the price.

We assume that there are m kinds of resource and n agents and resources are not produced. We define $p = (p_1, \cdots, p_m)$ is price of resource vector, x_i is the total demand for resource i, $\bar{x}_\alpha = (\bar{x}_{\alpha 1}, \cdots, \bar{x}_{\alpha j}, \cdots, \bar{x}_{\alpha m})$ is the amount of an agent α and $\bar{X} = \{\bar{x}_{\alpha j}\}$ is the distribution matrix. The rule of trading is barter and $\bar{x}_i$ is constant.

We formalize the Non-Tâtonnement Process as:

$$\frac{dp_i}{dt} = K_i(x_i(p, \bar{X}) - \bar{x}_i), \qquad (i = 1, \cdots, m, \qquad K_i > 0) \tag{1}$$

$$\frac{d\bar{x}_{\alpha i}}{dt} = F_{\alpha i}(p, \bar{X}). \qquad (i = 1, \cdots, m, \qquad \alpha = 1, \cdots, n) \tag{2}$$

(1) shows that the demand for a resource is reflected in the price at any particular time and the allocation of all agents and that price changes depend on excess demand. If demand exceeds supply, the price increases. If supply exceeds demand price decreases.

$F_{\alpha i}$ is called the transaction rule. Agents trade resources amongst each other following the transaction rule when demand and supply are imbalanced. Transaction rule is based, in principle, on equivalent barter. The kind and the amount of resource exchanged depend on $F_{\alpha i}$. Unlike the Tâtonnement Process, allocation $\bar{X}$ changes dynamically through (2). Each agent acts to improve its utility u_α by (1) and (2).

The Tâtonnement Process is defined as a special case of the Non-Tâtonnement Process, where $F_{\alpha i} \equiv 0$. However, the allocation of the Non-Tâtonnement Process at equilibrium differs from that of the Tâtonnement Process even if the initial endowment and utility function are the same. Therefore, if we choose the allocation yielded by Tâtonnement Process as the goal the allocation given by the Non-Tâtonnement Process does not always reach the goal though the allocation given by the Non-Tâtonnement Process is Pareto optimal.

The Tâtonnement Process is stable if resource has the property of gross substitution, i.e., $\frac{\partial x_j(p)}{\partial p_i} > 0 (i \neq j)$. In other words, for any different resources i and j, the demand $x_j(p)$ increases when price p_i goes up. Otherwise, the Non-Tâtonnement Process is also stable under gross substitution[4]. We note that some typical transaction rules such as the *Edgeworth process* researched by Uzawa[5], and the *Hahn process*, researched by Hahn and Negishi[1] are quasi-stable without the assumption of gross substitution.

The *Edgeworth process* and the *Hahn process* do not define F concretely but describe the characteristics of markets and agents, and specify transaction rule F.

2.2   Calculation Based on Non-tâtonnement Process

A calculation based on the Non-Tâtonnement Process is described as follows:

1. Calculation begins.
2. The auctioneer sends price vector and distribution matrix to consumer agents. The distribution matrix is made from transaction rule.
3. Consumer agents change their allocation after observing the distribution matrix.
4. Consumer agents send demand to the auctioneer.
5. The auctioneer renews the price according to the balance between allocation and demand, and calculates a new distribution matrix.
6. The market repeats from 2. to 5. until the allocation reach equilibrium.

We consider a distributed allocation method where agents negotiate with each other instead of the above centralized allocation. In this case, we change 5. to "Each agent calculates their demand by price, and negotiates with other agents. If agents can trade, they barter resources."

2.3   Comparison of Tâtonnement Process and Non-tâtonnement Process

In Figure 1, we show an example of the difference between demand and allocation in a dynamic environment. In Figure 1(a), the curved line shows demand while the rectangles show the supply at that time. Let T denote the time to calculate the equilibrium allocation in each iteration. Because the allocation does not change until the calculation reaches equilibrium in the Tâtonnement Process, the allocation is constant between (a') and (b') in the figure. It needs time T to reach equilibrium and the allocation reflects the old environment (a).

The Non-Tâtonnement Process allows agent to trade resource to settle excess demand at each of the iteration. In Figure 1(b), the change of the demand is drawn with a broken line and the allocation is drawn with a solid line changes. If we define the loss as the same in Tâtonnement Process, it is represented by shadowed region.

Next, we chose the ratio of the indirect utility of agents $\frac{u(\tilde{x})}{u(x)}$, which is the utility for demand to the utility for the allocation at that time, as the criterion of evaluation. There is the one-to-one relation between the utility ratio and the loss of allocation. If this ratio is small, the loss is large and the allocation is not preferable. On the other hand, if this ratio is large, the loss is small and the allocation can be said to be suitable to the demand. When the allocation agrees with the demand the ratio reaches 1.

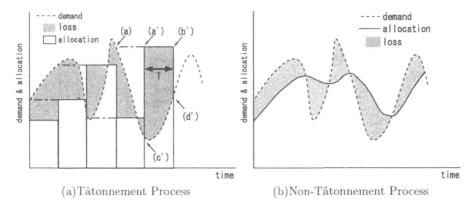

(a)Tâtonnement Process   (b)Non-Tâtonnement Process

Fig. 1. The loss generated by the difference between the allocation and the environment

In the static environment where the utility functions of agents does not change, the ratio of utility changes as they are illustrated in Figure 2. In this figure, the broken line shows ideal behavior of utility ratio. In region (a)(b)(c) in Figure 2, Tâtonnement Process cannot improve the quality of allocation because the calculation does not finish. On the other hand, Non-Tâtonnement Process renews allocation. Therefore, Non-Tâtonnement Process is preferable. In region (c)(d)(e) in Figure 2, Tâtonnement Process reaches equilibrium and the allocation by Tâtonnement Process is better than that by Non-Tâtonnement Process. When T is small (a)(b)(c) becomes small and (c)(d)(e) becomes large. In this case, Tâtonnement Process is preferable. On the other hand, when T is large (a)(b)(c) becomes large and (c)(d)(e) becomes small. In this case, Non-Tâtonnement Process is preferable.

In the static environment, we can say:

- If the T is smaller than the time to calculate the allocation by Non-Tâtonnement Process Tâtonnement Process is preferable.
- If the T is larger than the time to calculate the allocation by Non-Tâtonnement Process Non-Tâtonnement Process is preferable.

In dynamic environment, the ratio of utility changes is illustrated in Figure 3 by an example. In Figure 3(a), because the environment changes just after the Tâtonnement Process reaches equilibrium the region equivalent for (b) in Figure 2 is cut off and the allocation by Tâtonnement Process is not so good. On the other hand, in Figure 3(b), the allocation by Non-Tâtonnement Process can adapts to the environment.

If the environment changes faster, the allocation by Tâtonnement Process cannot adapts to the environment because it becomes obsolete by the change. On the other hand, the allocation by Non-Tâtonnement Process can adapts to the environment.

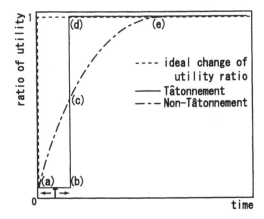

Fig. 2. The ratio of the indirect utility in static environment

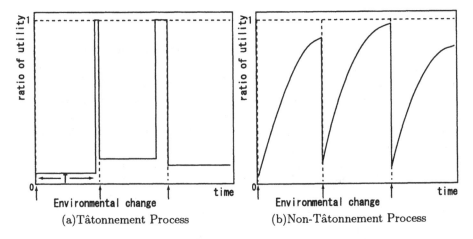

Fig. 3. The ratio of the indirect utility in dynamic environment

3   Experiments

We examine the allocation based on Tâtonnement and Non-Tâtonnement Process in the static and dynamic environment. We show one example of transaction rule of Non-Tâtonnement Process and compare it to Tâtonnement Process. In the experiment, we see

- In a dynamic environment, the allocation based no Non-Tâtonnement Process is more suitable to agents' preference than that based on Tâtonnement Process.
- And in a static environment, the quality of the allocation depends on the time to calculate. Particularly, in this experiment, the allocation based no

Tâtonnement Process is more suitable to agents' preference, because the implementation of Non-Tâtonnement Process needs more time to calculate than Tâtonnement Process.

3.1   Configuration

We use CES utility function as agents' utility, which has necessary characteristics. The utility function of the agent α is (3),

$$u_\alpha(x_{\alpha 1}, x_{\alpha 2}, \cdots, x_{\alpha m}) = \left(\sum_{i=1}^{m} a_{\alpha i} x_{\alpha i}^{\frac{\rho}{\rho-1}} \right)^{\frac{\rho-1}{\rho}}. \tag{3}$$

On (3), $a_{\alpha i}$ is the value of resource i. ρ is the marginal rate of substitution of resource. In this experiment, we set ρ as $1/2$ and $a_{\alpha i}$ as random numbers. $a_{\alpha i}$ is decided when agents are generated and it keeps until the environment changes. The environment alteration is defined as changing $a_{\alpha i}$.

To undergo the Non-Tâtonnement Process, we need to specify *transaction rules*. We implemented the one-to-one exchange rule, where two randomly-selected agents barter two kinds of resources if these agents can decrease excess demand by doing so. To compare the Non-Tâtonnement Process to the Tâtonnement Process, we implemented the Tâtonnement Process as follows:

- Calculate excess demand.
- If the excess demand of all kinds of resources is not 0, price equilibrium is not achieved and thus calculation is continued without changing the allocation.
- If the excess demand is 0, price equilibrium is achieved. At that time an auctioneer allocates resource and restarts calculation.
- Until price reaches equilibrium the allocation is the same as the one formerly calculated.

The parameters in this experiment are the number of agents, the number of kinds of resources, *transaction rules* and the time needed to calculate price and allocation. *Transaction rules* are above-mentioned "one-to-one exchange" and "Tâtonnement Process." The number of agents and kinds of resource can be set arbitrarily. The time needed is set in advance.

The parameter "time needed to calculate price" is set to m, because the time complexity of calculation of price is proportional to the number of kinds of resource. "Time needed to calculate allocation" is set to 0 in the Tâtonnement process because agents' don't trade and the time needed to calculate the allocation is set to $m^2 n^2$ in one-to-one exchange rule, because with m kinds of resource and n agents the calculation needs $O(m^2 n^2)$ time.

We chose the ratio of the indirect utility of agents, $\frac{u(\bar{x})}{u(x)}$,as the evaluation criterion.

We conducted two experiments as follows:

1. In order to investigate the effect of the number of agents and the number of kinds of resources on the time needed to achieve convergence, we assumed that there were 3 agents and 10 resources. These numbers are chosen as typical parameters of both few agents/resources and many agents/resources. With these parameter settings we assumed that the environment does not change. We conducted experiments five times in each parameter setting and evaluated how well the returned allocations reflect agents' preference.

2. To estimate the performance of each approach, we measured the ratio of utility in the several interval of environmental change. In this experiment, we assume the number of agents and resources are 3.

3.2   Results

The results of the first experiment are shown in Figure 4.

In Figure 4, the horizontal axis is the time needed in calculation, which is described in 3.1. The vertical axis is the utility ratio.

In the Tâtonnement Process the ratio of utility rose abruptly and intermittently (Figure 4). It is because:

- In Tâtonnement Process the ratio of utility becomes 1 at allocation of resource.
- The shown ratio of utility is the average of results in many experiments.

In Figure 4, utility improved remarkably at early stage of calculation, in the one-to-one exchange based on Non-Tâtonnement Process. When there are only few kinds of resource, the ratio of utility (i.e. adaptability) is 95%. When there are many kinds of resource, the utility also improved remarkably at early stage of calculation, but the elapsed time is relatively long.

In the early stage of experiment using Non-Tâtonnement Process, the calculation did not converge and initial endowment was used as allocation. The utility did not improve considerably because the allocation was not changed. Little increase of the utility happened because the demand is computed by the price at that time. On the other hand, when equilibrium allocation was obtained, the allocation agreed with the demand and the ratio of utility became 1. The time to calculate allocation was 100 in few agents and few kinds of resource case.

Next, we show the result of the second experiment. Considering 4, we assumed the time to converge is 100 and we set the interval to change environment 50, 100, 150 and 200.

We assumed there are 3 agents and 3 kinds of resource in market since in Tâtonnement Process the number of agents and the number of kinds of resource do not affect the time to calculate so much, and in Non-Tâtonnement Process increase of agents and the kinds of resource causes increase of the time to calculate.

As an environmental change, we adopted change of agent utility. We changed only the utility of one agent and the results shown below are the results of the chosen agent.

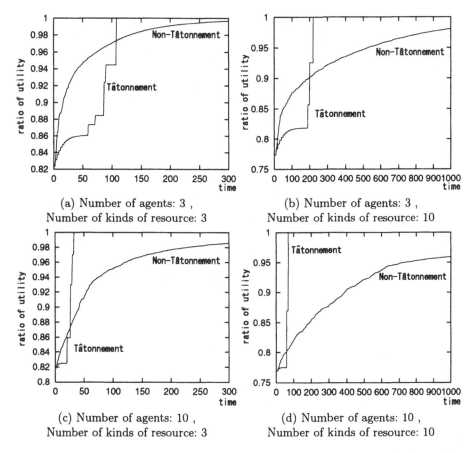

Fig. 4. The result of experiment depending on the number of agents and the number of kinds of resource.

The result of this experiment is shown in Figure 5 and the result when environment does not change is the same as Figure 4(a).

The difference between the case that the interval of environmental change is 50 time units and other cases is found in Figure 5. When the interval of environmental change is 50 time units, the allocation in Tâtonnement Process is not suitable to agents' preference because it needs about 100 time units to reach equilibrium. For this reason, the utility ratio is low in Tâtonnement Process. On the other hand, in one-to-one exchange based on Non-Tâtonnement Process the utility ratio falls at the change of environment, but it increases monotonously until next environmental change.

In the cases where the interval of environmental change is 150 or 200 time units, the utility ratio became 1 in Tâtonnement Process because it reaches equilibrium before environmental change and the allocation is suitable to agents' preference.

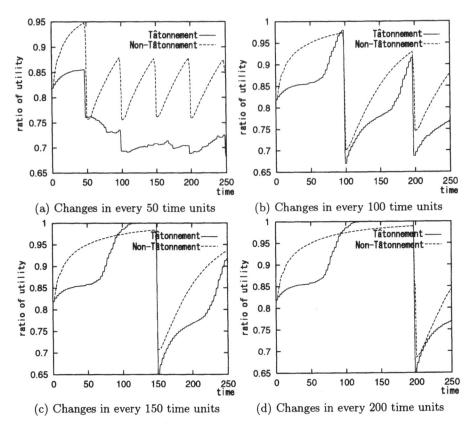

(a) Changes in every 50 time units   (b) Changes in every 100 time units

(c) Changes in every 150 time units   (d) Changes in every 200 time units

Fig. 5. Relation between environment change and the time of calculation.

3.3 Discussion

Let us compare Tâtonnement Process with Non-Tâtonnement Process using
Figure 4. It can be said that:

- In early stage of computation (before about 100 time units[1],) Tâtonnement
  Process does not reach equilibrium and it cannot improve utility. On the
  other hand, one-to-one exchange based on Non-Tâtonnement Process improves utility remarkably at the beginning. Therefore, one-to-one exchange
  is superior to Tâtonnement Process in early stage.
- In late stage of computation (after about 100 time units) Non-Tâtonnement
  Process does not improve utility up to much. On the other hand Tâtonnement Process reaches equilibrium and the allocation agrees with demand.
  Therefore, Tâtonnement Process is superior to one-to-one exchange in late
  stage.

---

[1] One computation can be exactly done in one time unit in the experiments.

On the whole of the process, it can be said that:

- In the case where the environment changes faster than Tâtonnement Process reaches equilibrium as illustrated in Figure 5(a), the allocation given by Tâtonnement Process is not suitable to agents' preference. On the other hand, the allocation given by one-to-one exchange based on Tâtonnement Process follows the change of agents' preference in this case. Therefore, one-to-one exchange is superior to Tâtonnement Process in fast fluctuation.
- In the case where the environment changes slower than Tâtonnement Process reaches equilibrium as illustrated in Figure 5(c)(d), the allocation given by Tâtonnement Process agrees with the demand. On the other hand, the allocation given by one-to-one exchange based on Tâtonnement Process does not always agree in this case. Therefore is Tâtonnement Process superior to one-to-one exchange in slow fluctuation.
- In slow fluctuation and in the static environment, the trade-off depends on the time to calculate. If we use the transaction rule which reach the equilibrium faster than one-to-one exchange, Non-Tâtonnement Process will be superior to Tâtonnement Process.

In the above discussion, we use the utility ratio to evaluate the adaptability to users' preference. Next, we examine the loss of allocation. To make clear the loss, we present Figure 6 of the average of loss in 0-400 times of calculation.

From Figure 6, when the environment changes fast, the loss of one-to-one exchange based on Non-Tâtonnement Process is smaller than that of Tâtonnement Process. The superiority of one-to-one exchange decrease as the interval of environmental change increases, and when the interval is 175, the loss of Tâtonnement Process becomes smaller than that of Non-Tâtonnement Process. Therefore, we can say:

- The loss of both Tâtonnement Process and Non-Tâtonnement Process decreases when the interval of environmental change becomes longer.
- When the interval of environmental is small the loss of Non-Tâtonnement Process is small. In this case, Non-Tâtonnement Process is preferable.
- On the other hand, when the interval of environmental is large the loss of Tâtonnement Process is small and Tâtonnement Process is preferable, because the time to reach the equilibrium by one-to-one exchange is larger than that by Tâtonnement Process.

In this paper, we implemented one-to-one exchange as transaction rule on Non-Tâtonnement Process. Using this rule, the time needed to calculate increases in proportion to square of number of agents and square of number of the kinds of resource. If more effective rule than one-to-one exchange is used as transaction rule, the allocation based on agents' preference can be given rapidly in large network where a lot of agents and resource exist.

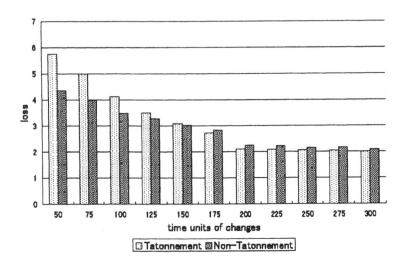

Fig. 6. Average loss.

4   Conclusion

In this paper, we compare Non-Tâtonnement Process to Tâtonnement Process
in static and dynamic environment, and we introduced one-to-one exchange based on Non-Tâtonnement Process to market-based network resource allocation
and clarified that the allocation based on Non-Tâtonnement Process adapts to
dynamic environment effectively in initial stage of process

In market-based network resource allocation, usually the approach based on
Tâtonnement Process is used and the characteristic of Non-Tâtonnement Process
has not been investigated enough.

In this paper, first we clarified that the approach based on Tâtonnement
Process does not adapt to change of agents' preference in dynamic environment.
Second, we introduced Non-Tâtonnement Process into network resource alloca-
tion by describing the calculating process. And we showed that:

– Non-Tâtonnement Process adapts to dynamic environment just after the
environmental change.
– When the environmental change is faster than the time to calculate the
allocation based on Non-Tâtonnement Process is more suitable than that
based on Tâtonnement Process because the latter changes the allocation at
the beginning of process.

– When the environmental change is slower than the time to calculate the quality of allocation depends on the calculating time. If the time to calculate the allocation by Tâtonnement Process is smaller than that by Non-Tâtonnement Process, Tâtonnement Process is preferable. If the time to caluculate the allocation by Tâtonnement Process is larger than that by Non-Tâtonnement Process, Non-Tâtonnement Process is preferable.

So far, the approach based on Tâtonnement Process is hard to apply to networks that have dynamic environment. On the other hand, Non-Tâtonnement Process illustrated in this paper can allocate resource based on users' preference at the beginning of the environmental change in those networks. The contribution of this paper is introduction of a new method in the market-based network resource allocation.

Subjects left to future are as follows:

– In Non-Tâtonnement Process transaction rules decide the efficiency, but transaction rules has not been formulated so far. In this paper, we show one example of transaction rule. But, it is needed to discover efficient transaction rules and evaluate them.
– The method based on Non-Tâtonnement Process for network resource allocation is shown in this paper, but the application to other problems of distributed resource allocation is not implemented. Application and evaluation of the method is needed.

References

1. Hahn, F. H. and Negishi, T.: A Theorem on Non-Tâtonnement Stability, *Econometrica*, Vol. 30, No. 3, pp. 463–469 (1962).
2. Kurose, J. F. and Simha, R.: A Microeconomic Approach to Optimal Resource Allocation in Distributed Computer Systems, *IEEE Transactions on Computers*, Vol. 38, pp. 705–717 (1989).
3. Negishi, T.: On the Formation of Prices, *International Economic Review*, Vol. 2, No. 1, pp. 122–126 (1961).
4. Negishi, T.: *General equilibrium theory and international trade*, North-Holland, pp. 207–227 (1972).
5. Uzawa, H.: On the Stability of Edgeworth's Barter Process, *International Economic Review*, Vol. 3, No. 2, pp. 218–232 (1962).
6. Wellman, M. P.: A Market-Oriented Programming Environment and Its Application to Distributed Multicommodity Flow Problems, *Journal of Artificial Intelligence Research*, Vol. 1, pp. 1–22 (1993).
7. Yamaki, H., Wellman, M. P. and Ishida, T.: A Market-Based Approach to Allocating QoS for Multimedia Applications, *The Second International Conference on Multi-Agent Systems (ICMAS-96)*, pp. 385–392 (1996).
8. Yamaki, H., Yamauchi, Y. and Ishida, T.: Implementation Issues on Market-Based QoS Control, *The Fourth International Conference on Multi-Agent Systems (ICMAS-98)*, pp. 357–364 (1998).
9. Ygge., F. and Akkermans., H.: On Resource-Oriented Multi-Commodity Market Computations, *Third International Conference on Multi-Agent Systems (ICMAS)*, pp. 365–371 (1998).

Autonomous Cooperative Factory Control

David Vasko[1], Francisco Maturana[1], Angela Bowles[2], and Stephen Vandenberg[2]

1   DAVasko@ra.rockwell.com
FPMaturana@ra.rockwell.com
Architecture and Systems Development
Rockwell Automation
1 Allen Bradley Drive
Cleveland, OH, 44124, USA

2   Bowles.Angela.AME@ bhp.com.au
Vandenberg.Stephen.SJ1@bhp.com.au
BHP Services
Market Development
600 Bourke Street
Melbourne, Victoria, Australia 3000

Abstract. In a highly flexible manufacturing line, the ability of the control system to react to and predict changes will ultimately determine the productivity of that line. This paper describes an Autonomous Cooperative System (ACS) for flexibly control a manufacturing line. The system allows each section of the line to have autonomy for controlling the operations of the underlying physical equipment. Autonomous decisions are carried out while the overall operations are optimized through cooperation among the controlled sections. ACS provides the ability to compensate for product changes, equipment wear and equipment failure. ACS was applied to a steel-rod production line. The operation of the line was observed during conditions of process and product changes. The results show how ACS reduced the impact of change and increased the productivity and flexibility of the line.

1 Introduction

The key to the creation of flexible automation is to use inherent redundancy in the capabilities of the system being controlled. This requires the control system to be continuously self-configurable under varying conditions. This behavior is expensive and difficult to accomplish using conventional control practices.

Programmable controllers were developed as a means of providing an alternative to hardwired relays in industrial applications. The relay ladder logic that was executed provided a flexible mechanism to make changes to the operation of machines in the factory without rewiring relays. Typically, a single programmable controller was used to control a machine or a group of related machines. However, as technology

C. Zhang and V.-W. Soo (Eds.): PRIMA 2000, LNAI 1881, pp. 156-169, 2000.

progressed, the execution speed and I/O capacity of the programmable controllers increased, but not without a cost. As the applications became larger, the cost of development and maintenance of programs over their lifecycle increased [1].

The introduction of computer networks in the factory floor allowed the creation of modular control in automated cells. This permitted the geographic distribution and reduction in the size of control software. However, the modular approach only transformed the problem of dealing with complexity. In this scenario, control engineers confronted a major problem of coordinating the operations of many small controllers. The coordination of these distributed controllers relied on interlocks of data or I/O points in hierarchical structures of master controllers. The proper operation of linked controllers depends on the accuracy of the preplanned interrelated operations. Consequently, the expansion, maintenance and development of such systems are tightly coupled and their associated lifecycle cost remains a concern.

As we look to the future, we see indications that the frequency of change in the factory is increasing and becoming a critical factor to successful operation. This manifestation is accompanied by rigorous quality and delivery performance measures [2][3][4]. To cope with these changes, the underlying control system will need to effectively tackle the numerous changeovers in the mainline configuration, tooling, material distribution, process steps, and quality. The control system will have to configure its nodes into effective virtual control clusters within a short period.

The focus of flexible change research in the factory floor has shifted away from the network and processor technology [5][6]. The solution to flexible change in industrial environments depends on effective information partitioning and coordination protocols for automated units. In this context, flexibility is the capability of the control system to act and in accordance with the system needs while organizing the available resources efficiently.

1.1 Technology to Enable Flexibility

Various research efforts have studied distributed behaviors in biological systems [7]. For example, ant colonies exhibit autonomous cooperative behavior. When ants search for food, they do so autonomously by randomly searching in an unknown and large terrain. When ants find food, they drop pheromones to create a trail to be sensed by other ants. Ants drop more pheromone as they continue to find food.

Natural systems provide important insights into how autonomous and cooperative solutions learned from nature could be adapted to factory operations. In the factory, autonomous machines can organize themselves to enhance system throughput. The needed data encapsulation, required by each autonomous unit, is achieved using object-oriented technology [8].

In the Distributed Artificial Intelligence (DAI) area, we find similar contributions to the study of distributed systems. Important developments in cooperation techniques have simplified the distribution of knowledge among dissimilar and specialized systems [9][10]. These expert systems can be created to drive solutions toward pre-established goals. Models that facilitate interaction and decision-making tasks among distributed components have been proposed [11][12]. These contributions provide tools to create intelligent control systems.

DAI research has proposed a new view of information technology based on Intelligent Agents [13], which will help create flexible and highly granular information systems. Intelligent agents are self-contained software entities capable of communicating and making individual decisions. They work autonomously, handle goals, maintain beliefs, and cooperate to create solutions.

Within agent-based control systems, intelligent agents will support the process of controlling every node in the system [14]. Examples of such applications have been reported in the Agile Infrastructure for Manufacturing Systems (AIMS), which contributed with an open information infrastructure to access agile production services [15]. Also, the integration of humans with computers in large distributed systems has been demonstrated in the Intelligent Agent (IA) framework [16]. Important standardization work for the use of intelligent agent technology in industry has also been carried out by the Holonic Manufacturing Systems (HMS) consortium [17]. This latter research has provided important results to build inexpensive, expandable autonomous systems.

1.2 The Autonomous Cooperative System

ACS is an adaptive agent-based architecture, which addresses five fundamental areas: Autonomy, Cooperation, Communication, Fault tolerance, and Learning.

Autonomy: Each agent makes its own decisions and is responsible for carrying out its decisions toward successful completion.

Cooperation: Agents combine their capabilities into collaboration groups to adapt and respond to events.

Communication: Agents share a common ontology to express their beliefs and intentions. Agents use a job description language to exchange information.

Fault tolerance: Agents prevent the propagation of faults. Agents reprocess committed plans to allocate other available resources.

Learning: Agents use past behaviors to direct responses and reduce computing overheads.

ACS is an emerging technology that provides an efficient solution to flexibility requirements and contributes with a method for bringing together the different pieces of complex distributed control systems. In ACS-based control, several networked controllers merge into virtual organizations to accomplish favorable plans. In this paper, we describe a methodology for using ACS in a steel-rod production line and present results from the factory implementation.

There are important research efforts in the area of intelligent-agent manufacturing systems that resemble the ACS architecture. This researches concentrate upon the integration of the overall manufacturing enterprise. Recent examples of these are in the AARIA (Autonomous Agents for Rock Island Arsenal) [18] and MetaMorph II [19] architectures. The AARIA architecture uses intelligent manufacturing agents for scheduling and simulation of manufacturing activities. In ACS, ACUs are intelligent software to represent equipment in a control environment. The ACUs are tested in PC-based simulations and subsequently connected to the real equipment on the factory floor. The MetaMorph II architecture integrates the enterprise activities into a mediator-centric system. Intelligent agents represent the manufacturing activities. The ACS architecture addresses enterprise integration by incorporating enterprise and control ACUs. These ACUs capture capabilities from both levels and integrate these into cooperative clusters. The Metamorph II architecture also uses an agent clustering approach, in which the clusters are coordinated by dynamic mediators.

2 Architecture of an Autonomous Cooperative System (ACS)

Machines and resources on the plant floor are represented by Autonomous Cooperative Units (ACUs) in a computing environment to cooperate with other units via messages across networks. The ACUs are connected to the machines through a common network to support cooperation environments. Each ACU performs two simultaneous activities: organizational coordination and machine-activity coordination. These activities concentrate the two major information-processing responsibilities needed for the control of the manufacturing environment. Organizational coordination helps interconnect resources logically. The logical relationship among the resources depends on the system conditions and activity requirements. Machine-activity coordination is the internal logical relationship of an ACU.

2.1 Physical Architecture

The manufacturing environment contains two main ACUs: Product and Equipment, as shown in Figure 1. There can be *n*-number of Product and Equipment ACUs. The relationship between Product and Equipment ACUs does not represent a hierarchy. The Product ACU does not need to know how a task is performed by the Equipment ACUs. The Equipment ACU subcontracts capabilities from other ACUs, whenever its capabilities do not suffice to complete a plan. Directory facilitators support the subcontracting process.   The required communication links are established dynamically.

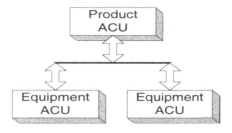

Fig. 1: Autonomous Cooperative Architecture

Each ACU understands the whole or a portion of a task. Generally, the ACUs combine capabilities to plan and execute tasks. This combined responsibility is an important property of ACS, which helps create highly flexible systems.

2.2 Product ACU

Figure 2 shows the architecture of a Product ACU. This ACU acts as a stand-in or agent for the product (i.e., steel rod) to be produced. It understands the goals and requirements of the product and converts the production requirements into process steps for using the available resources.

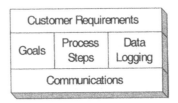

Fig. 2: Product ACU

Product ACUs announce jobs and receives plans for job announced. Plans can succeed or fail. Upon receiving successful plans, Product ACUs assign individual tasks to the executing resources, which in this case are represented by Equipment ACUs.

2.3 Equipment ACU

Equipment ACUs are wrappers around the physical equipment, as shown in Figure 3. Equipment ACUs act on behalf of the physical equipment during the construction of process steps. They understand how to perform one or more processes and how to communicate with peer ACUs. Equipment ACUs learn about their peers through a process of exchanging intermediate constraints. This activity is particularly important in continuous processes such as the rod mills.

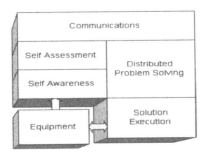

Fig. 3 Equipment ACU Architecture

A distributed problem solving technique is used to find solutions that best meet the system's goals. The technique is comprised of 2 steps. The first step consists of discovering the physical relationships among Equipment ACUs. The second step involves developing feasible plans that satisfy both local and shared constraints. Equipment ACUs are provided with self-awareness and self-assessment capabilities to create beliefs about themselves and the surrounding environment.

During the execution of a task, Equipment ACUs use an induction technique to synchronize the equipment activity. In this way, the unit automatically senses the product (steel rod) entering its section and applies a preplanned operation on it.

2.4 ACU Interaction

The Equipment ACUs interact in virtual control clusters. The clusters are created and dissolved dynamically. Each virtual control cluster corresponds to a contract-net node [16]. Within these clusters, the Equipment ACUs cooperate to obtain near-optimal solutions, while considering both local and system conditions.

The ACS architecture permits to create hierarchical decision-making trees and to link several contract-net nodes. Each node carries out the bidding process concurrently. The contract-net nodes can be distributed among multiple computing platforms.

In Figure 4, the ACUs collaborate by exchanging bids and responses. The sequence of communication is as follows:
1) The Product ACU multicasts the Equipment ACUs with a production request.
2) The Equipment ACUs cooperate to decide on different process steps.
3) The Equipment ACUs respond the Product ACU with a production plan.
4) The Product ACU uses its application knowledge to select the best plans toward goal satisfaction.
5) The Product ACU informs the Equipment ACUs to prepare for execution of a plan. This task assignment provokes a change of settings in the equipment.
6) The Equipment ACUs acknowledge the task assignment.

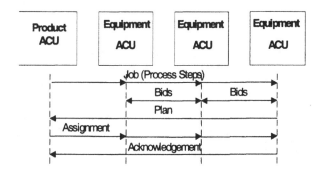

Fig. 4: ACU Interaction Diagram

3 Application of ACS to a Factory

The ACS architecture was tested in a real factory. We examined 17 different industrial test beds, including discrete manufacturing and material handling. The steel-rod mill application was selected because it presented a requirement for increased reliability during change. Also, the availability of process models, historical data logs and production support on site made this application a good environment for improving operation flexibility.

In applying ACS to the rod mill, we were able to create a flexible control system that permitted the production of steel rods at a desired quality and for a varied set of conditions. These results took into account the natural wearing of the machinery due to the thermal and mechanical conditions of the mill. This allowed us to test the results of ACS for changing products, equipment wear, and equipment failure.

3.1 Rod Mill

A modern rod mill typically has 4 functional sections, as shown in Figure 5. The functional sections are: 1) Billet re-heating furnace, 2) Roughing, 3) Intermediate and finishing rolling mills, 4) Water cooling boxes, 5) Air cooling conveyors.

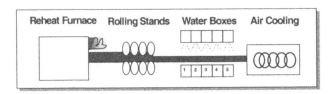

Fig. 5: Rod Mill Diagram

3.2 Steel Rod Production

Each functional section of the rod mill contributes to the quality of the steel rod produced. For instance, the reheat furnace raises the temperature of a steel billet so it can be rolled. The rolling stands gradually reduce the diameter of the billet to transform it into the final rod diameter. The water boxes provide bulk cooling to the rod and the air cooling section cools the rod at a precise rate to create the desired microstructure.

The rod mill typically produces a wide variety of steel rods. Custom rods of diverse diameter and quality for individual customers are common. The ability of the rod mill to change among the different products quickly and effectively is crucial to its economic success.

The rod mill is a dynamic environment with a lot of constraints and hazards that complicate operations. It is affected by multiple unplanned perturbations that reduce the production rate and quality of the products. Such perturbations include nozzle and roller deterioration, equipment unavailability or breakdowns, and changing chemical composition of the raw steel billet.

To cope with the complexity of the scenario above, Product and Equipment ACU were provided with compensation strategies to solve unexpected perturbations.

3.3 Compensation through Cooperation

For most products, each section of a rod mill has excess capacity and is able to indirectly compensate for missing capacity in other sections. The following outlines some typical compensation strategies:

- The reheat furnace is able to change the bulk temperature of the steel billet, which can compensate for a lack of cooling in a downstream section.
- The rolling stands are able to change the rate at which they operate. In slowing the production rate, the cooling power in downstream sections becomes more effective. Intermediate cooling may also be available to allow for extra cooling compensation.
- Water cooling boxes compensate for cooling in other water boxes or some of the cooling effect in the air cooling section.
- The air cooling section can compensate for the cooling in the water boxes.

The key to the development of flexible automation systems is to use this inherent excess capability to produce products under variable conditions.

4 Simulation Results

A simulation environment was built to closely emulate the rod mill. This environment provided an opportunity for extensive testing of ACS-based control under controlled conditions. This allowed us to eliminate or control error factors found in the real factory. Typical error factors are as follows:

- Signal noise
- Sensor error or failure
- Actuator error
- Sensing and actuation delay
- Process-model error and operator response

Over 1200 tests were performed during lab simulation to ensure that ACS was capable of handling the case scenarios observed in the plant floor environment. Figure 6 shows the simulation model. Product ACUs communicate a request to Equipment ACU. This request includes process steps and the expected quality. Equipment ACU (that is, Reheat Furnace, Rolling Mill, Water Box, and Air-Cooling ACUs) cooperate to find the best actuator settings.

Each partial plan reflects goals and satisfies the physical limitations of adjacent Equipment ACU. The process concludes with the scheduling of the partial plans for production. The execution of the plans starts when a billet is pushed out into the system. Thus, Equipment ACUs execute their preplanned task. The simulated factory takes in consideration the production parameters, induced noise, and equipment wear to simulate the equipment during the plan execution. To limit the effectiveness of working ranges, the Equipment ACUs use constraints to modify both intermediate and internal variables.

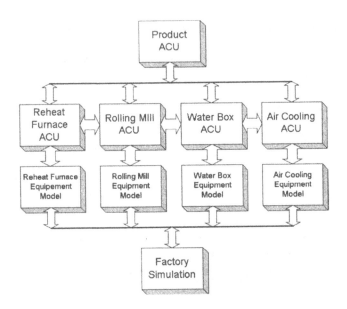

Fig. 6: ACS Simulation Environment

4.1 Simulation Testing

Evaluations were made using 10 different tests, on 3 product types over a wide variety of conditions obtained from the rod mill under study. The tests were designed to assess the ACS's ability to react to different working conditions such as equipment wear and equipment failure.

4.2 Equipment Wear

Equipment ACU assimilate wear through internal or external compensation:
- *Internal Compensation:* As products are rolled in the Rolling Mill, the Water Box nozzles progressively wear, which results in an increase of the nozzle diameters and a loss of cooling power. Figure 7 shows the behavior of the Water Box for different nozzle diameters. Note that as the nozzle size increases, the overall flow rate is increased to compensate.

- *External Compensation:* Figure 7 also shows that the effect of the nozzle wear will eventually exceed the capability of the Water Box to internally compensate.   In such a case, adjacent units will provide the needed process compensation.

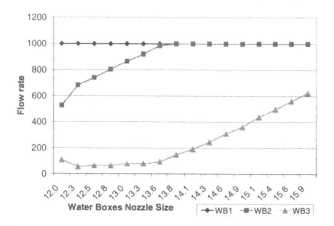

Fig. 7: Water box ACU internal compensation

Figure 8 shows the resultant cooperative behavior between the Rolling Mill and the Water Box. That is, the exit speed of the Rolling Mill is reduced to increase the efficiency of the water cooling in spite excessive nozzle wear. Note that as the water nozzles increase in size, the exit speed of the rolling mill is reduced.

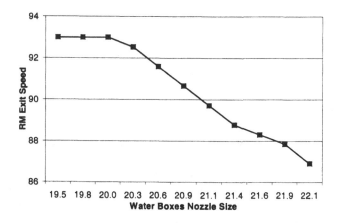

Fig. 8: External Compensation

The external compensation is good from the flexibility viewpoint; however, is it not good from the throughput rate. Slower production increases cost of operation and could harm the customer preference.

At some point, excessive nozzle affects the ability external compensation. At this point, the ACU failed to create acceptable plans. The operators were alerted to relax the quality, by switching to a lower tolerance product or to perform maintenance by replacing the water nozzles.

4.3   Equipment Failure

The ability of a system to continue functioning under equipment failures reduces unscheduled downtime and production delays.

To simulate failure in the Water Box unit, the flow rate to individual nozzles was disable. Figure 9 shows the behavior of the Water Box ACU in the process of compensating cooling power. Note that the individual flow rates for each functional nozzle was increased. Altogether, ACS still generated solutions to all experiments with various combinations of nozzle failure, except for cases of excessive failures. In this latter situation, the target tolerance of the rod could not be achieved.

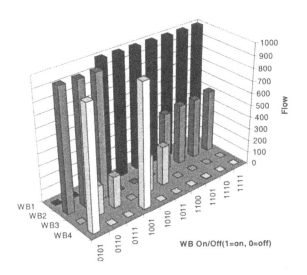

Fig. 9: Compensation for water box failures

The combination of water nozzles and flow rates per nozzle depended on the steel properties. Figure 9 only shows the final flow setting points. The Water Box ACU tried several combinations of these flows into the cooling process model to match the properties of the steel with the desired properties. In some cases, the flow rate combinations required the reduction of the Rolling Mill unit speed. In other cases, it was required to increase the Rolling Mill unit speed.

5 Field Trial Results

After testing the above conditions, the trials were moved to the real mill. The actual equipment replaced the equipment models and factory simulations. The experimental environment was constructed; so steel billets could be made with either the conventional control system or the ACS-based control system. This was allowed by simply changing positions on a selector switch.

Over a three months period, 52 experiments were performed during change events (product change, equipment failure, equipment wear, and equipment degradation) in the mill. In 25 of the experiments, the performance of the conventional control system was monitored. In 27 of the experiments, performance of ACS-based control was monitored.

Intermediate temperatures, real-time sensor readings, and resultant quality was collected for all experiments. During these experiments we were able to duplicate the results observed in the laboratory simulation environment.

To monitor the quality of steel during production, a measurement of the steel rod temperature is normally taken directly prior to entering the circular coiling apparatus in the mill. This apparatus is known as a laying-head; it is typically located between the water box and the air cooling units. Laying head temperature is a key real-time indicator of quality in a rolling mill. The closer the laying head temperatures are to the center of the target region, the more consistent the quality of the product is.

The experimental result demonstrated that ACU generated plans within the target laying-head temperature ranges. Figure 10 shows the frequency of the laying-head temperature deviation versus the laying-head temperature error. Note that all ACS controlled values are grouped within the target tolerance band. Testing of water box failures, variation in rolling mill speed and reduction of the water box flow rates produced comparable results. All results were within the target tolerance band.

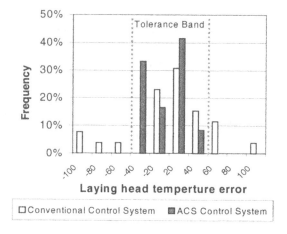

Fig. 10: Quality distribution (As measured by deviation in target laying head temperature)

6 Conclusion

The sample tests demonstrated that ACS could be used as a tool to partition information and achieve functional cooperation in a complex manufacturing line. ACS facilitated the integration of planning, scheduling and control levels into a flexible and adaptable system. This allowed the creation of control decisions that were consistent with variable conditions in the mill and in the simulated environment.

ACS-based control alternated between internal and external compensation strategies to meet system goals. These strategies were achieved through discovery, self-assessment and cooperation. Other important findings are:

- The results obtained from field experimentation serve to strengthen the findings observed during extensive simulation testing. ACU were capable of building acceptable plans to accomplish target quality. This was valid for multiple products, varying mill conditions, and failures.
- ACS-based control helped operators decide on alternative products that could benefit from the equipment conditions. This is a good indicator of the degree of flexibility added to steel rod production.
- Finally, further enhancements are required to generalize the architecture to expanded operational situations in other industrial environments.

7 References

1. Brooks, F.: Mythical Man Month, Addison-Wesley Publishing Company, (1975).
2. Agile Precision Sheet Metal Stamping Proposal, Advanced Technology Program, National Institute of Standard and Technology, April 11th, (1995).
3. Proceedings of the 4th Technical Advisory Committee Meeting, NSF Engineering Research Center for Reconfigurable Machine Systems, May 6-7th, (1998).
4. Proceedings of Auto Body Consortium, Inc.: Near Zero Stamping, Inc. Kickoff Meeting, December 1995.
5. Microprocessor Report, http://www.chipanalyst.com/q/@2271248bqwrrv/report/mpr.html
6. Gigabit Ethernet, http://www.gigabit-ethernet.org/
7. Steels, L.: "Toward a Theory of Emergent Functionality" From Animals to Animats: Proceedings of the 1st International Conference on Simulation of Adaptive Behavior. MIT Press, (1991).
8. Rumbaugh, J., Blaha, M., Premerlani, W., Eddy, F., and Lorensen, W.: Object-Oriented Modeling and Design, Prentice-Hall, Englewood Cliffs, NJ, (1991).
9. Bond, A. and Gasser, L.: Readings in Distributed Artificial Intelligence, Morgan Kaufmann Publishers, (1988).
10. O'Hare, G. and Jennings, N.: Foundations of Distributed Artificial Intelligence, John Wiley/Sons, (1996).
11. Clearwater, S.: Market-based control: A paradigm for distributed resource allocation, World Scientific, (1996).
12. Rosenschein, J. and Zlotkin, G.: Rules of Encounter: Designing for Automated Negotiation among Computers, The MIT Press, (1994).

13. Wooldridge, M. and Jennings, N.: Intelligent agents: theory and practice. *Knowledge Engineering Review*, 10(2), 115-152, (1995).

14. Davis, R. and Smith, R.G.: Negotiation as a metaphor for distributed problem solving. Artificial Intelligence, 20:63-109, (1983).

15. Park, K.H. and Cutkosky, M.: A.B., Conru, and S.H., Lee, An agent based approach to concurrent cable harness design, Artificial Intelligence for Engineering Design, Analysis and Manufacturing Journal, 8(1), 45-61, (1993).

16. Tenenbaum, J.M., Gruber, T.R., and Weber, J.C.: Lessons from SHADE and PACT. In Petrie, C. (Eds), Enterprise Modeling and Integration. McGraw-Hill, New York, (1992).

17. Christensen, J.H.: Holonic Manufacturing Systems: Initial architecture and standards direction, First European Conference on Holonic Manufacturing Systems, Hanover, Germany, 20pp, (1994).

18. Parunak, H.V.D., Baker, A.D., and Clark, S.J.: The AARIA Agent Architecture: An Example of Requirements-Driven Agent-Based System Design. IN Proceedings of the First International Conference on Autonomous Agents, Marina del Rey, CA., (1997).

19. Weiming S., Maturana, F., and Norrie, D.: MetaMorph II: An Agent-Based Architecture for Distributed Intelligent Design and Manufacturing, Journal of Intelligent Manufacturing, 11(3), 237-251, (2000).

Delegation of Responsibility in an Agent-Based Process Management System

John Debenham

University of Technology, Sydney,
School of Computing Sciences,
PO Box 123, NSW 2007, Australia
debenham@socs.uts.edu.au

Abstract. A multi-agent system manages high-level business processes. The conceptual agent architecture is a three-layer BDI, hybrid architecture. During processing the responsibility for a sub-process may be delegated. The delegation problem is the problem of choosing an individual to delegate responsibility to so as to achieve some corporate goal. An approach to the delegation problem uses an estimate of the probability that each individual is the best choice. This estimate is based on the values of observed parameters. These values are based on historic information, and are accepted as long as they are statistically stable. If variations in these observed values lie outside specified limits then the system attempts to deduce why this is so. If a reason for an unexpected value is quantifiable then that reason is used to revise subsequent values while that reason remains significant. The architecture has been trialed on a process management application in a university administrative context.

1 Introduction

The term *business process* includes here processes that take place at the higher levels of organisations. These processes are distinct from production workflows [1]. These business processes are opportunistic in nature whereas production workflows are routine. These processes are inherently distributed and involve asynchronous parallel work. What amounts to a „satisfactory conclusion" of a process may not be known until the process is well advanced. Further, the activities involved in a process are typically not predefined and emerge as the process develops. Those activities may be carried out by collaborative groups as well as by individuals. For example, in a manufacturing organisation such a high-level process could be triggered by „lets introduce a new product line for the US market".

In the system described here each human user is assisted by an agent. The term *individual* refers to a user/agent pair. Each business process has an individual, called the process *patron*, who is responsible for that process. That individual may choose to delegate the responsibility for a process, or for a sub-process within a process, to another individual. Here *delegation* is the transfer of the responsibility for a sub-process from one individual to another. Such delegation could be the transfer of the responsibility for achieving a sub-goal of a process. The *delegation problem* is the

C. Zhang and V.-W. Soo (Eds.): PRIMA 2000, LNAI 1881, pp. 170–181, 2000.

problem of deciding which individual to delegate responsibility to so as to achieve some corporate goal.

Process management is an established application area for multi-agent systems [2]. One valuable feature of process management as an application area is that 'real' experiments may be performed with the cooperation of local administrators [3]. The process agent architecture has been trialed on process management applications within university administration.

2 Process Management

The problem addressed here is the management of 'emergent processes'. This poses difficulties that are not typically found in the management of production workflows. *Emergent processes* [1] are opportunistic in nature whereas production workflows are routine. Emergent processes are inherently distributed and involve asynchronous parallel work. What amounts to a „satisfactory conclusion" of an emergent process is not generally known until the process is well advanced [5]. Further, the tasks involved in an emergent process are typically not predefined and emerge as the process develops. Those tasks are typically carried out by collaborative groups rather than individuals. So an emergent process management system may operate in a distributed environment.

Following [6] a *business process* is „a set of one or more linked procedures or activities which collectively realise a business objective or policy goal, normally within the context of an organisational structure defining functional roles and relationships". Implicit in this definition is the idea that a process may be repeatedly decomposed into linked sub-processes until those sub-processes are „activities" which are atomic pieces of work. [viz (op.cit) „An *activity* is a description of a piece of work that forms one logical step within a process."].

A particular process is called a (process) *instance*. So a process might be to „consider a request for overseas travel" and an instance might be to „consider my request to go to India for two weeks leaving on the 14th April". An instance may require that certain things should be done; such things are called *tasks*. A task—for example, a round table meeting—may lead to the generation of *process knowledge*.

Two classes of business process are identified: goal-driven processes and knowledge-driven processes:
- A *goal-driven process* is a business process that has two properties. First, it is *not* associated with a unique, valid decomposition. So in a goal-driven process, there is a choice of process decomposition. Second, the sub-processes in each decomposition terminate when a specific goal is realised. No matter how carefully a decomposition is chosen, the next activity may not achieve the next sub-goal. The reason for this may be that, due to fluctuations in a dynamic environment, that activity has become—maybe temporarily—an inappropriate way of achieving that sub-goal.
- A *knowledge-driven process* is a business process for which the termination of at least one sub-process in its decomposition is not determined by the realisation of a specific goal. This de-coupling of process termination and goal achievement admits processes whose goals are vague or may mutate. Emergent processes typically contain knowledge-driven sub-processes.

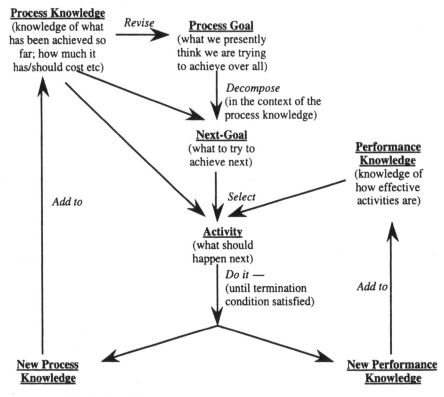

Fig. 1. Knowledge-driven process management (a simplified view)

The management of goal-driven sub-processes and knowledge-driven sub-processes pose problems that are not typically found in the management of production workflows. A goal-driven process may invoke an knowledge-driven sub-process, and vice versa. A simplified view of knowledge-driven process management is shown in Fig. 1.

The implementation of a management system to directly support all but the activities, as shown in Fig. 1, would be an enormous task. For example, the management of a growing body of process knowledge poses a complex belief revision problem. So the process knowledge is held by the process patron. The process management system assists with—but does not take responsibility for—the retention of this process knowledge, and manages the negotiation and subsequent commitments that players make to each other during a process instance. The system represents performance knowledge—this is described below. The system represents—but does not „understand"—the process goal. It represents next-goals and deals with the attendant communication surrounding the delegation of responsibility for achieving next-goals and the delivery to the patron of any new process knowledge.

The delegation problem is the problem of determining which individual should be delegated responsibility for a sub-process. Solutions to this problem may be based on various paradigms such as: authoritarian, free-market and so no. Practical solutions to this problem in manual systems can be quite elementary. The use of a multi-agent system to manage processes expands the range of feasible strategies for delegation from the authoritarian strategies described above to strategies based on negotiation between individuals. Negotiation-based strategies that involves negotiation for each process instance are not feasible in manual systems for every day tasks due to the cost of negotiation. In agent-based systems the agents are responsible for this negotiation and so a system in which the delegation of each task is determined by negotiation is feasible.

3 The Multi-agent System

The variety of process management described in Sec 2 is open and dynamic with a high degree of inherent distribution and a high degree of personalisation. This indicates that a multi-agent system may be appropriate.

Mission. The *mission* of the system is to support the management of processes as described in Sec. 2 in line with corporate priorities.

System Organisation. The system organisation consists of one process agent for each (human) user. There are no other agents in the system. A blackboard is used to announce the availability of agents. The agents play the *role* of an assistant to their user.

Interaction Protocol. If an agent wishes to delegate responsibility to another agent then a form of Contract Net is used. This form is Contact Nets with focussed addressing [7] in which the members of a subset of all suitably qualified individuals are invited to bid for work. Estimates of the time—total time to completion of the work—and cost—such as total time actually spent on the work—are asked for as part of each bid. The evaluation of bids is based on estimates of: the time that the individual will actually take, the cost that the individual will actually incur, the value that the individual will add to the process, and the likelihood that the individual will actually complete the work with the process constraints. Information supplied as part of a bid addressed the constraints of each process instance. These constraints could include the total budget for an instance, and the latest acceptable completion time for the instance.

Measuring value may be a purely subjective matter. In some cases value may be measured in terms of an eventual outcome. For example, the value added by a bank loans officer may be measured in time by observing whether the judgements made by that officer lead to good or bad loan outcomes.

Communication Protocol. In its direct communication with its user an agent:

- manages its user's web-based 'In Tray',
- clears its user's 'Out Tray',
- manages the storage and retrieval of documents, and
- communicates with its user.

If a process agent wishes to communicate with its user then it may do so either by modifying the user's 'In Tray' or by sending the user a message—perhaps by email. A user communicates with their agent by placing a document in the 'Out Tray'; this may, for example, be achieved by 'clicking' a software 'button' in a document. If a document is placed in the 'Out Tray' then this will be realised as one of the agent's incoming messages, and so it may then become a belief. In addition to its direct communication with users the multi-agent system manages the documents, performs automatic document checking and so on. Agents communicate with other agents by sending messages that are not seen by users. These messages are represented in KQML (Knowledge Query and Manipulation Language) [8].

Architecture. The conceptual architecture is adapted from the INTeRRAP conceptual architecture described in [9]. The process agent architecture is intended specifically for process management applications. World beliefs are derived *either* from reading messages received from a user, *or* from reading the documents involved in the process instance, *or* from reading messages received from other agents. These activities are fundamentally different. Documents are „passive" in that they are read only when information is required. Users and other agents are „active" in that they send messages when they feel like it. Beliefs play two roles. First, they can be partly or wholly responsible for the agent committing to a goal, and may thus initiate an intention (eg. a plan to achieve what a message asks, such as „please do xyz"). This is *deliberative reasoning*. Second, they can be partly or wholly responsible for the activation of a trigger that will directly effect the execution of an active plan. This is *reactive reasoning*.

Reasoning. As a hybrid architecture the process agent architecture exhibits both deliberative and reactive reasoning [10]. Deliberative reasoning is managed within a belief-goal–plan–intention framework [11]. Reactive reasoning is effected with triggers. Theses two forms of reasoning are balanced by giving reactive reasoning precedence over deliberative reasoning. That is, an attempt is made to fire all triggers before each deliberative cycle commences.

Reactive reasoning play three roles: first, a plan is aborted if its specified abort condition is satisfied, second, data is passed to partly executed plans for goals an agent is committed to achieve, and third, urgent messages are dealt with. Of these two roles the first takes precedence over the second. For example, the third role for reactive triggers handles messages of the form „stop what you are doing and do this"; this third role has yet to be implemented for emergent process management.

Implementation. The process agent is implemented in Java. It is implemented as an interpreter of high-level agent specifications. This interpreter enables agents to be built quickly. It also simplifies maintenance, which only has to deal with high level specifications of goals and plans. Fig. 2 shows the screen for entering a plan into an agent's plan library. The LiveNet workspace system [12] is used to handle virtual discussions.

4 Delegation Strategy

The *delegation problem* is the problem of deciding which individual to delegate responsibility to so as to achieve some corporate goal. A solution to the delegation problem is expressed as a *delegation strategy* that determines the individual to whom responsibility is delegated. In the system described in Sec. 3 each human user is assisted by an agent [13]. An „individual" is taken to be a user/agent pair. The notation $\{X_1,...,X_i,...,X_n\}$ is used to denote n individuals to whom responsibility for a sub-process could be delegated. A *delegation strategy* at time τ is specified as $S = \{P_1,...,P_i,...,P_n\}$ where P_i is the probability of delegating responsibility for a given sub-process at time τ to individual X_i chosen from $\{X_1,...,X_i,...,X_n\}$.

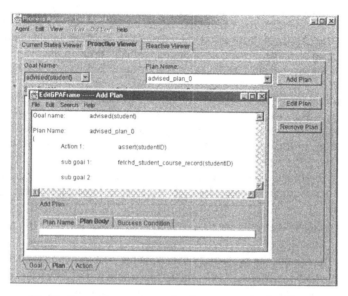

Fig. 2. Screen for entering a plan into an agent's plan library

The interaction protocol described in Sec. 3 employs Contract Nets with focussed addressing. So the delegation problem is partly solved by the specification, for each process type, of the set of individuals from whom bids are invited. It is assumed here that the set of individuals who are invited to bid for each process type is specified outside the process management system. The interaction protocol asks for bids, downgrades the value of bids—or eliminates bids—that do not satisfy the process constraints, and then evaluates the remaining bids if any. The evaluation of the bids takes account of the expected cost of the individual, the expected value that the individual is expected to give to the process instance and the extent to which the individual already has taken responsibility for process instances of the type under consideration in the recent past. This last factor is included to take account of sentiments such as „oh, don't give me *another* one of those today", or corporate strategies that could specify that individuals should receive process instances of the same type in a concentrated period of time and then given a break from receiving instances of that type for a while.

A bid consists of four real numbers (*Con, Workload, Cost, Value*), where *Con* means „the aggregated value of the constraint parameters", *Workload* means the number of processes of the type under consideration that the individual has „recently" taken responsibility for, *Cost* means „the estimated cost that will be incurred by delegating responsibility to that individual" that is an estimate of the actual cost of doing the job, and *Value* means „the estimated gross value added to the sub-process by delegating responsibility to that individual". The reduction of a bid to four numbers may appear to be rather restrictive, but when the choice is made between bids there must be some mechanism for deciding:
- the extent to which a bid should be downgraded—or not considered at all—because of the values of its constraint parameters;
- how to compare acceptable bids, and

• how concentrated the delegation strategy has been.

To make the discussion here simple we assume that this reduction to four single quantities is done as part of the construction of the bid. Consider *Value*, this could be estimated on the basis of how good the individual is, *Cost* could simply be a combination of an estimate of the cost of the individuals' time on the sub-process and an estimate of the overall time taken to deal with the sub-process—ie including the „waiting time".

The extent to which the delegation strategy is expressed in terms of the expected total overall payoff may reflect corporate culture [14]. Three examples are given. In the first example, the corporate culture states that the people in an organisation should continually be given the opportunity for improving what they do. In which case the delegation strategy S_1 ignores expected payoff and is $P_i = \backslash F(1,n)$. In the second example, the corporate culture states that each task should be allocated to the individual who is available to do the best job at the time. In which case the delegation strategy S_2 is:

$P_i = \backslash B \backslash LC \backslash \{(\backslash A \backslash CO1 \backslash AL \backslash VS0(\backslash F(1,m)$ *if* X_i is such that $Pr(X_i \grave{E})$ is maximal, , 0 *otherwise*))

where $Pr(X_i \grave{E})$ means „the probability that X_i is the best individual in some sense" and m is such that there are m individuals for whom $Pr(X_i \grave{E})$ is maximal. The strategy S_2 maximises overall expected payoff. Using this second strategy an individual who performs poorly may never get work. A desirable strategy should be able to balance (A) maximising "expected payoff for the next delegation"—such as in the second example S_2 above—with (B) improving available skills in the long term—such as in the first example S_1 above.

To balance expected payoff for the next delegation with the improvement of available skills requires an estimate of *how* individuals are expected to improve if they are allocated the responsibility for sub-processes [15]. This could be done but is not considered here. Instead, an *admissible* delegation strategy is defined as having the properties that:

• *if* $Pr(X_i \grave{E}) > Pr(X_j \grave{E})$ *then* $P_i > P_j$
• *if* $Pr(X_i \grave{E}) = Pr(X_j \grave{E})$ *then* $P_i = P_j$
• $P_i > 0$ (:i)

So the two strategies S_1 and S_2 given above are *not* admissible. An admissible strategy will delegate more responsibility to individuals with a high probability of being the „best" than to individuals with a low probability. Also with an admissible strategy each individual has a chance of being given responsibility. The strategy S_3 is $P_i = Pr(X_j \grave{E})$. This strategy is admissible and is used in the system described here [16]. It provides a balance between favouring individuals who perform well with giving occasional opportunities to poor performers to improve their performance. This strategy is *not* based on any model of process improvement and so it can *not* be claimed to be optimal in that sense. There is an infinite variety of admissible strategies; for example, any strategy of the form: $S = \alpha \_ S_1 + \beta \_ S_2 + \gamma \_ S_3$ will be admissible if $\alpha + \beta + \gamma = 1$ and if $\gamma > 0$. Strategies S_2 and S_3 rely on some estimate being available of the probability that an individual is the „best" in some sense.

5 Choosing the 'Best' Individual

The probability that an individual is the „best" in some sense may be derived from the values of parameters for how „good" each individual if those parameters are normally distributed. The parameters that are treated here are: the expected cost that an individual will incur in accepting responsibility for a sub-process, the expected total (elapse) time from the delegation of responsibility to the end of the work, the expected value that the individual will give to the sub-process, and the probability that the individual will complete the work if given the responsibility for it. It is „not unreasonable" to expect that the first three of these are normally distributed. The fourth is binomially distributed, and may be approximated by a normal distribution under standard conditions. So any hybrid parameter defined in terms of these four basic parameters should also be „approximately" normally distributed. So we assume that the measure of how „good each individual A is", p_A, is normally distributed.

Suppose that for each individual there is an estimated of the mean, $\backslash O(x,^\wedge)_A$, and the standard deviation, $\backslash O(s,^\wedge)_A$, of that „goodness" parameter.

The probability that individual A is „better" than individual B is the probability that $(p_A - p_B) > 0$. This quantity is the area under that normal distribution with mean $= \backslash O(x,^\wedge)_A - \backslash O(x,^\wedge)_B$ and standard deviation $= \backslash r(\backslash O(s,^\wedge)\backslash O(^2{}_{,A}) + \backslash O(s,^\wedge)\backslash O(^2{}_{,B}))$ for $x^3 0$. This method for choosing between two individuals may be extended to a method for choosing between three individuals, and may be generalised to a method that chooses between any number of individuals.

6 Parameters Estimates

The ideas in the previous section rely on the availability of estimates of the expected „goodness" of individuals. That measure is assumed to be normally distributed and will be combined from estimates of: the expected cost that an individual will incur in accepting responsibility for a sub-process, the expected total (elapse) time from the delegation of responsibility to the end of the work, the expected value that the individual will give to the sub-process, and the probability that the individual will complete the work if given the responsibility for it. Estimates of the *Workload* parameter are also part of the Contact Net bid. The *Workload* parameter may be used to directly influence the delegation of responsibility and so it is *not* reasonable to assume that it will be normally distributed. So some method is required for estimating these parameters. As the estimates for each of these parameters should be updated each time any responsibility is delegated the method for estimating them should be chosen to simplify these update calculations.

The *Workload* parameter is estimated by noting the amount of work delegated in each—discrete—time period. Suppose that $\{w_i\}\backslash O(_{i=1},^n)$ are the previous amounts of work delegated in previous time periods, where w_1 is the most recent previous time period. A weighted estimate places more emphasis on recent delegations. The geometric mean gives such an estimate of prior workload:

$$\backslash f(\backslash O(\textstyle\sum_{i=1}^n,\,)\,\alpha^{i-1}\_w_i, \backslash O(\textstyle\sum_{i=1}^n,\,)\,\alpha^{i-1})$$

where the constant α lies in the range $(0, 1)$. A current estimate for the *Workload* parameter is obtained by adding the number of delegations made in the present time period to the estimate of prior workload. This leads to the very simple update formula: *Workload* = $(1 - \alpha)$ _ (number of delegations made in the present time period) + α _ (value of *Workload* at the end of the previous time period). The value of α is chosen to reflect the expected time that it takes to deal with delegated work. If work is normally dealt with in one or two time periods then the value of α should be low, say 0.3. For work of a type that takes longer to deal with the value should be higher.

Estimates for the mean of the (assumed) normally distributed parameters time t, cost c and value v are made similarly. The estimate of the standard deviations uses the „folded" distribution. For example, to estimate the standard deviation $\backslash O(s,^\wedge)_A$. If the same assumptions hold that were required to estimate $\backslash O(x,^\wedge)_A$ above then over n observations:

$$\backslash r(\backslash f(\pi,2))\_\backslash f(\backslash O(\textstyle\sum_{i=1}^n,\,)\mid t_i-\backslash O(x,^\wedge)_A\mid,n)$$

is a point estimate for the standard deviation $\backslash O(s,^\wedge)_A$. As for the point estimate of the mean, the weighted mean places more emphasis on recent behaviour:

$$\backslash f(\backslash O(\textstyle\sum_{i=1}^n,\,)\,\alpha^{i-1}\_\mid t_i-\backslash O(x_A,^\wedge)\mid,\backslash O(\textstyle\sum_{i=1}^n,\,)\,\alpha^{i-1})$$

and this is used here as the point estimate for $\backslash r(\backslash f(2,\pi))\_\backslash O(s,^\wedge)_A$. So:

$$\backslash O(s,^\wedge)_{A_{new}} = (1-\alpha)\_\mid t_1-\backslash O(x,^\wedge)_{Aold}\mid + \alpha\_\backslash O(s,^\wedge)_{Aold}$$

To commence this iteration some initial value $\backslash O(s,^\wedge)_{A_{init}}$ is required; a value of say 0.3 is a cautiously optimistic starting point.

The estimation of *value* is rather more problematic due to the inherent difficulty of estimating the actual value added to a process, although some progressive organisations have staff whose job it is to evaluate the work of others. These evaluations are then used by the process management system.

The probability that an individual will complete the work if given the responsibility for it is binomially distributed which reduces to the normal distribution under standard criteria.

One advantage to using the statistical method described above for determining which individual to delegate a sub-process to is that the method provides a theoretical basis for identifying anomalies. By making measurements $\{e_{i_A}\}$ for individual A the method estimates a mean and standard deviation for the four parameters p (likelihood of success), t (time), c (cost) and v (value). So for some parameter q—which could be defined as a combination of any of these four parameters—and for some individual A, the method calculates $\backslash O(x,^{\wedge})_{A_{old}}$ as an approximation to the mean, $\backslash O(x,^{\wedge})_A$, and $\backslash O(s,^{\wedge})_{A_{old}}$ as an approximation to the standard deviation, $\backslash r(\backslash f(2,\pi))\_\backslash O(s,^{\wedge})_A$. Then the next measurement for A, e_{1_A}, should lie in the confidence interval: $(\backslash O(x,^{\wedge})_A \pm \alpha\_\backslash O(s,^{\wedge})_A)$ to some chosen degree of certainty. For example, this degree of certainty is 95% if $\alpha = 1.645$. The set of measurements $\{e_{i_A}\}$ can progressively change without e_{1_A} lying outside this confidence interval; for example, an individual may be gradually getting better at doing things. But if e_{1_A} lies outside this confidence interval then there is grounds, to the chosen degree of certainty, to ask why it is outside.

The above method is based purely on historical data; it does not take account of *why* that choice behaved the way that it did. Inferred explanations of *why* a selected path through a plan behaved as it did may sometimes be extracted from observing the interactions with the users and other agents involved in that path. For example, an agent may note that „Person X" was very slow in attending to a certain process instance yesterday" and that a sub-process for which X had taken responsibility failed; a simple interchange with other agents may reveal that „Person X was working on another sub-process instance concerned with the company's annual report yesterday; that instance is scheduled for completion within six days" and that that appeared to be a reason for sub-process failure. Inferred knowledge such as this gives *one possible cause* for the observed behaviour; so such knowledge enables us to *refine*, but *not* to *replace*, the historical estimates of parameters.

The measurement e_{1_A} may lie outside the confidence interval for four types of reason:

1) there has been a permanent change in the environment or in the process management system—the measurement e_{1_A} is now the expected value for $\backslash O(x,^{\wedge})_A$ —in which case the estimates $\backslash O(x,^{\wedge})_{A_{old}}$ and $\backslash O(s,^{\wedge})_{A_{old}}$ should be re-initialised.

2) there has been a temporary change in the environment or in the process management system and the measurements $\{e_{i_A}\}$ are expected to be perturbed in some way for some time—in which case the reason, Γ, for this expected perturbation should be sought. For example, a new member of staff may have been delegated the responsibility—temporarily—for this sub-process. Or, for example, a database component of the system may be behaving erratically.

3) there has been no change in the environment or in the process management system and the unexpected measurement e_{1_A} is due to some feature γ that distinguishes the nature of this sub-process instance from those instances that were used to calculate $\backslash O(x,^{\wedge})_{A_{old}}$ and $\backslash O(x,^{\wedge})_{A_{old}}$. In other words, what was thought to be a single sub-process type is really two or more different—but possibly related—process types. In which case a new process is created and the estimates $\backslash O(x,^{\wedge})_{A_{old}}$ and $\backslash O(x,^{\wedge})_{A_{old}}$ are initialised for that process.

4) there has been no change in the environment or in the process management system and the nature of the most recent process instance is no different from previous instances—the unexpected measurement e_{1_A} is due to—possibly combined— fluctuations in the performance of individuals or other systems.

In option 2) above the reason Γ is sometimes inferred by the system itself. This has been achieved in cases when a user appears to be preoccupied working on another task. If the reason Γ is to be taken into account then some forecast of the future effect of Γ is required. If such a forecast effect can be quantified—perhaps by simply asking a user—then the perturbed values of $\{e_{i_A}\}$ are corrected to $\{e_{i_A} \mid \Gamma\}$ otherwise the perturbed values are ignored.

Consider a formerly reliable individual A. Suppose that the value of $\backslash O(x,^\wedge)_{A_{old}}$ is 0.9 and of $\backslash O(s,^\wedge)_{A_{old}}$ is 0.2. Then suppose that individual A fails to meet commitments, and $e_{1_{A_{observed}}} = 0$. Suppose that the reason is that A is working on the company's annual report and that this is seen to be largely responsible for the observed behaviour. Suppose that this reason is seen to be of roughly of linearly decreasing relevance up to time $\tau = 6$ days. Then the measurement e_{1_A} is corrected to allow for this explanation:

$$e_{1_{A_{corrected}}} = \backslash O(x,^\wedge)_{A_{old}} + [e_{1_{A_{observed}}} - \backslash O(x,^\wedge)_{A_{old}}] \_ f(\tau), \quad \text{where:}$$

$f(\tau) = \backslash B \backslash LC \backslash \{ (\backslash A \backslash CO1 \backslash AL \backslash VS0(\text{ undefined if } \tau < 0, 0.4 + 0.1 \_ \tau$

$\text{if } 0 \, 2 \, \tau \, 2 \, 6, 1.0 \text{ if } \tau > 6))$

This mechanism provides a way of refining the measurements by taking *one reason* for path performance into account.

7 Conclusion

High-level business processes are analysed as being of two distinct types [17]. The management of these two types of process has been described. A multi-agent system is designed to manage these processes. The conceptual agent architecture is a three-layer BDI, hybrid architecture. During a process instance the responsibility for sub-processes may be delegated. The delegation problem is the problem of choosing an individual for such delegation in line with corporate priorities. An approach to the delegation problem estimates the probability that an individual is the best choice. This estimate is based in turn on the values of certain observed parameters. These values are based on historic information, and are accepted as long as they are statistically stable. If variations in these observed values lie outside specified limits then the system attempts to deduce why this is so. If a reason for an unexpected value is quantifiable then that reason is used to revise subsequent values while that reason remains significant. The architecture has been trialed on a process management application in a university administrative context.

References

[1] Dourish, P. (1998). Using Metalevel Techniques in a Flexible Toolkit for CSCW Applications. ACM Transactions on Computer-Human Interaction, Vol. 5, No. 2, June, 1998, pp. 109—155.

[2] A. P. Sheth, D. Georgakopoulos, S. Joosten, M. Rusinkiewicz, W. Scacchi, J. C. Wileden, and A. L. Wolf. „Report from the NSF workshop on workflow and process automation in information systems." SIGMOD Record, 25(4):55—67, December 1996.

[3] Debenham, J.K. „Supporting Strategic Process", in proceedings Fifth International Conference on The Practical Application of Intelligent Agents and Multi-Agents PAAM2000, Manchester UK, April 2000.

[5] Muth, P., Wodtke, D., Weissenfels, J., Kotz D.A. and Weikum, G. (1998). From Centralized Workflow Specification to Distributed Workflow Execution. In Journal of Intelligent Information Systems (JIIS), Kluwer Academic Publishers, Vol. 10, No. 2, 1998.

[6] Lawrence, P. (1997). Workflow Handbook. Workflow Management Coalition. John Wiley & Son Ltd, 1997.

[7] Durfee, E.H.. (1999): „Distributed Problem Solving and Planning" in Weiss, G. (ed). Multi-Agent Systems. The MIT Press: Cambridge, MA.

[8] Finin, F. Labrou, Y., and Mayfield, J. (1997). KQML as an agent communication language. In Jeff Bradshaw (Ed.) Software Agents. MIT Press (1997).

[9] MŸller, J.P. (1996) „The Design of Intelligent Agents" Springer-Verlag.

[10] Debenham, J.K. (1997) „Strategic Workflow Management", in proceedings International Workshop Distributed Artificial Intelligence and Multi-Agent Systems DAIMAS'97, St Petersberg, June 1997, pp103—112.

[11] Rao, A.S. and Georgeff, M.P. (1995): „BDI Agents: From Theory to Practice", in proceedings First International Conference on Multi-Agent Systems (ICMAS-95), San Francisco, USA, pp 312—319.

[12] Hawryszkiewycz, I.T. (1999). Supporting Teams in Virtual Organisations. In Proceedings Tenth International Conference, DEXA'99, Florence, September 1999.

[13] Debenham, J.K. (1998) „A Multi-Agent System for Emergent Process Management", in proceedings Nineteenth International Conference on Knowledge Based Systems and Applied Artificial Intelligence, ES'99: Applications and Innovations in Expert Systems VII, Cambridge UK, December 1999, pp51-62.

[14] Debenham, J.K. (1998) „Knowledge Engineering: Unifying Knowledge Base and Database Design", Springer-Verlag, 1998

[15] Koriche, F. (1998): „Approximate Reasoning about Combined Knowledge" in Intelligent Agents IV, Singh M.P, Rao, A. and Wooldridge, M.J. (Eds), Springer Verlag, 1998

[16] C. Bussler, S. Jablonski, and H. Schuster. „A new generation of workflow management systems: Beyond taylorism with MOBILE." SIGOIS Bulletin, 17(1):17—20, April 1996.

[17] Debenham, J.K. (2000) „Three Intelligent Architectures for Business Process Management", in proceedings 12th International Conference on Software Engineering and Knowledge Engineering SEKE2000, Chicago, 6-8 July 2000.

Author Index

Lecture Notes in Artificial Intelligence (LNAI)

Lecture Notes in Computer Science